THE ROAD TO IP TELEPHONY:
HOW CISCO SYSTEMS MIGRATED FROM PBX TO IP TELEPHONY

Stephanie L. Carhee

Cisco Press

800 East 96th Street

Indianapolis, Indiana 46240 USA

The Road to IP Telephony:
How Cisco Systems Migrated from PBX to IP Telephony

Stephanie L. Carhee

Copyright© 2010 Cisco Systems, Inc.

Published by:
Cisco Press
800 East 96th Street
Indianapolis, IN 46240 USA

Printed in the United States of America. This book is printed digitally on demand.

First Printing May 2010

Library of Congress Cataloging-in-Publication Number is on file

ISBN: 1-58720-420-7

Trademark Acknowledgments

All terms mentioned in this book that are known to be trademarks or service marks have been appropriately capitalized. Cisco Press or Cisco Systems, Inc. cannot attest to the accuracy of this information. Use of a term in this book should not be regarded as affecting the validity of any trademark or service mark.

Warning and Disclaimer

This book is designed to provide information about the migration process from a PBX-based to an IP Telephony environment. Every effort has been made to make this book as complete and as accurate as possible, but no warranty or fitness is implied.

The information is provided on an "as is" basis. The author, Cisco Press, and Cisco Systems, Inc. shall have neither liability nor responsibility to any person or entity with respect to any loss or damages arising from the information contained in this book or from the use of the discs or programs that may accompany it.

The opinions expressed in this book belong to the author and are not necessarily those of Cisco Systems, Inc.

Feedback Information

At Cisco Press, our goal is to create in-depth technical books of the highest quality and value. Each book is crafted with care and precision, undergoing rigorous development that involves the unique expertise of members from the professional technical community.

Readers' feedback is a natural continuation of this process. If you have any comments regarding how we could improve the quality of this book, or otherwise alter it to better suit your needs, you can contact us through e-mail at feedback@ciscopress.com. Please make sure to include the book title and ISBN in your message.

We greatly appreciate your assistance.

Corporate and Government Sales

Cisco Press offers excellent discounts on this book when ordered in quantity for bulk purchases or special sales.

For more information, please contact: U.S. Corporate and Government Sales 1-800-382-3419 corpsales@pearsontechgroup.com

For sales outside the U.S., please contact: International Sales at international@pearsoned.com

Publisher	John Wait
Editor-in-Chief	John Kane
Executive Editor	Jim Schachterle
Cisco Representative	Anthony Wolfenden
Cisco Press Program Manager	Nannette M. Noble
Acquisitions Editor	Amy Moss
Production Manager	Patrick Kanouse
Senior Development Editor	Christopher Cleveland
Development Editor	Debbie Hart
Project/Copy Editor	Karen A. Gill
Technical Editors	Steve Mergist, Paul Molyski, Alex Oldham
Team Coordinator	Tammi Barnett
Book and Cover Designer	Louisa Adair
Composition	Mark Shirar
Indexer	Tim Wright

CISCO SYSTEMS

Corporate Headquarters
Cisco Systems, Inc.
170 West Tasman Drive
San Jose, CA 95134-1706
USA
www.cisco.com
Tel: 408 526-4000
      800 553-NETS (6387)
Fax: 408 526-4100

European Headquarters
Cisco Systems International BV
Haarlerbergpark
Haarlerbergweg 13-19
1101 CH Amsterdam
The Netherlands
www-europe.cisco.com
Tel: 31 0 20 357 1000
Fax: 31 0 20 357 1100

Americas Headquarters
Cisco Systems, Inc.
170 West Tasman Drive
San Jose, CA 95134-1706
USA
www.cisco.com
Tel: 408 526-7660
Fax: 408 527-0883

Asia Pacific Headquarters
Cisco Systems, Inc.
Capital Tower
168 Robinson Road
#22-01 to #29-01
Singapore 068912
www.cisco.com
Tel: +65 6317 7777
Fax: +65 6317 7799

Cisco Systems has more than 200 offices in the following countries and regions. Addresses, phone numbers, and fax numbers are listed on the
Cisco.com Web site at www.cisco.com/go/offices.

Argentina • Australia • Austria • Belgium • Brazil • Bulgaria • Canada • Chile • China PRC • Colombia • Costa Rica • Croatia • Czech Republic Denmark • Dubai, UAE • Finland • France • Germany • Greece • Hong Kong SAR • Hungary • India • Indonesia • Ireland • Israel • Italy Japan • Korea • Luxembourg • Malaysia • Mexico • The Netherlands • New Zealand • Norway • Peru • Philippines • Poland • Portugal Puerto Rico • Romania • Russia • Saudi Arabia • Scotland • Singapore • Slovakia • Slovenia • South Africa • Spain • Sweden Switzerland • Taiwan • Thailand • Turkey • Ukraine • United Kingdom • United States • Venezuela • Vietnam • Zimbabwe

About the Author

Stephanie L. Carhee has worked at Cisco Systems for nearly five years. Prior to moving to the IP communications enterprise services marketing team, she worked as an IP Telephony implementation team lead within the strategic program management group of Cisco IT voice services. Her primary role was to lead the campus-wide migration of Cisco IP communications solutions. In May 2001, Stephanie led the conversion that completed the largest deployment of IP Telephony in industry history. Her efforts were to lead a cross-functional team of top project managers, design engineers, support team, CCIEs, technical marketing engineers, systems engineers, and IP Telephony partners who completed the conversion of the Cisco San Jose, California campus to IP Telephony, in which 20,000 users and devices were converted to the Cisco IP Phone.

Stephanie is an experienced, dynamic speaker who is acknowledged as a subject matter expert in the processes and procedures of deploying an IP Telephony solution, delivering hundreds of customer briefings around the county (including Networkers 2002, 2003, and 2004). Stephanie's best practices have been featured in Cisco publications, such as *IQ* and *Packet* magazine. Her areas of expertise include enterprise technology adoption, voice practice business development, governance, process re-engineering, organizational change management, and program management. Stephanie is frequently asked to consult on customer engagements and various presales activities, where she consults with some of the top Cisco customers to duplicate the success Cisco has had.

Stephanie also architected the recent relaunch of the Cisco Steps to Success IP Telephony Engagement Guide website, for which she earned the Cisco excellence award. Steps to Success provides Cisco partners with a step-by-step resource for selling and delivering IP Telephony services and support throughout the planning, design, implementation, operations, and optimization (PDIOO) project life cycle. Steps to Success is based on a proven methodology built on Cisco research, experience, and development, as well as knowledge gathered from successful Cisco solution engagements.

Today, Stephanie is leveraging her knowledge within the Cisco customer advocacy services organization, where she develops IP communication partner enablement programs and customer services and support programs. Stephanie is a senior project manager with more than 10 years of project management experience in managing, developing, and implementing projects in the areas of IT network engineering, operations, system administration, advanced technology, marketing, and sales. She holds a bachelor of arts degree in business management and communications. Stephanie can be reached online at scarhee@cisco.com.

About the Technical Reviewers

Steve Mergist, CCIE No. 4853, is the enterprise network practice manager for Avnet Enterprise Solutions (AES). He is responsible for solution development for Avnet's IP Telephony and IT security practices and supports the national sales organization. Steve is also part of an overall team within Avnet that drives the strategic direction for technology solutions and defines go-to-market activities when deploying these solutions to the field sales team and end customers. Steve has been with Avnet for nearly five years and has worked as a network engineer and advanced technology manager for eight years.

Paul Molyski is a project manager for the Cisco IT infrastructure department. He managed the retrofit of the Cisco LAN infrastructure for the San Jose, California main campus in preparation for the deployment of IP Telephony. Recently, Paul was the project manager for the deployment of an early field trial (EFT) Unity unified messaging test environment that supported in excess of 700 users. Paul has worked in various capacities in computing and networking for more than 30 years. He has been at Cisco for over five years, spending most of that time on network infrastructure projects.

Alex Oldham, CCIE No. 4652, is a network consulting engineer for Cisco advanced services. He is responsible for implementation and technical design of IP Telephony products across various customer environments. Alex has been at Cisco since 1999 and has worked in the networking field for 15 years.

Dedications

To My Family

Issac, my father, for his unconditional love.

Mary, my mother, for her wisdom and support

Stephen, my twin brother, for his big heart and love

Stanley, my baby brother, for his willingness to back up his big sister

And a special dedication to my Aunt Ina Mae Lawson, who passed away right before I finished this book and was my loudest cheerleader

Acknowledgments

I'd like to give special recognition to Debbie Hart, my copy editor, development editor, and all around partner in crime in the development of this book. Debbie, your professionalism and commitment never wavered, and the success of this book can certainly be attributed to your contributions. Most importantly, you were never afraid to tell me like it was and keep me on the path, and we always had the same vision: to make a good book. You are truly a good friend.

Thanks to Manny Rivelo for being the first person to say "Yes, I will support you" in writing the Cisco story. David Tucker and Anne Smith: Thanks for cheering me on all the way. Don Proctor and team: Thanks for your support. Thanks also to Brad Boston and Lance Perry for their kind words of encouragement. Mark Bonfoey, and Rune Olslund, I appreciate your bringing me into my new Customer Advocacy family. Dale Seavey: You were my first believer. Thanks for the ice cream. Finally, thanks to Doug McQueen (and the entire SPM and IT Voice Services team), who allowed me to spend the necessary time (two years) writing and researching this book.

A big thank you goes out to the entire Cisco AVVID Tiger Team, without which the success of this project and book would not have been possible. As with any large endeavor, many people contributed to this book. Thanks for offering your quotes and words of wisdom, sharing your experience, and lending your expertise. I hope this book reflects how much I appreciate and honor you by delivering a true and honest account of our experiences.

Mike Telang, you are my hero. Without your contributions to Chapter 5, "Day 2 Handoff and Support," this book would not have been complete. Tracy Mercer, your contributions on the Cisco Support Center section were pivotal. Del Hays and Chad Ormondroyd with STS International, you both were incredible to work with and quite possibly the best IP Telephony Support leads in the business.

Dennis Silva, Bill Lowers, and Anthony Garcia are truly my favorites. The contributions that the three of you have made in the development of IP Telephony are truly staggering. Dennis, thanks for always being brutally honest and committed to this project. Anthony, working side by side with you was truly an honor. Bill, I'm still waiting for you to open up "Bill's University of IP Telephony." I'll be your press agent and first student. Your kindness and willingness to pick up the phone no matter what time it was will keep you in my prayers forever.

And William McDade, I look forward to our new journey together. You will always have a special place in my heart. Thanks for being there.

Lastly, I'd like to thank John Chambers and Cisco Systems. When I entered the doors of this amazing company, who knew the journey I would take would lead me here. This is truly the best place in the world to work and thanks for giving me the ride of my life.

Contents at a Glance

Foreword   xxiii

Introduction   xxvi

Chapter 1   A Cisco Evolution   1

Chapter 2   Before You Begin   13

Chapter 3   The Migration Strategy   83

Chapter 4   Implementation   137

Chapter 5   Day 2 Handoff and Support   219

Chapter 6   Final Piece of the Conversion   251

Chapter 7   Moving Forward: Continuing to Be Cisco's First and Best Customer   309

Appendix   Customer Concerns   353

Glossary   357

Index   365

Contents

Foreword   xxiii

Introduction   xxvi

Chapter 1   **A Cisco Evolution   1**
Operational Benefits of Cisco IP Telephony 2
ROI 5
Where It All Started 8
Cisco Architecture in the Beginning 8
Cisco Architecture Evolution 9
Summary   10

Chapter 2   **Before You Begin   13**
Importance of a Cross-Functional Team   14
AVVID Tiger Team   15
Roles and Responsibilities   15
Executive Sponsor   16
Steering Committee   16
Team Lead   17
Tiger Team Program Manager   17
Core Tiger Team   17
Third-Party Partners   18
Ad Hoc Team Members   18
The Four Project Tracks   19
Technology Track   19
Support Track   21
Financial Track   22
Theater Track   22
Best Practices: Building a Cross-Functional Team   23
Executive Management Sponsorship   24
Best Practices: Executive Management   25
Managing Change   27
Organizational Culture   28
Change Readiness   29
Voice of the Client Survey   31
"Must Have" Features   31

Know Your Users/Manage Expectations   32

A Word About Communication   33

Best Practices: Managing Change   35

Best Practices: Cultural Standards for Managing
   Organizational Change   36

Best Practices: Communicating Change   37

Best Practices: Know Your Users and Manage
   Expectations   38

Where Do You Begin? The Engineering Story   38

Understand Your Infrastructure   39

   PBX Infrastructure   40
   Data Infrastructure   40

IP Telephony Readiness   41

Plan the Dial Plan   42

Plan for Growth   43

CallManager Server Location and Placement   44

   Environmental Concerns   44
   Security Concerns   45
   Floor Plan Concerns   45

Best Practices: Evaluating the PBX Infrastructure   46

Best Practices: Evaluating the Data Infrastructure   47

Best Practices: Plan the Dial Plan   48

Best Practices: CallManager Server Location   49

CallManager Today   49

Resources   52

Summary   52

**Appendix 2-A: AVVID Tiger Team Roles and
   Responsibilities   53**

Executive Sponsor   53

Steering Committee   53

Tiger Team Lead   54

AVVID Program Manager   54

Core Tiger Team   55

AVVID Engineering   57

LAN Team   57

Theater Implementation Managers—Corporate, Americas,
Field Sales Offices, EMEA, Asia Pacific   58

Remote Field Office-Theater Implementation PM
Responsibilities—Countdown to Cutover   59

Support Track Lead   61

Finance Track Lead   62

Appendix 2-B: Project Planning Flowchart   62

Appendix 2-C: Voice of the Client Survey   63

**Appendix 2-D: General Preimplementation Considerations
Checklist   66**

Design Considerations   66

If You Have Legacy PBXs   67

Call Flow   67

Sites   68

User Population   68

LAN   70

WAN   72

Analog Connectivity   74

Digital Connectivity   74

Dial Plan   75

Third-Party Special Features   76

Features   77

Voice Mail   79

Chapter 3   **The Migration Strategy   83**

Hold Planning Workshop   84

A Phased Approach   86

New Employees   87

Relocations (Adds, Moves, Changes)   87

Existing Buildings   88

New Buildings   88

Best Practices: A Phased Approach   90

Optimize Project Pace and Schedule   90

Establish Milestones   91

Work Closely with Technology Team   91

Remove Obstacles   92

Develop Vendor Relationships   93

Identify an Operations Center   93

Best Practices: Optimize Project Pace and Schedule   94

The Communication Plan   95

Develop the Communication Strategy   96

Initiate a Project Website   96

Create E-Mail Aliases   97

Best Practices: Communication Plan   99

Identify Business-Critical Phone Users   100

Business-Critical Phone Users   101

Call Center Agents   101

Best Practices: Business-Critical Phone Users   102

Converting "Executive Row"   103

Engage Your Sponsor   104

Visual Confirmation of Phone Configuration   104

Plan the Schedule   105

Provide Additional Support   105

Best Practices: Converting Executive Row   106

User Training   108

Use the Operations Center   109

Best Practices: User Training   110

Identify Operational Policy Changes   111

Modem/Analog Policy   112

Bill's "Clean Network" Theory   112

Operational Security Policy   113

Emergency Phone Lines   113

Best Practices: Operational Security Policies   114

Best Practices: Operational Policy Changes   114

The Good, the Bad, and the Ugly   115

Top Ten Things That Can Go Wrong During the
Retrofit   115

Top Ten Things That Will Improve as a Result of the
Retrofit   116

Resources   118

Summary   118

Appendix 3-A: Planning Workshop Template   120

    Executive Requirements and Expectations   120

    Technical Requirements and Expectations   121

    Existing Network Review   122

    Applications and Features   125

    Planning and Strategy   128

    Support   129

Appendix 3-B: Sample Users Conversion Notice   130

Appendix 3-C: Phone Configuration Template   132

Appendix 3-D: Executive Row Checklist   132

Appendix 3-E: User Frequently Asked Questions   134

    IP Phone Support Information   134

    Cisco IP Phones   134

    Troubleshooting   135

Chapter 4   **Implementation   137**

Planning the Implementation: Steps to Success   138

    Step 1: Implementation Planning Phase   138

        Hold Implementation Planning Meeting   139

        Develop Response and Escalation Plan   139

        Verify Customer To-Do List and Action Plan   140

        Prepare Installation Documentation   140

        User Training   140

    Step 2: Project Monitor and Control   141

        Status Reporting   141

        Change Management   141

        Issue/Risk Management   141

        Quality Control   141

    Step 3: Site Preparation   142

        Validate Site Specification   142

        Complete Site Survey   143

        Prepare Site   143

        Site Verification   143

    Step 4: Install and Configure   143

        Stage Hardware/Software   143

        Install Server Software   144

        Load, Configure, Integrate, and Test Client Software   145

        Network Implementation Plan Acceptance   145

Step 5: Test and Acceptance   146

  Test the Solution   146

  Conduct a Prelaunch Test   146

  Network Ready-for-Use Acceptance   146

Step 6: Knowledge Handoff   147

  Train the Administrator   147

  Perform End-User Training   147

  Hold Cisco TAC or Day 2 Handoff Meeting   148

Step 7: Closeout   148

  *Perform an Internal Review to Determine Lessons
  Learned   148*

  Create TAC Transition Documentation   148

  Project Acceptance   149

The Cisco LAN Infrastructure   149

Standardization   150

QoS on the Cisco IT Network   151

Inline Power   153

Security   154

The Results   154

Best Practices: LAN   155

Preparing the WAN   156

Bandwidth   156

Software and Hardware Upgrades   157

Best Practices: WAN   158

Category 5/Category 3 Wiring, Cabling Requirements   159

  Cable Distance and Wall Phones   159

  A Simplified Process   160

Power, Rack Space, and Ordering Circuits   161

Best Practices: Network Provisioning   162

Provisioning the VLAN   162

Best Practices: Provisioning the VLAN   163

Connecting to Voice Mail   163

Site Survey   164

Best Practices: Site Survey   165

The Implementation   165

Boss/Admin Phone Configurations   166

System Admin Tools   167

Exporting Existing Phones   167

Bulk Administrative Tool/Scanner   168

Phone Installation Test Procedures   169

Removal of Stations from PBX   170

Postponing Adds, Moves, and Changes   170

Retrofit Implementation Guide   171

Staffing Required for Retrofit Team   172

    Move Team   172

    Retrofit Team   173

Implementation Schedule   174

Project Risk Assessment   175

Best Practices: Implementation   176

Customer Service   177

Best Practices: Customer Service   179

Resources   179

Summary   180

Appendix 4-A: Project Planning Flowchart   181

Appendix 4-B: Implementation Planning Template   182

Appendix 4-C: Site Survey Template   182

Appendix 4-D: LAN Upgrade Test Procedures   182

Appendix 4-E: Implementation Checklist   183

Appendix 4-F: Retrofit Implementation Guide   184

General Phone Information   185

Cutsheet Requirements   185

    Analog Phones   185

    IP Phones   186

    IP Phone Naming Standards   186

    Analog Phone Naming Standards   187

    Call Restriction Standards   187

Operations Retrofit Process   187

    Documents Prior to Walkthrough   187

    Walkthrough   188

    Spreadsheet Cleanup   189

    Friday Switch Work   189

    PBX Cleanup   190

Add IP Phone   190

Add Analog Phone   191

Phone Tests   191

    Outgoing Call Tests   *191*
    Incoming Call Tests   *192*

IP Phone Spreadsheet Creation Procedures   192

    Cutsheet Cleanup   *192*
    BAT Users Worksheet Creation   *192*
    BAT Phones Worksheet Creation   *193*

BAT Import Procedures   193

    Create BAT Phone Import Files   *193*
    User BAT Phone Import Files   *194*
    Running BAT   *194*

Restricted Phone Configuration Procedures   195

Miscellaneous Phone Installation Notes   195

    Floor Walkthrough Checklist   *195*

Wall Phone Wiring Punchdown   196

Headset Support   196

Boss/Admin Phone Configurations   196

    Standard Boss/Admin: Two Phones with One Line Ringing on Both Phones   *198*
    Standard Boss/Admin in Two Locations (Four Phones Total)   *199*
    Known Boss/Admin Feature Limitations   *199*

Voice-Mail Only Configurations   200

Troubleshooting Cisco IP Phones   200

War Room FAQ   201

Retrofit Project FAQ   201

Sample Retrofit Issues Log Report   202

Appendix 4-G: Cisco IP Phone Test Procedure   203

Appendix 4-H: IP Telephony Retrofit Efficiency Report   204

Appendix 4-I: IP Telephony Retrofit Project Gantt Chart   205

Appendix 4-J: Sample Project Plan   212

Appendix 4-K: Sample Project Schedule   212

Appendix 4-L: Project Risk Assessment Table   217

Chapter 5   **Day 2 Handoff and Support   219**
In Mike's Own Words...   220
The Support Team   221
   Tier 1   221
   Tier 2   223
   Tier 3   224
   Support Manager   225
   Training   226
   Certification   226
   AVVID Boot Camp   227
   Documentation   228
   Best Practices: The Support Team   229
The Support Process   229
   Tiered Support   230
The Support Tools   232
   Best Practices: The Support Process   232
   Network Management   232
   Clarify Reporting   234
   CallManager Monitoring/EMAN   235
   Monitoring Tools   237
      Microsoft Performance Monitor   237
      Microsoft Event Viewer   237
      CallManager   238
      Sniffer Trace   238
   Troubleshooting   238
Power Backup   239
Serviceability—Five 9s   240
   Device File Backups and Recovery   242
Support Frequently Asked Questions   244
Resources   245
Summary   245
Appendix 5-B: Cisco CallManager 3.2 Software Upgrade
   Checklist   246

Chapter 6   **Final Piece of the Conversion   251**

But We're Not Done Yet   253

Change Management   253

    Critical Steps for Creating a Change Management
        Process   255

        Planning for Change   255
        Managing Change   256

    High-Level Process Flow for Planned Change
        Management   256

        Scope   257
        Risk Assessment   257
        Test and Validation   259
        Change Planning   261
        Change Controller   262
        Change Management Team   263
        Communication   264
        Implementation Team   264
        Test Evaluation of Change   265
        Network Management Update   266
        Documentation   266

    High-Level Process Flow for Emergency Change
        Management   267

        Issue Determination   268
        Limited Risk Assessment   269
        Communication   269
        Documentation   269
        Implementation   270
        Test and Evaluation   270

    Performance Indicators for Change Management   271

        *Change Management Metrics by Functional
        Group   271*
        Targeting Change Success   272
        Change History Archive   272
        Change Planning Archive   272
        Configuration Change Audit   272
        *Periodic Change Management Performance
        Meeting   273*

    Quarter End Freeze   273

Best Practices: Change Management   274

Software Upgrades   274

Best Practices: Software Upgrades   276

Disaster Recovery   277

Best Practices: Disaster Recovery   278

PBX Lease Returns   280

Best Practices: PBX Lease Returns   281

Vendor Rules of Engagement   282

Best Practices: Vendor Rules of Engagement   283

Nonleased Equipment Disposal   283

Retrofit Cleanup   285

Preparing Your Network for the Future   286

Operate Phase   288

Step One: System Management   289

Step Two: Change Management   291

Step Three: Performance Management   292

Optimize Phase   293

Step One: Optimization Planning   293

Step Two: Optimization Execution   294

**Cisco IP Communications Services and Support
Programs   295**

Lessons Learned   302

Communication   302

Team/Relationships   302

Planning/Strategy   303

Strategic Placement of Equipment   304

Understand Current Environment   305

Technology   305

Operations   306

Resources   306

Summary   307

Chapter 7   **Moving Forward: Continuing to Be Cisco's First and
Best Customer   309**

Looking Back and Moving Forward   310

PBX Removal Complete   312

   What's Next for Cisco   314

Cisco IP Contact Center Migration   317

   How We Started   318

   Site Deployment Design   321

   Implementation Approach   322

   Challenges   324

   Design Solutions   325

   Results   325

   Benefits   326

Cisco Wireless LAN Migration   328

   Pilot Testing   329

   Architectural Standards   329

   Results   330

   Next Steps   331

Maintaining Five-9s on the New Network   334

Cisco Unity Voice Mail Migration   335

   Global Implementation Strategy   336

      Global Implementation—Phase 1   336

      Cisco Unity Architecture Summary   337

   Cisco Unity Architecture (Pre/Post)   338

Conclusion   340

   What It Has Meant to Me… A Few Words from the
     Author   340

   And Now… A Word from Our Sponsors   341

   Lessons Learned   342

      Communication   342

      Team/Relationships   342

      Planning/Strategic   342

      Strategic Placement of Equipment   342

      Understand the Current Environment   343

      Migration Strategy   343

      Technology   343

      Process   343

      Operations   344

      Optimize   344

      Get the Project Team Thinking   344

Appendix 7-A: Stephanie's Checklist of Questions to Ask the Project Team   344

Planning   345

Design   347

Implementation   348

Operate   349

Optimizations   351

Appendix A   Customer Concerns   353

Glossary   357

Index   365

Icons Used in This Book

 Communication Server

 PC

 PC with Software

 Sun Workstation

 Macintosh

 Access Server

 Token Ring

 Terminal

 File Server

 Web Server

 Cisco Works Workstation

 Modem

 Printer

 Laptop

 IBM Mainframe

 Front End Processor

 Cluster Controller

 Third-party H.323 Server

 Gateway

 Router

 Bridge

 Hub

 DSU/CSU

 FDDI

 Catalyst Switch

 Multilayer Switch

 ATM Switch

 ISDN/Frame Relay Switch

 Cisco CallManager

Network Cloud

Line: Ethernet

Line: Serial

Line: Switched Serial

 Voice mail server
MOH server
SW conference bridge
MTP
Microsoft NetMeeting

Stations

 Cisco IP Phone

 Gateway
Gatekeeper
HW Conference bridge
Transcoder
Analog gateway
H.323 gateway
DHCP
DNS
Voice-enabled router

POTS Phone

Cisco IP Phone 30 VIP

Foreword

IP Telephony: The Next Frontier in the Emergence of IT

In a world where cost reduction and doing more with less have become the norm, organizations continue to seek ways of increasing efficiencies and enhancing employee productivity while sustaining ever-higher standards for customer satisfaction. That is a tall order, but one made much easier with the right tools, products, services, best practices, and methodologies all working in concert.

In a recent study sponsored by Cisco (Net Impact Study, found at http://business.cisco.com), it was found that Internet business solutions helped the 2000 U.S. organizations surveyed to increase revenues by approximately U.S. $444 billion and reduce costs by U.S. $155 billion in the past three years. This astonishing discovery was attributed to improvements in customer care as well as back-office Internet solutions that introduced production and distribution efficiencies, reducing both logistical and labor costs.

Internet technology has become the greatest business enabler of our time, and one that Cisco has embraced since its inception. Cisco has always made a practice of using its own technology, and in 2000, we began migrating our existing PBX systems to a converged voice and data network to test and strengthen what we felt was a technology that would change telecommunications. Overlaying IP Telephony over an already robust system while incorporating applications such as e-learning, videoconferencing, and communications was simply the next logical and necessary frontier.

The phased migration was rolled out worldwide to 40,000 Cisco employees. The San Jose campus—consisting of nearly 20,000 employees—was completed within just 12 months. During the course of the deployment, we learned three fundamental lessons that led to the success of this massive project. First, we treated IP Telephony not as a phone replacement, but as another vertical application that would fit into our overall IT strategy and complement a compliant, common infrastructure. Second, using mostly existing staff, we created a cross-functional implementation team that consisted of key constituents representing not only IT, but also each of our business units, sales, global theaters, services and support, and others who were recognized as stakeholders. Finally, we focused on what was really behind the deployment—the people—and how IP Telephony would impact them.

Although the needs of every enterprise are different, some things are universal. Planning, communication, teamwork, and understanding your user's requirements are as important as technical expertise. The purpose of this book is not to tell you how to technically architect your own network. The intent is to provide best practices learned throughout the Cisco experience with phased migration to a converged voice and data network enabled by the interoperability of Cisco Architecture for Voice, Video and Integrated Data (AVVID) IP Telephony.

—Lance Perry, vice president of Worldwide IT infrastructure, Cisco Systems, Inc.

How the Cisco Story Benefits You

Learning from those who have already climbed the mountain makes the journey much easier for those who are still scaling the wall. Integrating our own products and technologies throughout our organization underscores our commitment to the Cisco technology and enables us to help our customers with solutions that provide maximum benefit. Whether it is migrating our entire organization to an e-business strategy, implementing wireless LAN into all corporate facilities, piloting our SN5420 storage router, or installing our IP contact center solution into Cisco locations around the world, we have mandated that we will always be our own first and best customer.

In October 2000, an enterprise-wide deployment of IP Telephony began at the San Jose campus. Within the next 12 months, 55 buildings and nearly 20,000 users spread out over a 2-mile radius were converted. This was the largest deployment of LAN infrastructure and IP Telephony in industry history. The program charter was to implement our own AVVID technology solution 12 to 18 months ahead of our external customers to develop business models that would demonstrate return on investment (ROI), complete technology proof of concept, and processes for support and deployment of IP Telephony.

Cisco IP Telephony offers an immediate ROI by reducing total cost of network ownership through one converged network. Savings are even further realized through reduced equipment and infrastructure cost, increased productivity, and much easier network management. The financial impact of the internal Cisco initiative encompasses significant annual savings in competitor-leased equipment and PBX maintenance cost, to name just a few.

However, to extract the maximum benefit from an enterprise-wide IP Telephony initiative, careful and comprehensive planning before the actual implementation are critical. Whether it involves 200 phones or 20,000 phones, planning, communication, teamwork, and knowing where the "gotchas" are hiding will divert problems before they occur, reducing unnecessary costs and headaches that can hinder a successful implementation.

The voices in this book come from an experienced team of project managers, engineers, operations personnel, and support teams who completed the conversion of the Cisco San Jose, California campus to IP Telephony. This book focuses not on the technology, but on the planning and business processes associated with a large IP Telephony implementation. Our hope is that by sharing our experience, we can help our customers plan and realize the value of a converged, IP-enabled network.

—Manny Rivelo, senior vice president of worldwide field process and operations, Cisco Systems

Introduction

New technology can challenge even the most technically savvy users. In the case of IP Telephony, as with any new technology that Cisco offers, we test its usage, prove its value, and experience first hand what our customers will experience by deploying it throughout our own organization.

In 2000, I was assigned the role of team lead project manager and tasked with developing a plan to migrate the 55 Cisco buildings and more than 20,000 phones located on the San Jose Campus—within 12 months!

IP Telephony was new technology at the time, and as such, I had no one's previous experience to lean on that could help me prepare for what I needed to do. There were no best practices, templates, or guides that offered a framework on how to get started. Our team learned as it went along, and during the migration process, I kept copious notes of the processes the team created. I knew that one day customers would want to know how Cisco did what it did and what was learned along the way.

After we completed the migration, we began to receive numerous requests to share our story and offer best practices that would help customers with their own impending migration. The message was consistent. Concerns centered less on the technology than on the business processes and support services, such as how to get the organization onboard, where to begin, how to build a team, and what could be done to ensure things were done right the first time.

The motivation for writing *The Road to IP Telephony: How Cisco Systems Migrated from PBX to IP Telephony* begins and ends with our customers. This book tells the story of the Cisco experience of migrating from a PBX circuit-switched network to IP Telephony. It provides a comprehensive view of a successful IP Telephony network deployment from the early planning stages through the final retrofit cleanup. It documents our experience; provides tips; and delivers templates, tools, and resources that became invaluable to the migration team as Cisco began the journey into the new world of IP Telephony. You will learn what you need to address even before you begin the planning process.

We offer strategies for building the right project team, explain the importance of setting the pace and schedule, and show you how to get your users on board. You will be able to identify a migration strategy, learn how to manage user expectations, and develop a training and communication plan. For post-implementation, you will learn how we developed a services and support model that included Day 2 handoff and how to plan your network for the future. Finally, you will learn how we handled the final PBX decommission.

We hope you will use this book to learn from our mistakes, leverage our best practices, and customize the tools and templates we have created to make your own migration a smooth one. There is no better path to successful implementation than to follow in the footsteps of those who have already been there, learned what worked and what did not work along the way, and developed a methodology that has proven successful.

Goals and Methods

"Just get it done" no longer works in today's complex world—a world with limited resources where business operatives depend on technological solutions that achieve productivity, efficiency, and customer satisfaction goals. Working smarter, not harder is the new directive.

The purpose of any enterprise-wide initiative is to ensure that it is consistent with the goals of the organization. Doing it right and keeping those goals in sight is even more critical than adhering to a tightly orchestrated schedule with little room for flexibility.

The implementation team successfully upgraded the company's entire desktop LAN infrastructure, removing 22 Expansion Port Network (EPN) PBXs and 10,000 old-world phones that we counted, packaged, and returned along with 2500 ancillary parts and components. Five CallManager clusters with 8 servers each, along with 500 Catalyst 6000 and Catalyst 3500 switches, were installed during the initial upgrade.

We knew that we would run into issues that were inherent with introducing any type of new technology or process change. We knew that users would experience emotions ranging from anxiety and confusion to resistance and refusal. Finally, we knew that without the right planning—including the right skill sets, tools, and processes—the initiative could quickly spiral out of control.

By taking the time upfront to plan the implementation strategy, understand the impact that the technology would have on its users, and put together a carefully chosen deployment team, the initiative was one of the greatest successes for Cisco.

This book will help you to develop the right planning strategy to deploy new technology. It offers a winning formula for success. The following are key highlights and benefits of *The Road to IP Telephony: How Cisco Systems Migrated from PBX to IP Telephony.*

- "Must-have" reference book for the entire project team on how to deploy IP Telephony

- An A to Z account of everything you should know about deploying IP Telephony

- Easy-to-read chronicle of steps that both a beginner and an expert could follow and find value in

- More than 200 best practices and lessons learned that every IP implementation team lead should know

- An honest summary of the good, the bad, and the ugly of deploying IP Telephony, written from an IT project manager's point of view

- Real-world proven solutions that adhere to a PDIOO model

- Key business processes and deployment methodologies that do not cover the highly technical elements that have been documented in other books

- Real customer concerns in which 200+ presentations/interviews on the subject were derived

- Invaluable guidance from an experienced team of people who have undertaken the world's largest IP Telephony migration in the industry

This book is a collaboration of the top project managers, design engineers, support team, CCIEs, technical marketing engineers, and systems engineers at Cisco Systems.

Who Should Read This Book?

The voices in this book come from an experienced team of project managers, engineers, operations personnel, and support teams who completed the industry's largest IP Telephony conversion in the world. The Cisco internal IP Telephony deployment taught the project team a valuable lesson. We learned early that a successful IP Telephony deployment was not just about the technology; rather, it was about the people and the process. Also, regardless of whether your deployment includes 200 phones or 20,000 phones, the same commitment to standards and processes apply. This book attempts to uncover the many questions that keep decision makers, executives, and project managers up at night. It was designed for the following audience:

- Voice network decision makers: CEO, CFO, CTO, COO, CIO, and other members of senior management, planning, design, implementation, and operations (telecom managers, PBX engineers, LAN network teams, senior project management, and members of the voice services team).

- Any required knowledge/experience assumed: Basic understanding of voice networks.

- Level of experience: This book was designed for easy reading and includes information that anyone, from a beginner to an expert, can comprehend and use.

- Audience:

  — **Primary**—Small, medium, and large enterprises, small and midsize business owners, service providers of all types, and Cisco partners and resellers who are considering or have decided to migrate to the Cisco IP Telephony solution

  — **Secondary**—Telecom consultants, IP Telephony software developers, and any other IT or telecom professional who is looking to buy, implement, or sell IP Telephony solutions

  — **Other**—Sales teams, account managers, and voice specialists who are delivering the IP Telephony solution and need a better understanding of how the implementation will affect an organization, along with the processes and tools that should be in place

How This Book Is Organized

Reading this book cover to cover will provide the entire voice services team with an end-to-end view of the complete migration strategy. However, this book was designed to be flexible and allow team members to move easily between chapters and sections of chapters that cover just the material that is relevant to them. Each of the seven chapters addresses an evolution within the process.

Chapter 1, "A Cisco Evolution," includes the background on why Cisco decided to migrate to an all-IP network, features a discussion on ROI, and describes the architectural evolution from the beginning of the migration.

Chapter 2, "Before You Begin," discusses items that you need to address before you begin the planning process. It addresses the importance of procuring executive sponsorship, discusses the elements that enabled the Cisco team to effectively manage change, provides a preliminary engineering overview, and introduces the Cisco cross-functional AVVID Tiger Team.

Chapter 3, "The Migration Strategy," covers the planning process. It takes you through the Cisco experience of developing the migration strategy and project plan, setting the pace and schedule for the implementation team, overcoming the challenges and cautions of converting senior management's "executive row," discovering the importance of a comprehensive communication plan, and identifying and addressing user training and operational policy changes. This chapter also highlights the top ten things that can go wrong without proper planning, as well as the top ten things that will improve as a result of the retrofit.

Chapter 4, "Implementation," provides the tactical elements of the implementation, including LAN infrastructure requirements, identification of wiring and cabling requirements, phone configurations, ordering of circuits, the Retrofit Implementation Guide, and other helpful system admin tools that the Cisco team employed.

Chapter 5, "Day 2 Handoff and Support," covers the operations and support phase. In this chapter, you will learn how the Cisco tiered support model provides 24×7 support, which support tools to use, how to monitor the network, and what happens during the Day 2 handoff. In addition, this section addresses the auxiliary VLANs and power backup, managing and maintaining the network, troubleshooting tips, and support FAQs.

Chapter 6, "Final Piece of the Conversion," uncovers the optimization phase and the final piece of the conversion. Here, you will learn about software upgrades, disaster recovery planning, PBX lease returns, and the final retrofit cleanup. Also included is a discussion on preparing your network for the future. Chapter 6 concludes with a collection of lessons that members of the Cisco IP Telephony Tiger Team learned.

Chapter 7, "Moving Forward: Continuing to be Cisco's First and Best Customer," discusses how all well-planned technological initiatives are continuous evolutions. This chapter discusses the changes that were made in the year since the conversion was completed. It brings Cisco forward by outlining the additional technologies that Cisco has rolled out as a result of its initial IP Telephony migration and the benefits of a converged, IP-enabled network. In addition, Chapter 7 includes key questions for your project team.

The Road to IP Telephony: How Cisco Systems Migrated from PBX to IP Telephony will provide you with more than 200 tips, lessons learned, best practices, and resource links, along with several appendixes that you can download and tailor to meet the specific needs of your implementation requirements. You will find references to various Cisco tools, templates, sample documents, website links, and other resource materials that Cisco used and that you might find helpful in your own conversion.

| NOTE | To help you keep track of all the various steps involved in managing your migration, we have provided a link to a PDIOO poster to serve as a visual reminder of the steps to success you should consider throughout your IP Telephony engagement. The poster exists online under the original ISBN: ciscopress.com/1587200800 under the downloads link. This is a "must-have" tool for every member of the project team. To make it easier for the reader, the poster also outlines where within the book you can find additional details concerning the various steps. |

CHAPTER 1

A Cisco Evolution

IP Telephony replaces standard public switched telephone (PSTN) networks (PBX), using the Internet to send audio between two or more users in real time and allowing users to communicate via an IP telephone. Replacing conventional circuit-switched technology with a more cost-effective and efficient packet-based architecture, the Cisco Architecture for Voice, Video and Integrated Data (AVVID) transmits data, voice, and video over a single network infrastructure.

With 23 Expansion Port Network (EPN) PBXs coming up for renewal throughout the various Cisco facilities, the organization needed to make the decision whether to renew the leases or to migrate its phone system to IP Telephony. After conducting a return on investment (ROI) analysis and determining that it would be much more cost effective to migrate, Cisco began to put the team together to develop the processes that would ensure a smooth transition.

The Cisco AVVID network infrastructure is the foundation that is essential for rapid and seamless deployment of emerging technologies such as IP Telephony and other new and evolving Internet business solutions across the enterprise. Built on the Cisco AVVID network infrastructure, the AVVID IP Telephony solution brings the promise of high-quality IP voice and fully integrated communications to fruition by allowing data, voice, and video to be transmitted over a single network infrastructure.

Cisco has always been its own "first best customer," integrating its own technologies typically at least 18 months ahead of market requirements as well as using that opportunity to test and build new feature requirements.

Operational Benefits of Cisco IP Telephony

From a user's standpoint, Cisco looked to IP Telephony to increase personal and workgroup productivity, improve its ability to respond to customers, and reduce operational costs. Because the IP phone registers itself whenever it is moved, users can take their phones with them, creating a virtual office by plugging into spare data wall jacks and receiving calls regardless of their current location. They can access and self-manage their own set of phone services while maintaining one phone number. Also, because IP Telephony uses the same standards as data communications, both PCs and phones can access voice mail, check e-mail, view video broadcasts, and enable other IP Telephony applications on the same shared network.

For network managers, the process of managing a converged voice and data network becomes a much simpler task. Centralized voice services provide the ability to extend the functionality of the corporate IP voice, video, and data solutions to remote office locations without having to invest heavily in additional infrastructure and software for the remote offices. This gives the central office (CO) a greater degree of control over what is added to the network and ensures greater systems integration and security.

In addition, the cost of relocating a phone or changing phone numbers when an employee moves—a significant expense that can cost up to U.S. $90 per phone—is eliminated. Also, because IP Telephony is a software application, enhancing its capabilities in a production environment is a matter of upgrading software on the server platform, thereby avoiding expensive hardware upgrade costs.

Table 1-1 demonstrates the cost reduction and operational savings generated by the streamlined process of managing and facilitating IP telephone adds, moves, and changes.

Table 1-1 *IP Telephony Impact on Adds, Moves, and Changes: San Jose Campus IT/ Telecom Savings: Fiscal Year 2002 (August Through June)*

Type	Volume	Unit*	Savings
Project moves	3,625	$3.00	$11,244
Individual moves	784	$50.00	$6,150
Adds (new hires/configurations)	5,852	$50.00	$440,300
	5,852	$0.00	$0.00
			$457,694
WPR Savings**			
Reduction of contracted services to support MACs			
	Fiscal Year 2001	Fiscal Year 2002	
Type of Service	**Average $/Move**	**Average $/Move**	**Savings**
Disconnect/reconnect systems support	$39.38	$3.62	$153,503
(Approximately 91 percent of expense reduced)			
Other Benefits	Move process time shortened Zero downtime of phones Higher client satisfaction Integration of resources		

*Cost variance between IP and non-IP MACs
** WPR = WorkPlace Resources

Cisco calculated efficiencies in both resource and cost savings based on the following time-division multiplexing (TDM) market assumptions:

- From 250 to 10,000 phones at one site per month

- PBX maintenance—U.S. $3.50 to U.S. $2.50 per port with 33 percent ports, not phones

- Move/add/change activity—U.S. $90 per move/add/change (110 percent of phones at Cisco move each year)

- Voice mail support—U.S. $2.20 to U.S. $0.90 cents per phone

- Software upgrade support—U.S. $0.44 cents per phone

- PSTN support and coordination—U.S. $0.50 cents per phone

- LAN/WAN support—U.S. $5.00 to U.S. $0.25 cents per phone

Factoring in the preceding assumptions, the IP Telephony Remote Network Management (RNM), the service that monitors the IP Telephony network remotely, was identified as further reducing ongoing total cost of ownership due to IP Telephony eliminating support overhead and combining LAN/WAN, PSTN, and PBX support, as shown in Table 1-2.

Table 1-2   *Impact on Total Cost of Ownership*

PBX Support Comparison	Traditional TDM PBX Support	IP Telephony-RNM Telephony
PBX maintenance	Maintenance fees	Cisco SMARTnet
Upgrade support	Sold separately	Cisco SAS
PBX management	Dispatch or labor	Included
Move/adds/changes	Dispatch or labor	Included
PSTN management	Not included	Included
LAN management	Not included	Included
Remote site management	Not included	Included
Infrastructure changes	Not included	Priced separately

Ongoing support is made much easier with the migration to IP Telephony, and relative costs are reduced significantly. Figure 1-1 provides a view of the expected ongoing support costs for PBX versus IP Telephony.

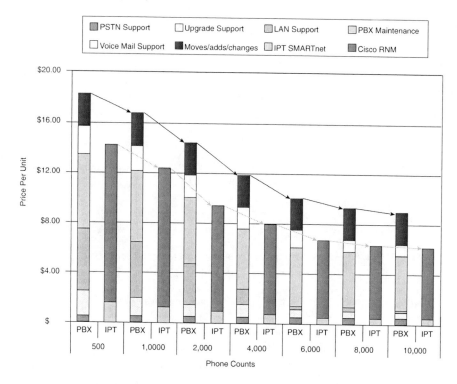

Figure 1-1   *Ongoing Support Costs for PBX and IP Telephony*

ROI

One of the first and possibly most difficult questions that companies face when determining whether to invest in a new technology is whether there will be sufficient benefits and returns for the required investment and, if so, how much impact they will have. Like most companies, Cisco requires a positive business case or financial justification for funds to be approved for any major investment.

However, ROI calculations should be only one aspect of the measurement system. Other factors, such as business, operational, and adoption impact, must be taken into consideration as well. In addition, reporting only on metrics that directly relate to the initiative's success is critical. IT organizations sometimes measure projects in ways that do not directly assess the project's contribution to business goals, making it difficult for senior management to assess the value of the initiative and provide the necessary sponsorship for its success.

Cisco developed a simple ROI measurement system that enabled IT to assess the viability of the IP Telepohony implementation. The measurement system included the following factors:

- **Financial**—Reduction of wide-area facility requirements; fewer devices to manage and maintain; simpler adds, moves, and changes; and lowered overhead cost associated with simplified and converged infrastructure

- **Operational metrics**—Availability, performance, and error rates

- **Business metrics**—Cost savings, satisfaction, cycle-time acceleration, transaction response times, availability, and error rates

- **Adoption metrics**—Adoption rates and overall employee satisfaction with the new system

"An important part of any ROI objective is to weigh the risks of implementing the initiative versus not implementing it," said Lynnee Jimenez, Cisco IT finance manager. "We weighed the benefits—strategic and financial—and asked ourselves what the overall justifications were versus the alternatives we considered."

This necessary emphasis on frugality leads to renewed importance on the performance of ROI calculations. Chris Kozup, a senior research analyst for Meta Group, points out that in the generous economic environment of past years, executives would cite general ROI expectations for technology implementations. Now, says Kozup, executives are pressed to pinpoint more specific ROI targets, such as those for a 12-month or 24-month period, with a clearly stated "time to ROI" target.

In an effort to identify specific ROI factors, Cisco began by committing all new building openings to one set of wiring standards. All upcoming PBX leases were terminated when they came up for renewal, and all new employees were issued an IP phone right from the start.

Cisco addressed several variables during the IP Telepohony deployment to calculate ROI. Each variable was categorized by either hard or soft cost factors. Hard cost factors included areas where quantifiable "account balance" results could be identified and measured. Soft cost factors, although not as quantifiable in measurable dollars, still impact savings realized through efficiencies and increased productivity. Table 1-3 documents the hard and soft cost factors identified during and after the migration.

Table 1-3   *Hard Cost Factors and Soft Cost Factors for IP Telephony Deployment*

Hard Cost Factors	Soft Cost Factors
Drastically reduces cabling requirements for new site openings.	Increased proficiencies—Adds, moves, and changes are simple, quick, and efficient.
Incurs less cost and time to perform adds, moves, and changes, as well as fewer personnel to support.	New employee IP phone allocations are efficient and easy to manage, despite enormous growth.
Eliminates PBX maintenance cost.	Increased productivity—Employees use the technology to be more self-sufficient.
Eliminates leased equipment cost.	Increased mobility—Workplace sharing ratio enables employees to plug in and work wherever they happen to be—at home, in multiple offices, in conference rooms, and so on.
Eliminates PBX system cost (phones, line cards, trunk cards, system software, user licenses, and so on).	Leveraged resources—Both voice and data staff provide IP Telephony support.
Reduces toll-bypass and network carrier costs.	
Eliminates costly hardware PBX expansion port cost to accompany fast growth.	
Encourages virtual office space design because of maximum use of real estate space.	

You can use the Cisco ROI calculator to calculate the ROI for your Cisco IPT solution. You can find the calculator at http://www.cisco.com/warp/public/779/video/iptv/roicalc/.

Where It All Started

The greatest challenge for Cisco throughout the entire IP Telephony deployment was probably that the technology at that time was new to the industry, and voice running over the data network was still new to Cisco. "This originally started out when Cisco acquired Selsius Systems, a company that provides network PBX systems for high-quality telephony over an IP network," says Dennis Silva, voice services senior network design and engineer. "The scariest thing for us back then was that, not only was it new to us, there had never been an IP Telephony deployment that involved more than 50 phones in production anywhere in the world. The technology was still in development, and most of the Selsius deployments had all taken place in a lab environment."

Silva and his team were tasked with learning the technology quickly and then conducting a pilot within Cisco. "We tested the technology and then deployed about 100 phones within the IT department to run a carefully monitored trial for a period of time."

Cisco Architecture in the Beginning

The first challenge the team identified was the lack of voice mail integration. Minimizing user discomfort during the migration was of utmost importance, and being able to keep the user's existing phone number and voice mail was high on the "must have" list. "To accommodate this, we came up with a Simple Message Desktop Interface (SMDI) because we knew Selsius supported SMDI," Silva says. "Although they had never used SMDI and had never integrated with Octel, they did have that particular type of interface. So we purchased an Octel 350, dedicated it with a CallManager, and assigned all new employees to this dedicated CallManager." This prevented the necessity of integrating with the PBX and Octel systems.

"Then we decided to put new users on the CallManager software release 2.3 and use the SMDI integration to an Octel 350, under the assumption that we were going to break this system at, say, 500 users," Silva continues. "We had a commitment from the business unit that we could put 500 users on there. However, by the time we got to 500 users, no doubt we'd be on CallManager 3.0, which was the latest software upgrade; we'd have an Octel solution, and all of our problems would be solved."

But like many best-laid plans, that did not happen. The rollout had begun with the first test success, and by the time the team could catch its breath, it was managing 2500 users. "It kind of got out of hand because of Cisco's rapid growth. All new employees were being given IP phones when they started," Silva says. "So here we were with a new system that had never been tested for more than 200 people, and now we had over ten times that."

However, the development team was able to work through the challenges, and with careful monitoring and management of software releases, the initiative to deploy an IP Telephony solution throughout Cisco hit the ground running and never looked back.

Cisco Architecture Evolution

Figures 1-2 and 1-3 represent the evolution of the Cisco architecture and the migration of the technology. Figure 1-2 provides a view of how the network architecture looked in 2001 at the beginning of the migration. Figure 1-3 demonstrates how calls come in to the network, how they tandem through the PBX, and how voice mail and intercluster calling are performed.

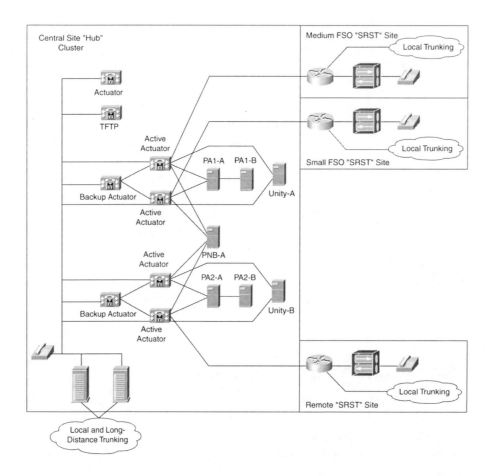

Figure 1-2   *Traffic Flow Example of Voice Mail and Intercluster Calling*

Summary

This chapter provided the background on why Cisco decided to migrate to an all IP network, included a discussion on ROI, and described the architectural evolution from the beginning of the migration to IP Telephony. The chapters that follow will provide you with the knowledge and tools to plan, design, implement, operate, and optimize your IP network.

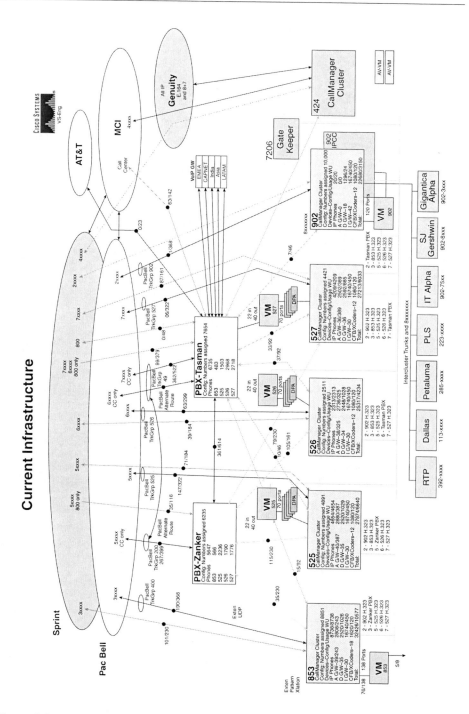

Figure 1-3   *Cisco 2001 San Jose Campus Environment*

CHAPTER 2

BEFORE YOU BEGIN

This chapter details the importance of developing a solid foundation that lays the groundwork for a smooth transition to a converged IP-enabled network. Often the most neglected part of any initiative is the preplanning. Chapter 2 identifies the key elements of successful change management, offers insights on how to overcome barriers, and provides the baseline from which Cisco took the first step. You can find best practices developed from the Cisco experience at the end of each section.

Importance of a Cross-Functional Team

Many components work in combination to effect a well-orchestrated migration to a new technology. However, probably the greatest contributor to the success of the initiative is a cross-functional team that represents all four corners of the organization and includes the requisite skills and technical expertise.

A cross-functional team serves the obvious purpose of ensuring the rapid delivery of initiatives that optimize a company's investments. It also serves the less obvious but equally important purpose of creating an environment that helps to build an organization where cross-functional program management is a core competency.

A cross-functional team is truly the only way to successfully implement a large initiative, especially one involving new technology. Cisco manages its voice network to a five-9s quality standard, which requires that the system be operational 99.999 percent of the time. Because a voice network performs one function—the switching of calls—it is much easier to manage to that high quality standard. Introducing data into the picture can sometimes make this quality standard much more challenging because availability is designed into a distributed system rather than a box.

Because of this multifunctionality, a cross-functional team armed with the proper tools and staffed with team members who understand voice and data and application systems becomes even more critical to sustain the high level of quality that Cisco and its customers demand.

AVVID Tiger Team

The creation of the Architecture for Voice, Video and Integrated Data (AVVID) Tiger Team was in direct response to the company's decision to develop and sell IP Telephony solutions. The Cisco cross-functional Tiger Team led the conversion to Voice over IP (VoIP) with team members chosen for their expertise in various disciplines and functions and representing users in each of the areas impacted by the implementation. For example, a representative from each of the Cisco global offices was chosen to act as team lead to represent the needs of that location.

The Tiger Team lead, whose responsibility was to provide overall direction for the initiative, was also manager of the Cisco voice services operations and held the position of director of strategic program management. In that role, it made logical sense for that individual to also take the lead on helping to build a global cross-functional team that would allow us to step into the role of being the Cisco first, best customer with this new technology.

After the team identified the skill sets that were needed and chose the members of the team, it kicked off the initiative by clearly defining the objective and overall goal of the project and then identifying the tasks that would help meet those goals. The team identified change management challenges and began to develop the components of an enterprise-wide, comprehensive communication plan.

The global team met on a weekly schedule to share status, discuss issues, and create solutions, communicating project updates, roadblocks, and project wins with senior management on a consistent basis.

Roles and Responsibilities

The AVVID Tiger Team was made up of four components:

- The executive sponsor
- The steering committee
- The team managers (consisting of a team lead and a program manager)
- The core team tasked with implementing the rollout

In addition to their roles as team members, employees still held their "day jobs" and needed to maintain their daily operational duties and roles within Cisco. This was challenging, and the dual roles required a high degree of organizational skills and tactical expertise. However, commitment, close adherence to the goals, and priorities were established early on, and a comprehensive communication process made the job easier and more manageable. Figure 2-1 illustrates the AVVID Tiger Team structure.

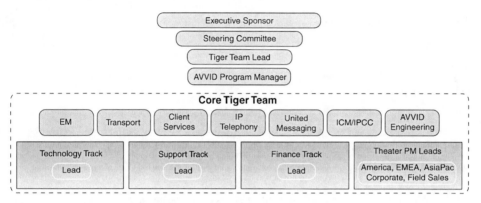

Figure 2-1 *AVVID Tiger Team*

Executive Sponsor

The executive sponsor is typically the highest ranking member of the organization, such as the CEO, president, or other level of authority who will help you resolve high-level issues and gain buy-in from those impacted by the change. It is the executive sponsor's responsibility to communicate the vision, incorporate the objectives of the project with the goals of the company, demonstrate public support for the initiative, and commit the resources required for implementation.

A more in-depth discussion of the importance of an executive sponsor follows this section.

Steering Committee

The steering committee was made up of senior-level executives who could influence the deployment of the project and help resolve issues that arose as a result of the conversion. Members of the AVVID Tiger Team steering committee were vice presidents of IT, marketing, and sales—all individuals who had decision-making authority and helped to keep the project moving forward. The steering committee acted as the centralized customer voice and made certain that user input was prioritized in the rollout.

"Of primary importance is maintaining open and honest communication between the users and the program team," says Manny Rivelo, senior vice president of WW field process and operations. "The steering committee's job was to ensure that that occurred."

Team Lead

The Tiger Team lead focused on building a global cross-functional team that represented voice and data expertise, support, and all the other disciplines required to further the initiative. Working with the Cisco cross-functional IT departments to provide a converged support staff was a paramount concern and primary focus for the Tiger Team.

In stepping into the role of first customer, we partnered closely with the business units to understand what our users needed, prioritize feature requirements, and identify "severity one" problems—those that could take the system down or compromise operations—before the system went live.

Tiger Team Program Manager

The primary role of the Tiger Team program manager was to ensure that product issues, resource issues, and client expectations were addressed and to coordinate all high-level issues that could potentially jeopardize the full conversion of traditional voice to IP Telephony. "Every stage of the process was given a certain priority, depending on product availability and user readiness," comments the Tiger Team program manager. "All of that was compared to the features needed to be successful in the user's daily job."

Core Tiger Team

The core team held responsibility for setting the pace for the deployment as well as carrying out the implementation. The members of the core team needed a high level of organizational skills because they were being asked to balance their primary day-to-day responsibilities with the needs of the team.

Within the core team, four tracks made up the IP Telephony, including technology, support, financial, and global theaters. A track lead was assigned to each track and held accountable for his particular area of responsibility. (See "The Four Project Tracks" later in this chapter for a more in-depth explanation.)

Third-Party Partners

The development of any e-business implementation puts a premium on flexibility and key business competencies within an IT organization. Like many companies, Cisco chose to out-task selected functions, retaining key IT competencies and partnering with third parties to provide those services. The "plug and play" function (also known as the phone installation phase) was outsourced to one of our third-party partners. Not only were they responsible for conducting site surveys and managing moves/adds/changes, but they also coordinated special user configurations.

Ad Hoc Team Members

Some members of the Tiger Team participated only as the need for those resources became necessary. The ad hoc members typically did not attend the weekly project meetings but were added to the distribution list so that they would receive the status reports and remain current with the process and progress of the initiative. The ad hoc team consisted of the following:

- **WorkPlace Resources (WPR)**—Although the members were not experts on the infrastructure, WPR was well versed on the individual buildings on the San Jose campus, as well as the users within those buildings. WPR developed a floor-by-floor spreadsheet of all the users, their phone numbers, and their locations so that we could consolidate it with the data we pulled from the PBX configuration report, verify the information, and identify any gaps. The Tiger Team also developed an automated process and worked with WPR's external moving company to ensure that as the implementation team completed each building, the retrofit equipment was routinely relocated and ready for them when they arrived to begin the implementation of the next building.

- **Facilities Management (FM)**—The Tiger Team worked with FM and Security Operations to halt any adds, moves, and changes at least a week before the conversion so that the data used by the implementation team was current and clean.

- **Security Operations**—Cisco's internal security group worked with the implementation team prior to each building's scheduled implementation to provide access to locked offices and other sensitive areas where new IP phones were to be installed. We included security ops on the distribution update list so they would know ahead of time where the implementation team would be working on a week-by-week basis. This ensured that the "plug-and-play" phase would continue uninterrupted rather than halting the process to wait for the proper authorization.

 Refer to Appendix 2-A, "AVVID Tiger Team Roles and Responsibilities," for an in-depth review of each Tiger Team role, specific tasks, and responsibilities assigned to those roles. This appendix appears at the end of this chapter and is also available at http://www.ciscopress.com/1587200880.

The Four Project Tracks

To provide the required level of technical expertise, ensure that all stakeholders would be represented across the organization, provide a high level of support after handoff, and keep the budget in line, the Tiger Team was segmented into four project tracks as described in the sections that follow.

Technology Track

The technology track was responsible for the architecture and design of new products being introduced into a production environment. These individuals were experts on the Cisco current infrastructure and had a view to the key feature requirements that the organization required. As gatekeepers, they determined when a product was available and ready for implementation, how its functionality would fit into the current Cisco infrastructure, and provided a safe zone where new technology could be demonstrated and tested in a nonproduction (lab) environment.

The technology track team leads were the team's direct link into the business units, providing feedback on how the products could be improved to better fit the Cisco business and infrastructure requirements.

To ensure that the technology track team was well rounded and technically savvy, the eight technology track team leads were chosen for their solid understanding of old-world PBXs, design and engineering, LAN infrastructure, voice dial plans, NT/Windows 2000 expertise, and exposure to Cisco VoIP Telephony.

With the introduction of 12 new Windows 2000 systems running on Microsoft platforms, a Windows 2000 expert was critical. The technology track worked closely with the operations and support track to ensure synergy with architectural recommendations. The goal was to develop a standard template that each theater could follow, with buy-in from design and engineering and operations and support.

The LAN team installed and maintained the network infrastructure that supported IP Telephony and coordinated their schedule to align with the implementation team's highly aggressive schedule. This ensured that the infrastructure would be installed, tested, and operational by the time the implementation team came in to switch out the PBX phones. The LAN infrastructure team stayed one to two weeks ahead of each weekend conversion. Preparing for this in advance and reviewing the entire current infrastructure ahead of time ensured that there would be few surprises.

The design and engineering team consisted of individuals who were familiar with the features of the current PBX technology and voice traffic patterns, as well as the new IP Telephony architecture. This team maximized use of the technology as it was rolled out and developed adjustments to accommodate situations requiring additional infrastructure. On a weekly basis, design and engineering completed CallManager traffic reports and monitored trunking on the PBX and CallManager, a dual tone multifrequency (DTMF) and time-division multiplexing (TDM) load on PBX, and voice mail traffic on PBX.

"Based on the traffic reports, we removed PBX trunking to PSTN as we removed PBX users," said Anthony Garcia, IT AVVID engineer. "We added or removed PBX tie trunking based on the need and moved or managed voice mail facilities from the PBX to the CallManager by adding Digital PBX Adapter (DPA) ports to the CallManager."

The team also managed the load on the PBX Expansion Port Networks (EPNs), depending on the TDM and DTMF results, and then moved the PBX tie to the EPNs with low load. "One thing we learned throughout this process was the importance of traffic reports," Garcia said.

Support Track

The support track managed and implemented the operational support (Day 2 Support) requirements that ensured the ongoing stability and reliability of the network. This team consisted of representatives from design and engineering, transport, LAN and WAN, the product business unit and operations, and a Cisco support partner. The LAN and WAN teams were cross-trained on the principles of IP Telephony so that if an issue arose, individuals were available who were capable of determining if the problem was a LAN issue or a voice issue.

"All of the team members were engaged very early in the process," says Mike Telang, manager of AVVID infrastructure. "They were chosen because of their expertise in all areas of the network to ensure that troubleshooting would be as efficient and nondisruptive as possible."

The initial challenge was bringing the consolidated team up to speed on how to troubleshoot and maintain a converged network. All of our PBX experts were trained on the principles of IP Telephony and later became our strongest IP Telephony senior network engineers. Telephony server management and LAN and WAN IT teams had to converge and work closely because any change made to the network independently would now affect them all. Because the problem could be either LAN or voice, the team also had to understand how any change to one could affect both.

The support track was also responsible for developing the training requirements, identifying the different problem priorities, confirming the design standards dictated by the technology track, and developing an escalation path and a resolution grade. The Cisco support track ensured that the help desk systems, ticket generations, and accountability for all the problems were well documented and implemented.

"We made sure that GTRC (Global Technical Response Center) was involved in the details and ensuring that support prerequisites were built and documented," said Sandy Thompson, GTRC manager. "Their biggest contribution was acting as the client advocate and IT's support advocate, making sure both were considered during process and decision making." (See Chapter 5, "Day 2 Handoff and Support," for an overview of the Cisco support process.)

Financial Track

The Tiger Team financial analyst acted as the gatekeeper of the budget and all funds spent on the project. Because Cisco is such a large organization with more than 400 office buildings located around the world, the financial track ensured that no duplicate equipment or equipment that was not critical to the implementation was purchased, which could have greatly offset the budget.

Just-in-time IT product procurement ensured that inventory did not get out of hand and that depreciation costs were allocated during the process. You do not want 20,000 phones sitting in your warehouse for several months. The financial analyst made sure that budgetary spending stayed on track, the goals of the implementation were in line with the goals of the company, and that our return on investment (ROI) objectives were on target.

"We built financial models and prepared an ad-hoc scenario analysis for team members to make the process easier and more streamlined," says Shelby Roshan, IT financial analyst. "We also prepared and consolidated standard reporting on the program, which included data from each theater on their headcount, capital, and expenses."

Keeping an eye on depreciation factors, upcoming lease renewals, headcount, outside services expenditures, and equipment orders were the financial track's top priorities.

Theater Track

The theater track was the final track of the AVVID core Tiger Team. It maintained responsibility for the deployment of the technology in each theater of the global Cisco organization. The most important role of the theater project managers was to ensure that the needs of the users within their designated locations were met and that everyone followed the same standards, processes, and format.

Understanding and having the ability to analyze the business needs of each organization and communicate that to the rest of the team was also a key function. Meeting weekly with all the theater project managers ensured that best practices and lessons learned were shared across theaters. The meetings fostered a solid understanding of how issues are resolved within the organization and how to use the Cisco culture to drive the implementation locally.

The AVVID Tiger Team's purpose was to enable the overall conversion throughout Cisco to IP Telephony, develop global standards and support procedures, keep the budget in line and goals in sight, and ensure that participation and communication were consistent and effective. "Cisco is an amazing company when we are focused on providing a benefit to the overall organization," says James Robshaw, AVVID Tiger Team program manager. "Everyone rallies together to make even the most difficult times acceptable."

Best Practices: Building a Cross-Functional Team

The list that follows provides some best practices tips on building a cross-functional team:

- Build and retain a strong vision to ensure that everyone is working toward a shared goal.

- Form cross-functional teams composed of key stakeholders across the organization (end users, support, engineering, finance, executive leadership).

- Secure early buy-in from the cross-functional team. This leads to internalization, individual contributions to the goal, and strong individual ownership.

- Look for cross-functional dependencies and resources up front, build on them, and continually review. Utilize existing resources and count on their level of expertise to identify and deflect "surprises."

- Build a training program customized for each track of the Tiger Team to fill in any skill set gaps and increase speed to learning.

- Create organizational awareness of the project to garner broad commitment and prioritization by sharing the purpose, benefits, and goals of the project.

- Lead by example. The executive sponsor must walk the walk and ensure that the goals of the Tiger Team align with the strategic direction of the organization.

- Communicate each subteam's role and with whom they work to eliminate confusion, reduce duplication of effort, and enable a highly focused direction for members of the team.

- Measure results formally and informally, adjust and leverage resources based on measurements, and constantly monitor progress to keep the initiative on track.

- Alter your process procedures to integrate lessons learned.

- Establish explicit matrix management accountability and roles and responsibilities at the outset—especially between teams—to prevent gaps or overlap.

- Build a solid technical foundation of both internal and external contributors for the entire team so that the organization is not reliant on any one or two individuals.

- Include your deployment partners early to ensure that they are fully in the loop, they understand your needs, and they can hit the ground running.

- Build a strong communication program between users and the project team and between the team members to achieve milestones, eliminate ambiguity, and manage expectations.

- Pull in the support team early in the process so that they can understand the potential breakpoints in the hardware and software and the design requirements, or one-offs, that they will have to support.

- Try to keep the same team members throughout the project and maintain consistency with how the team communicates. This simple yet important step reduces constant review cycles and generates a comfortable rhythm for the team.

Executive Management Sponsorship

Sponsorship from top management is key to the success of every change initiative. The level of authority that will help resolve high-level issues and gain buy-in from those impacted by the change is critical. However, the lack of sponsorship or a champion at high levels in the organization will make it much more difficult to succeed.

John Chambers, Cisco CEO, took on the sponsorship role for the Cisco migration to a converged telephony network. The sponsor's main contribution is to set the tone for the project, visibly supporting the objectives, and encouraging the organization to get on board.

"As the executive sponsor of the AVVID Tiger Team," says John Chambers, Cisco CEO, "my goal was for Cisco to be our best first customer by showing worldwide leadership in the deployment of Cisco's IP Telephony." Chambers took every opportunity to talk about the project at town hall meetings, as part of executive announcements, and at his own staff meetings to raise visibility and create buy-in. That level of visibility and support from the executive sponsor made the Tiger Team's job much easier.

It is also the role of the executive sponsor to align the strategic vision of the company with the objectives identified by the Tiger Team. But the sponsor's role is not finished when the project kicks off. The sponsor must also ensure that the future strategic goals of the company include e-commerce initiatives that integrate the effective use of the technology to drive usage and adoption and continue to drive that message even after the migration is complete so that the organization's goals and objectives are optimized.

Although the role of a sponsor is to set the example, everyone—even senior management— works better if it is clear what he is being asked to do. The Tiger Team facilitated a session with members of the steering committee and core Tiger Team to develop the key message around the change and communicate the expected behaviors for both managers and employees. That process clearly defined what the team needed their sponsors to do and outlined the key activities that would assist in championing the change.

Best Practices: Executive Management

The list that follows documents some best practices for executive management sponsorship:

- Communicate the vision and provide a clear definition of what change must occur.

- Tie the business objectives of the company to that of the migration so that users are aware of the positive financial and productivity gains.

- Demonstrate public support and commitment to the transition, communicating the benefits of IP Telephony that make the change attractive.

- Meet privately with direct reports and other individuals or groups to convey strong personal support.

- Stay focused on the goal and reject inconsistent or short-term action.

- Commit the resources required for successful implementation.

- Design a plan that fits your own culture and company objective.

- Understand the scope of the effort that the implementation will have on the organization, know the size of the group affected by the change, and be sensitive to the human resource issues that major change often raises.

- Because sponsors deliver the message through their actions and words, a list of answers to frequently asked questions will help them maintain message consistency:

    - What is the purpose of this change?

    - What's in it for me?

    - How will this change affect me?

    - What's my role in the change?

    - What will I need to do differently as a result?

    - What are the benefits to the organization, customers, and so on?

    - How will the rollout take place? When? How long will it take?

    - Where can I obtain additional information concerning the new initiative?

Managing Change

"I think it's much more than just the technology that will determine winners and losers. It's as much about business processes and culture—changing them and managing through that change—as it is the bits and bytes."

—Bob Kelly, Cisco manager of technical marketing, enterprise solution

Resistance to change is normal and should always be anticipated as a natural human behavior. Most people find it extremely uncomfortable to face situations filled with ambiguity and are attracted to familiar situations because they allow them to feel that they are in control. However, the truth is that although people do not need to like the change, they do need to accept that it is taking place.

We managed this change by taking away the mystery—by being open and honest and providing frequent communication that was relative to the stakeholders. We also found that the ability to be flexible, be proactive, anticipate the glitches, and constantly improve the process along the way, tailoring it to the specific needs of the stakeholders, was critical. Managing user expectations is paramount to making the process smooth and accepting.

The importance of flexibility and responsiveness to stakeholders was never more apparent than when the Tiger Team began to switch out the phones at the company's San Jose campus buildings.

In an early version of Cisco CallManager, it was necessary to create a shared-line appearance between an admin and his manager, and the team sometimes had to give users new phone numbers. This was standard practice, and most users accepted it without a problem. However, when the team switched over the Corporate Headquarters building, it ran into some unexpected pushback.

The admin staff was seriously concerned about getting new phone numbers because it meant that some of them would have to alter their phone number distribution system to incorporate the new number within their streamlined, busy office. In the end, the team allowed the admin staff to pick their own numbers, even though it was an exception to the policy and to the automatic numbering system. Sometimes you have to be sympathetic to the individual's unique business needs rather than using a cookie cutter approach with every stakeholder.

Keep in mind that changing one's phone number is no longer required in the current version of CallManager. However, when an occasion to change a user's phone number comes up, being flexible and listening to their needs will make it a little less painful for the user.

We also found that meeting our stakeholders' needs might require adjusting the schedule on occasion. For example, conducting the conversion for a few key people on Thursday night instead of over the weekend allowed the admin staff, who handle heavy call volume, to become comfortable with the new phone system before the Monday morning rush.

Reducing the discomfort that is an innate part of change ensures buy-in from the users. Because we took the time to understand our audience and identify potential resistance or issues, we were able to respond appropriately.

Organizational Culture

Corporate culture is often defined as "the way we do things around here." Culture builds a common language and brings people together, enabling them to work toward a shared goal. Cisco CEO John Chambers consistently talks about the importance of culture, bringing it up in every meeting he holds and asking his leaders to do the same.

Culture is also about how your organization handles change. As with all successful companies, the primary objective of Cisco is to serve customers. This, of course, means that we have to deliver. An organization's culture can make or break the ability to reach that important goal.

Cisco employees are accustomed to fast-paced endeavors and trying out the latest technology. Typically, it is not necessary for us to spend a lot of time on training. Using our own web tools (online tutorials and Video on Demand [VOD] modules) to train employees is the Cisco way. In fact, whenever I tried to use the old method of holding live training sessions, only about 10 out of 500 people would participate. Our culture is too fast to slow down for scheduled training. Our employees prefer options that allow them to train themselves on their own schedule, not the Tiger Team's schedule.

Understanding and working with your organization's culture is critical to a successful implementation of new technology. Does your company encourage risk taking? Is change incorporated often, and does the company embrace it? Is the new technology embraced or rejected when it is first introduced? Do employees solve problems in a team environment?

Is communication a top priority? Is yours a virtual company with telecommuters or employees scattered across the globe? How has change been introduced and institutionalized in the past? Was the change successful or painful? All these factors are part of your organizational culture and can influence your ability to manage change.

Often when an organization considers change that impacts every employee, such as a large-scale IP Telephony implementation, the process tends to focus on hardware, software, and getting the technology up to speed as quickly as possible. However, remember that a company's infrastructure is composed not just of hardware and software, but also of its people. The successful conversion to Cisco IP Telephony was not just a question of viability or reliability. It was a careful combination of people, process, and organizational change.

Change Readiness

An Organizational Change Management Plan is produced after change impacts have been identified and organizational change readiness has been assessed. Business results cannot be delivered without change, and these changes must be managed to ensure that resistance to change does not create an impediment to realizing the targeted business results.

Cisco manages change by first considering the impact on its employees—paying close attention to details and being considerate of the timetable, ensuring that the switchover didn't take place during a quarter close or other critical event.

For example, a few days before our manufacturing building was scheduled to be migrated, my manager received a panic phone call asking him to hold off the migration because of a large customer-critical order that needed to be shipped that weekend. We immediately sent out word to the team about the change of plans. Not wanting to waste time or have our third-party partners stand around with nothing to do, we shifted them from implementation to cleanup of unidentified analog lines in previously migrated buildings. (See "Retrofit Cleanup" in Chapter 6, "Final Piece of the Conversion.")

In addition to user sensitivity, achieving the desired business results from the IP Telephony implementation typically requires significant business changes, staff training and education, and redesigned business processes, and it might even depend on fundamental changes within the organization. You must properly identify and manage all these changes, and coordinate and integrate change initiatives, to produce the intended results.

Implementing an effective Organizational Change Plan requires that all team members understand the process by which change occurs:

- Know the tools and methods that you can use to analyze and manage change.

- Plan and implement proactive change management to do the following:

    - Understand the nature and impact of change in the program environment.
    - Manage the negative implications of change.
    - Realign expectations.
    - Build commitment.

The Cisco Organizational Change Plan is a template (see Appendix 2-B, "Project Planning Flowchart") consisting of a set of questions covering four areas of organizational change risk: sponsorship, resistance, cultural alignment/communications, and skills.

The Organizational Change Plan is closely tied to the Communication Plan described in Chapter 3, "The Migration Strategy." You can address risks that you discover through this assessment in the Communication Plan, and your activity description can point to the Communication Plan. Items discovered when preparing the Communication Plan can also appear on the Organizational Change Plan. The Communication Plan should make the following considerations:

- Inputs

- Business outcome network

- Value case

- Program Risk Management Plan

- Identified change issues

- Deliverables

- Organizational Change Plan

 Refer to Appendix 2-B. Use the Organizational Change Template to identify and describe the actions to be taken for the low- and medium-change risk areas. The Organizational Change Management questionnaire can offer some assistance in determining proper actions. This appendix is available at http://www.ciscopress.com/1587200880.

Voice of the Client Survey

Voice of the Client is a program used within Cisco that consists of client-targeted surveys and focus groups used to benchmark and track user needs and satisfaction with Cisco IT services, products, and solutions. The feedback process gauges client needs and expectations and mitigates user discomfort, using design tools and processes that help to continuously improve the quality of the technology solutions that IT provides.

You can use the Voice of the Client survey as a tool to identify critical phone features, enable a smooth migration, and offer continued productivity. You can also use the survey as an opportunity to include those features that the new phone system will offer and determine the priority of which should be enabled. The Tiger Team used the survey to solicit user feedback, help the team develop action plans to leverage the appropriate technology and applications, and manage user expectations.

More than 6700 employees responded to the survey from around the world. One of the things we learned through the survey was that 81 percent wanted to migrate to the new Cisco system as long as key features were incorporated into the change. The survey gave the Tiger Team a report card that validated what they felt were key business needs, as well as acting as a gauge to see how responsive users were to the impending change. Risk tolerance was measured as well, and the team learned that the majority of users would tolerate a loss of some key features for up to three months. Because the product was still in the development stage, the team used this information to determine how fast and how vast the conversion should be.

The Tiger Team evaluated the responses to the Voice of the Client employee survey so that they could successfully identify potential problems, develop workarounds, meet client expectations, and focus on turning the input into world-class solutions.

"Must Have" Features

Some features are identified as "must have" and include those features that are critical to the business and enable users to do their jobs. Part of the Voice of the Client survey was dedicated to making sure that those critical features were represented but identified separately from the "nice to have" features.

Through the survey, the Tiger Team learned that keeping their existing phone numbers and voice mail was a "must have" to some users, particularly those who worked with customers and partners. The team worked closely with the design, engineering, and business units to ensure that a plan was in place to address that concern before the conversion. If we had conducted the conversion without first learning the concerns of our users, the project would have experienced a significant snag. Listening carefully to what users are asking for in advance helps ensure that solutions are identified to address these basic business requirements.

"The other side of that, though, is to level-set the expectations right up front," says Dennis Silva, voice services senior network design engineer. "Be honest about what they can realistically expect from an IP phone. You'll find that when you are upfront with people and help them create workarounds for those features—even if the features won't be the same as their 'old world' phones—they are much more adaptable to the change."

 Refer to Appendix 2-C, "Voice of the Client Survey," which attempts to identify the "must have" versus "nice to have" features that a user might require. Use the template to conduct a survey with your users so that you are able to determine the tolerance levels and user requirements for migrating to your new voice system. This data is critical to managing user expectations and design requirements. This appendix appears at the end of this chapter and is also available at http://www.ciscopress.com/ 1587200880.

Know Your Users/Manage Expectations

The more background you have on your users, the more surprises you take out of the picture. Moreover, the fewer surprises you have, the easier the conversion is. Because the Tiger Team included members of Cisco voice services operations, who knew each building's infrastructure as well as the type of users in that building, they were able to identify those users who had special requirements.

Most people don't know what their phone setup is. They just know that it works or it doesn't work, so we couldn't really rely on them to inform us of their existing phone setup. The team performed a dump of the PBX to review each user's setup and to ensure that their new phones would mimic their existing phone configuration.

When the voice services team reviewed the results of the executive staff conference room PBX dump, they alerted the conversion team to the special care requirements that needed to be taken to convert the conference room in the corporate building where shareholder conference calls were held. That room has a private phone line that is separate from the rest.

If voice services had not told us it was there, we would have converted the room the same as the others, potentially causing a public relations disaster if anything had gone wrong.

Each business has its own set of business-critical phone users. At Cisco, these include call center agents who manage the multitude of customer service calls that come in from around the world each day; administrative personnel who manage multiple phones and require special setups; and financial analysts who require special high-speed modems for fax transmission. Not knowing where the users are located or what their special needs are can lead to disruption of business and loss of productivity.

"We ran frequent reports that generated from the existing PBX switch, the voice mail system, and the directory listing," says Mary Tsang, service and support manager. "We consolidated lists and determined which users were working from home and which users would need a phone set in the office." Tsang also noted that it was important to get those lists from the various databases as early as possible. "Too many changes being made at the last minute or on [the] first day of production make it extremely painful for both the project manager and the end user," Tsang cautions.

One of the most important elements of setting expectations with end users is to help them understand exactly what they're getting. "You need to tell them what this is and what it means to them," Silva says. "Lay it on the table and let your users ask questions. Help them become familiar with what you're talking about." Failure to do that is a recipe for disaster.

The Tiger Team cautioned against inconsistent communication from a fragmented implementation team as well as nonstandard processes. "I think we've seen failures in various implementations because there were too many different groups claiming ownership," Tsang comments. "That's why the Tiger Team approach was so successful. You need a centralized team with the ability to make decisions—working from a standardized process—so that your users are getting consistent, reliable information."

A Word About Communication

Many failed change initiatives can be traced back to inadequate communication. Unfortunately, one of the most commonly overlooked aspects of managing any project is the communication plan. Throughout the IP Telephony implementation at Cisco, team leaders communicated effectively to manage quality and productivity levels, achieve the desired results of current and planned change initiatives, and maintain and strengthen leadership credibility.

"The open and honest communication among all the team members was what made this initiative the success that it was," says Manny Rivelo, senior vice president, WW field process and operations. "From day one, this was a Cisco effort and not an individual effort. In true Cisco fashion, it was a team, and it always felt that way."

Each organization and group has something to contribute. For example, voice services helped guide user requirements into the design and functionality of the solution. The LAN team addressed the sensitivity of voice traffic and helped provide a stable infrastructure upon which it runs. The Windows 2000 experts provided assistance in managing the application resources and the impact of making a systems change.

However, more than ever, it was critical to keep the communication flowing between all those teams. "I think our biggest challenge was when the LAN team performed their change management process, assuming that they weren't going to affect the telephone network," Silva recalls. "It turned out that every time they would do a routine change or a recalculation, we would lose thousands of phones. It took us awhile to understand the changes they were making and how they affected the voice network."

Addressing a solution to that challenge, the team developed a process that required any individual making a change to the network to open a change management request. (See Chapter 6 for a review on the Cisco change management process.) Core members of the Tiger Team were then assigned to review and either approve or reject the requests on a case-by-case basis.

Communication within the implementation team is only one piece of the puzzle. The people who will be impacted by the change must also understand *how* they will be affected, especially when the change involves a relatively unknown technology. In this case, the change impacted end users who had grown comfortable with their conventional PBX telephones. IP Telephony was a relative unknown, and the resulting anxiety was addressed through online tutorials posted on the Cisco intranet two to three weeks before the switchover began and again on day one.

Your stakeholders not only need to know what the change is, when the change is coming, and why it is being implemented, but also how it affects them and the behaviors—even the little ones— that need to be changed to institutionalize the new technology.

When we were using traditional PBXs and anyone moved from one location to another, voice services had to schedule the moves and physically move their phones for them. With the new IP phones, the infrastructure is in place that enables those employees to take their phones with them and simply plug them in at their new location. The system automatically knows who they are and what their configuration is. However, after the migration, our employees had to remember to go online and update the employee directory database with their new locations. This was a new behavior that we needed to institutionalize.

Handling change and evolving your business model have become an accepted part of doing business. Your culture dictates how fast and how vast your conversion process should be. People are often uncomfortable with change. But if you take the mystery out of the change and help people understand the value and the goals, how it will impact them, and the required behaviors, they will more easily come to accept the importance and respond appropriately.

Chapter 3 provides additional information on creating a comprehensive communication plan.

Best Practices: Managing Change

The list that follows documents some best practices tips for managing change:

- Build credibility and trust. Be honest and upfront; share the good, the bad, and the ugly. Return phone calls and e-mails quickly. Be sensitive to little things such as putting the user's new phone back in the same place as the original.

- Set expectations early on.

- Clarify roles and responsibilities so that everyone knows what is expected.

- Lead by example. The Tiger Team was the first group to participate in the conversion, followed by voice services and IT.

- In the survey, ask about training options. Most Cisco employees dislike hands-on training sessions, preferring web-based tutorials, online documentation, and hard copy booklets left near the phone.

- Know the features that are critical to your users and have solutions in place ahead of time.

- Be flexible and sensitive to users who have unique business needs.

- Always listen to the voices of your users to determine if you are going in the right direction. Use that feedback to identify critical phone features that meet user expectations, enable smooth migration, and ensure continued productivity.

- Design is an important component that must meet the needs of the users. Be sure to tie the user requirements with the design requirements so that user expectations are met.

- Culture and the previous successful training methods used within your organization dictate the most optimal training options. Use various tools such as hands-on training and online tools (such as tutorials and VODs) to conduct user training and choose the best option that offers a scalable and timely yet efficient solution.

Best Practices: Cultural Standards for Managing Organizational Change

The list that follows documents some best practices tips for fostering cultural standards within your Organizational Change Management Plan:

- **Empowerment**—Employees are encouraged to run with their ideas and make a difference.

- **Teamwork**—Teamwork is rated as one of the success factors against which employees are measured.

- **Trust**—Without trust, no team can be effective. Team members must know that they can count on each other to succeed.

- **Driving change**—The spirit of driving change and risk taking is rewarded in a formalized recognition program.

- **Constant communication**—Share information openly and informally, both good news and bad. Employees are empowered to ask questions, make suggestions, and raise issues, and they should expect a response within 24 hours.

- **No technology religion**—Promoting an open systems environment keeps system maintenance costs low, enables you to take advantage of new and improved technologies, and allows you to choose the right technologies for the right scenario. Employees are encouraged to be frugal and spend the company's money as if it were their own. This means always being mindful of expenditures and looking for opportunities to save.

Best Practices: Communicating Change

The list that follows documents some best practices tips for fostering better communication during major changes and especially during new technology conversions:

- Understand what communication-related changes need to take place, what the impact of those changes on each stakeholder group is, and what the required new behaviors are.

- Ensure that consistent messages are sent and delivered. It is critical that the senior leadership team develops the messages and provides for accountability—among themselves and with their direct reports—for delivery and actions to support the words.

- Set up communication vehicles between the cross-functional teams so that decisions aren't made in a vacuum.

- Create a project website and communication vehicles such as e-mail aliases that keep users informed of your schedule, progress, and next steps.

Best Practices: Know Your Users and Manage Expectations

The list that follows documents some best practices tips to manage user expectations and minimize the discomfort that a user might feel during the IP Telephony migration process:

- Know who your users are, how they use their phones, and how the initiative will impact them.

- Help users understand the differences between the old PBX phones and new IP phones.

- Generate PBX dumps, voice mail systems, and directory listings early enough to allow time to design solutions to unique configurations. Set up a change freeze to ensure that your reports are current.

- Be consistent and relevant with useful information, and direct users to the project website for answers to FAQs.

- Obtain buy-in from all members of the team to reduce inconsistent communication and reinforce their commitment.

Where Do You Begin? The Engineering Story

As with any type of initiative, especially one that can impact an employee's ability to do his job, you need to address the basics first. Start with the right team, familiarize yourself with the new technology, and understand how it will impact your current infrastructure. Also understand what your users need, and then manage the expectations so that users know what they're going to get.

Engineering is the cog that makes the wheel turn. We made sure that there were people on the team with the appropriate experience in both voice and data technology. Also critical was having someone on the team with the appropriate NT background who could support the servers.

As a data company, Cisco did not start out with comprehensive skill sets in voice. "Although we now offer services and support expertise to handle all of the IP Telephony requirements for deployment, we had to learn that from scratch," recalls Bill Lowers, voice services senior network design engineer. "When we started, we really didn't know that much about it, but we knew we'd better learn. So we sat down and read the manual from front to back—several times—becoming familiar with the CallManager, installation configuration, the admin guide, and all of the other resources that were available."

"It's necessary that you have members on the team who can learn and understand a dial plan," Silva adds. "If they don't understand it, they can't work on a network. If you don't understand the basic infrastructure, the basic communication technology, and how a voice and data network works, it will be much more difficult to understand the components of the CallManager."

Just as critical to the success of the implementation is the appropriate level of experience in telephony, programming, voice, and alternate route selection. A basic understanding of least-cost routing, modified numbering plans, and the Unified Dial Plans (UDP), Coordinated Dial Plans (CDP), and Modified Dial Plans (MDP) is also important.

Last but certainly not least, the engineering team must understand how the new application will impact the organization on a global basis. Any new technology, network, or application must be designed right from the start to be "world-ready." This involves setting and maintaining IT development standards that support multiple-byte character sets; multilingual input screens; various date, currency, and time formats; and address formats.

Understand Your Infrastructure

It all starts with a single step. You need to know where you're starting from before you can know where you're going. Knowing how your users use the system today, re-examining your existing LAN infrastructure to ensure that it is ready to deploy voice, and considering whether there are multiple or remote locations is critical.

"If they're all sitting in one city, it's easier," Silva says. "But maybe they want to call New York City from San Francisco in five digits. Or they want to call London using a modified numbering plan. All those things need to be considered when doing the numbering plan."

As daunting and overwhelming as all that sounds, put things into perspective and remember that IP Telephony is simply a new application running on your current network, not an entirely new network. "It's a different application," Silva says. "It's just an IP device using services on an existing LAN or multiservice backbone. You're not changing the network; you're riding another application across that same infrastructure."

PBX Infrastructure

Understand the grade of service that is currently being provided, and engineer a solution to aggregate traffic and trunking together to take advantage of a more efficient, cost-effective solution. The engineering team thoroughly evaluated its PBX infrastructure so it could understand the organization's current voice features and functionality. This information helped the engineering team to identify the required features that users would need as well as the PBX-to-IP Telephony connectivity requirements. As a result of this detailed understanding of the current infrastructure, the team was able to tailor the CallManager configuration to replace the existing PBX systems.

"If you look at an existing PBX with 'X' amount of trunks, 'X' amount of tie line trunks, and 'X' amount of local trunks for inbound, out-bound access, that's exactly the number I would throw onto the CallManager," Silva says. "You have to make sure you have enough facilities for people to receive phone calls and be able to call out. For example, if I have 20,000 phones on the PBX side, I know how many trunks that requires. If I move a quarter of those phones over to the IP environment, then I know I'm going to need at least 25 percent of the available facilities on the CallManager."

AVVID Readiness Audit provides the recommended baseline information. To view or take this audit, go to http://tools.cisco.com/Assessments/jsp/welcome.jsp?asmts. A Cisco.com login is required.

Data Infrastructure

Before adding voice to the network, you must design the data network properly. Cisco ensured the successful implementation of IP Telephony solutions by first considering their LAN infrastructure.

The LAN team also considered the location of servers and Gateways prior to implementation and identified them in the LAN infrastructure-planning phase. Considering the placement of these devices ensured that service availability would be consistent across the LAN infrastructure.

"We identified Gateway and server network locations for the TFTP, DNS, and DHCP servers, the firewalls, the NAT or PAT Gateways, and the CallManager and Gateway locations," Silva says.

After the team determined locations, it investigated network service availability, Gateway support, and available bandwidth and scalability to ensure readiness for the IP Telephony solution.

IP Telephony Readiness

To help prepare for the IP Telephony implementation and ensure that our network design would support IP Telephony and the Cisco IP Telephony solution, we used the Cisco web-based IP Telephony Readiness Assessment tool. The assessment requires about an hour to complete and includes approximately 100 questions. At the end of the assessment, a summary report is provided and a more detailed printable report card can be generated.

To access the IP Telephony Readiness Audit template, go to http://tools.cisco.com/ Assessments/jsp/welcome.jsp?asmt=VOIP. It requires a Cisco.com login.

A sample of the assessment follows.

Select a Deployment Plan

The Cisco IP Telephony solution currently supports three major deployment models:

- **LAN campus or multiple isolated LAN campus**—The first is called *LAN campus*. This might include multiple LAN campus environments where interconnectivity is provided by direct access to the public switched telephone network (PSTN). Many organizations will begin deployment of Cisco IP Telephony with LAN campus deployments.

- **WAN deployment with campus and centralized call processing for WAN sites**— The second deployment model is referred to as the *centralized call processing model*. In this model, the organization has multiple geographically dispersed sites with one centrally located Cisco CallManager or Cisco CallManager cluster. Additional questions are asked for this deployment model to cover WAN infrastructure, quality of service (QoS) issues, and call admission control for centralized deployments.

- **WAN deployment with campus and distributed call processing for WAN sites**— The third deployment model is referred to as the *distributed* or *decentralized call processing model*. In this model, the organization has plans for Cisco IP Telephony solutions at multiple WAN sites with Cisco CallManager servers located in multiple locations. Additional questions are asked for this deployment model to cover WAN infrastructure, QoS issues, gatekeeper support for call admission control, and distributed Cisco CallManager processing.

Plan the Dial Plan

When designing the large enterprise solutions for Cisco, it was critical to fully understand existing dial plan requirements and caveats that help in the transition to CallManager routing. Dial plan requirements are basic and encompass the ability to handle internal calls as well as external calls originating from the PSTN, applications, or other CallManager clusters. They need to be flexible enough to support abbreviated dialing, such as internal four- or five-digit extensions.

The key to any dial plan is finding the common denominator, which is typically the directory number (DN). The DN length must always be recognizable, routable, and unique enough for all services that use those devices. A dial plan must be flexible enough to accommodate future applications and growth to reduce the cost of ownership of the installed base.

Cisco proposed a global dial plan for its organization based on an underlying architecture of a seven-digit dial plan. These seven digits are broken down as a three-digit unique site code with a four-digit extension.

"All users are assigned this unique seven-digit extension," says Gert Vanderstraeten, IT engineer and member of the technology track. "But it is up to each location's preference whether that extension appears on the IP phone's display. The default display will show the seven-digit extension." This variance, as well as local office four- or five-digit dialing, is accomplished with translation patterns and voice mail field entries on the line appearance.

Voice application usage is one of the key roles of a dial plan. Voice mail was the most widely used application at Cisco, and the interplay of creating and forwarding messages based on the directory number was of primary importance.

"We made retention of existing four- or five-digit local dialing for phone-to-phone dialing within a site a priority," says Steven Hunter, IT engineer. Hunter cautioned that the design of the local dial plan should always accommodate this requirement through well thought-out use of translation patterns, dialing domains, and the # end-of-dial character.

Dial plans play another key role in the relationship of how a call is routed both internally and externally in CallManager. The standardizing of CallManager CSS/partitions was addressed in this track, as well as part of the architecture for the gatekeeper, extension mobility, and other voice applications that had an interaction with the dial plan.

Allowing interoperability of current systems/applications and future initiatives, the team developed the following best practices that helped set the foundation for common tools, maintenance, and monitoring. These best practices enabled users to travel from office to office without adjusting or reprogramming their portable device applications. Although not all the best practices are directly related to the dial plan, they all played a part in enabling Cisco to develop a standard, comprehensive, global dial plan.

Plan for Growth

A site survey conducted within all of Cisco's locations that were targeted for the IP Telephony solution helped to determine if that office had enough growth capacity and to avoid revisiting the office in a few months. Cisco planned each of its field offices to accommodate a three-year growth capacity, using the following questions to help determine scalability:

- Does the current PBX have analog or digital interfaces? If yes, what type of analog (FXO, FXS, E&M) or digital (T1, E1, CAS, CCS) interfaces does the PBX currently have?

- What type of signaling does the PBX currently use?

- What is the FXO/FXS: loop start or ground-start?

- Is the E&M a wink-start, delay-start, or immediate-start?

- Is the E&M a Type I, II, III, IV, or V?

- What is the T1: CAS, Q.931 PRI (user-side or network-side), Q.SIG, DPNSS, and proprietary d-channel (CCS) signaling scheme?

- What is the E1: CAS, R2, Q.931 PRI (user-side or network-side), Q.SIG, DPNSS, and proprietary d-channel (CCS) signaling, R2 scheme?

- What type of framing (SF/ESF/HDB3) and encoding (B8ZS/AMI/CRC-4) are currently in use?

- Does the field office require passing proprietary PBX signaling? If so, which timeslot is the signaling passed on, and is it HDLC-framed?

- Will the field office provide clocking, or expect the router to provide clocking?

- If PRI or QSIG signaling is being used, is the PBX acting as user-side or network-side?

CallManager Server Location and Placement

When selecting a suitable location to place the CallManager servers, the AVVID Tiger Team considered environmental elements including security, UPS, power generators, availability, and network connectivity. The network operations centers (NOCs) were considered the best site placements for the Gateways due to availability, backup power requirements, security, and access for the telephone company (telco) carriers. The sections that follow offer some questions to consider when identifying your CallManager server locations.

Environmental Concerns

- Where will you place the CallManagers? Cisco typically installs them in data centers because these rooms usually have the best environmental conditions, have optimal UPS requirements, and are the most secure.

- Are there environmental issues with the wiring closets or telco rooms?

- Are there plenty of dedicated power circuits and correct power outlets? Not all equipment uses standard 110 volts. For example, the Catalyst switches with inline power Ethernet blades use 208 volts.

- Do tie cables exist between the telco equipment and the new CallManager?

Security Concerns

An IP phone is a direct connection into your network. Lobby phones are phones made available to visitors in public areas of the organization. They can create a security breach if they are not managed properly. "If a visitor chooses to plug his or her laptop into the available IP phone or the wall jack that an IP phone is connected to, it can be a direct connect into the organization's data network," Silva cautions.

Making the wall jack that the IP phone is connected to a voice-traffic-only port is one way to safeguard a publicly displayed phone. "We had to make certain policy changes when deploying these phones in order to ensure security," Silva recalls.

Floor Plan Concerns

The entire installation team must be provided with up-to-date layouts of the office in which the CallManager is being installed. "It's important that everyone is working off the same versions of all documentation to prevent problems," says Shawn Armstrong, IT engineer. "Whenever possible, we assigned areas of responsibility to the installation team and made sure everyone's copies reflected those divisions."

Servers that are placed in diverse data centers on site equally balance load and fail-over redundancy. Gateways that are placed in main wiring closets enable diverse routing from the local and long-distance providers. Also consider UPS and generator backups.

Floor plans included the username and phone extension number, and any fax and modem numbers with the associated jack number identification. The Tiger Team worked closely with WPR and the facilities team to obtain current versions of employee locations and phone numbers and to request that they discontinue processing moves at least a week before the conversion. This ensured that their data was current and reflected all existing user locations. The networking equipment and patch panels in the closet were labeled with the jack number and identification for all fax and modems. Maintaining this data helps the support and operations team to troubleshoot problems in the future.

 Refer to Appendix 2-D, "General Preimplementation Considerations Checklist," which offers a baseline of core design requirements, outside of the phone features, that you should address in your network design. This appendix appears at the end of this chapter and is also available at http://www.ciscopress.com/1587200880.

Best Practices: Evaluating the PBX Infrastructure

Evaluating the PBX infrastructure helps you determine your new network design and infrastructure requirements. Use the following best practices to conduct a thorough review of your current infrastructure:

- Perform an analysis on the current traffic requirements to help migrate both DID/DOD and voice mail.

- Study current voice mail to determine requirements—which options are required, which are obsolete, and which are better suited in a different platform. When the team did this, it found that a current Octel "port assignment" was required to validate the PBX configuration and help move the ports as needed in the migration.

- Study current PBX trunking and analyze the current traffic requirements for T1 loading both for initial start as well as cutting over buildings during retrofit.

- Study the existing dial plans (shared and overlap) to understand the current requirements and identify what is needed to migrate to CallManager.

- Identify and understand the policy for the number plan, which is essential for developing the "master plan" of dial plan and number management.

- Understand the network disbursement.

- Understand feature names in CallManager versus PBX. Many basic terms from the same system might have a completely different meaning in the other system. Cisco used the same naming/concept in PBX because standardizing across CallManagers helps in "concept" learning from one system to another.

- Examine the existing blocking factor for potential capacity issues.

Best Practices: Evaluating the Data Infrastructure

Evaluating the data infrastructure helps determine your new network design and infrastructure requirements. Use the following best practices to conduct a thorough review of your current infrastructure:

- Review the device inventory, network design, and baseline information. Links and devices should have sufficient capacity for the additional voice traffic and might require upgraded links with high peak or busy hour utilization.

- Target devices with high CPU utilization, high backplane utilization, high memory utilization, queuing drops, or buffer misses for additional inspection and potential upgrade. Peak utilization characteristics in the baseline are valuable in determining potential voice quality issues.

- Evaluate the availability requirements for the IP Telephony network, and review network topology diagrams, feature capabilities, and protocol implementations.

- Review redundancy capabilities of the network to ensure that it meets your availability goals with the current network design (or a new design) recommended for IP Telephony.

- Evaluate current feature capabilities of the network and device characteristics, including chassis, module, and software inventory. This is useful in determining the IP Telephony feature capabilities in the existing environment.

- Evaluate the overall network capacity and impact to ensure that the network will meet overall capacity requirements and that there will be no impact on the existing network and application requirements.

- Evaluate the network baseline in terms of the impact on performance management requirements from an IP Telephony requirements perspective.

Perform an IP Telephony readiness audit to provide the appropriate baseline information. From this audit, the team made and implemented recommendations. To access the IP Telephony Readiness Audit Template, go to http://tools.cisco.com/Assessments/jsp/ welcome.jsp?asmt=VOIP. A Cisco.com login is required.

Best Practices: Plan the Dial Plan

Planning the dial plan best practices helps guide your new dial plan design requirements. Utilize these principles when creating your dial plan:

- Establish a unique 7-digit number for personal identification dialing as well as voice mail, personal assistant, and other applications, customizable to 4 or 5 digits for office location.

- Enable a common interoffice routing access code to imply end-to-end least-cost routing (8+).

- Enable a common mobile routing access code to imply end-to-end least-cost routing—in both directions—to and from mobile phones (7+).

- Use a common PSTN routing access code (9+ or 0+).

- Use the # sign in both CallManager and voice mail to signify the end of dialing, which excludes the need for region-/country-specific dial plans.

- Standardize on the core calling search space (CSS)/partition.

- Standardize on the core route patterns for all application and personal usage.

- Institute a gatekeeper for dial plan resolution for interoffice dialing.

- Use least-cost routing on fully qualified E164 numbers with PSTN fail-over. The carrier for a certain source/destination is chosen independently of the dialing habits of the user.

- Keep one dialing domain for all Unity servers within the organization.

Best Practices: CallManager Server Location

The list that follows provides some best practices tips for determining the best location for the CallManager server(s).

- Each cluster should have its own TFTP server. By using an alternate TFTP path directory, all clusters write to a single cluster so that all DHCP scopes throughout the site can have a single entry, preventing phones from registering all over the world.

- Use the dedicated TFTP server in conjunction with the publisher in a small cluster (around four or less servers). In larger clusters, the TFTP and publisher should be separated depending on the deployment size.

- Set option 150 on the local DHCP server so that the phones will register locally and not across the network.

- Use "Rogue" with auto registration turned on to one CallManager cluster. This forces the "Rogue" devices to register and saves TFTP from being continuously "hammered" by the devices that originate from the DHCP.

- If a reboot of a CallManager server is required, perform the reboot after hours to minimize hits to the DHCP and TFTP servers.

- Establish physical security. Creating a physical boundary for critical communications equipment is a fundamental foundation in building secure networks. Network designs and software configurations cannot protect a network whose assets are not physically protected from potential malicious threats.

CallManager Today

The topology in Figure 2-2 illustrates the complete overview of our entire San Jose Campus infrastructure as we were migrating. This document was used to track real-world entities such as traffic, trunking, and modified configuration as we migrated to the CallManager.

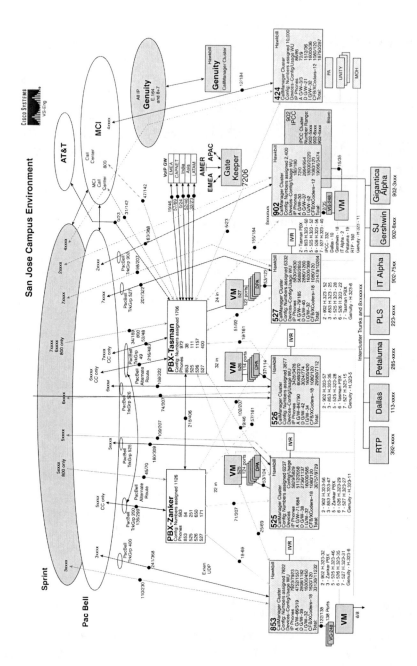

Figure 2-2 *Cisco CallManager Infrastructure Illustration During the CallManager First Phase Migration at the Cisco Systems Headquarters in San Jose, California*

Thanks to Bill Lowers for use of this topology figure.

NOTE   The Cisco Unity voice mail solution was not available at the time of the initial migration. Cisco is currently migrating to Cisco Unity and replacing the Octel voice mail solution. Refer to Chapter 7 for the update.

The network diagram in Figure 2-3 demonstrates the LAN architecture, CallManagers, and other related LAN infrastructure components, including the 6500s that support T1 and analog lines and the access layer switches.

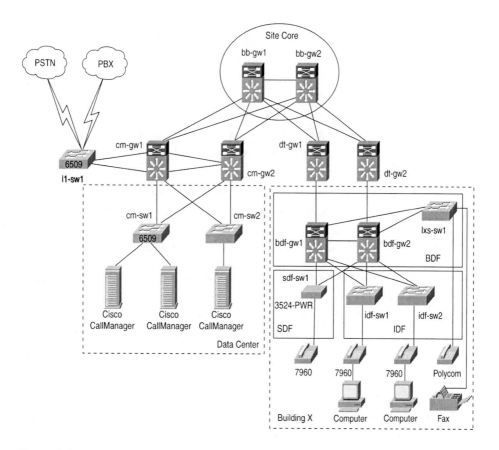

Figure 2-3   *Recent Network Diagram*

Thanks to Bill Lowers for use of this topology figure.

Resources

Throughout this chapter, you have seen references to several utilities made available for download at http://www.ciscopress.com/1587200880. You are encouraged to use these utilities for your own purposes during the preplanning phase.

- Appendix 2-A: AVVID Tiger Team Roles and Responsibilities

- Appendix 2-B: Project Planning Flowchart

- Appendix 2-C: Voice of the Client Survey

- Appendix 2-D: General Preimplementation Considerations Checklist

Summary

The importance of the preplanning phase cannot be overemphasized. Because time was spent to "plan the plan," the result was a transition in which obstacles were identified and dealt with ahead of time. Considering issues that revolved around the impact the initiative would have on users ensured buy-in and greater speed to competency. Putting together a cross-functional team with the right expertise and accountability resulted in a much more reliable, stable network and a support team that has been onboard since the beginning. Following is a short summary from each section of Chapter 2.

- **Importance of a cross-functional team**—The AVVID Tiger Team was made up of an executive sponsor, a steering committee, a team lead and program manager, and a core team that included four tracks representing expertise in technology, support, finance, and each of Cisco's global theaters.

- **Executive management sponsorship**—Executive sponsorship was instrumental to the team's ability to gain buy-in from the user community. The executive sponsor should be the highest-ranking individual within the corporation. The executive sponsor for Cisco was its CEO, John Chambers. Chambers' role was to champion the initiative, tie in the business objectives for the migration, communicate the vision and importance, and commit the resources required to complete the project.

- **Managing change**—Understanding user needs, communicating the who, what, where, when, and why, instilling a culture of openness to change within the organization, and managing expectations built acceptance by the user community.

- **Where do you begin: the engineering story**—Building the right team with experience in either voice or data helped fill the gaps, enabled a comprehensive understanding of the current infrastructure, and determined what it would take to evolve to a converged network. In addition, planning the dial plan, ensuring the ability to scale, and determining the best location for the infrastructure laid the groundwork for a successful migration.

Appendix 2-A: AVVID Tiger Team Roles and Responsibilities

This appendix provides an in-depth review of each Tiger Team role, specific tasks, and responsibilities assigned to those roles. This appendix is also available at http://www.ciscopress.com/1587200880.

Executive Sponsor

Expertise: CEO, president, or level of authority that will help you resolve high-level issues and gain corporate buy-in from those impacted by the change.

Roles and responsibilities:

- Communicate the vision and provide a clear definition of what changes must occur.

- Demonstrate public support and commitment to the transition.

- Commit the resources required for successful implementation.

Steering Committee

Expertise: Senior-level executives with decision-making authority.

Roles and responsibilities:

- Influence the deployment of the project, keeping it focused on organizational goals.

- Help resolve issues that arise as a result of the conversion to keep the project moving forward.

- Act as the centralized customer voice, ensuring that user input is prioritized in the rollout.

Tiger Team Lead

Expertise: Director of voice services; overall management of telecom department. Requires an understanding of PBX telecommunications requirements, IP Telephony, support, operations, and finance.

Roles and responsibilities:

- Communicate the initiative's global deployment objectives, policies, and processes.

- Ensure that worldwide implementation standards are set and adhered to.

- Provide status reports to steering committee, executive sponsor, and so on.

- Establish priorities and requirements for each theater.

- Work to build teamwork and maintain business unit contacts throughout the organization.

- Help to establish objectives and metrics within each theater.

- Highlight common and theater-specific resource requirements.

- Identify and justify resources for AVVID programs.

- Track and report budget and resource allocations.

AVVID Program Manager

Expertise: Has had technology-specific training leading to a high-level understanding of how to manage and drive areas of the technology development, support, operations, implementation, and finance. Maintain high-level view of AVVID technologies. Has comprehensive understanding of how the organization resolves issues and completes projects.

Roles and responsibilities:

- Gather, collect, refine, and report on key process, technology, team, and coordination issues.

- Identify priorities, milestones, deadlines, and tasks of the global team—both common and theater specific.

- Conduct weekly global track meetings.

- Define, maintain, track, and communicate the format and content of standard track deliverables.

- Identify key needs for resources, processes, measures, and tools for track processes.

- Provide measured business objectives (MBO) ratings to managers and individual contributors on performance.

- Communicate global technology deployment objectives and policies.

- Establish cross-functional team partnerships and strategies—internally and externally.

- Create, maintain, and build relationships with business units, internal teams, and customers.

- Assess integration and deployment practices and polices for technologies.

- Provide organization structures and process models within theaters.

- Manage AVVID budget, capital, expense, and resource allocations.

- Establish policies, priorities, and coordination requirements for technologies and theaters.

Core Tiger Team

Services/application program leads: IP Telephony, unified messaging, ICM/IPCC, transport, client services.

Expertise: Have a solid understanding and knowledge of applications and services provided through the deployment of a converged network. Be able to work with the Tiger Team to gather user requirements, resolve issues, recommend policies and support processes, and coordinate application deployment.

Roles and responsibilities:

- Acquire assigned dedicated resources for AVVID technology deployments and assessments.

- Establish objectives, metrics, timelines, tasks, and deliverables for teams and contributors.

- Provide MBO ratings, rewards, and assessments to assigned resources, managers, and individual contributors.

- Gather and organize business plans from internal and external stakeholders.

- Provide technology deployment objectives to cross-functional design, implementation, and operations teams that align with internal and external business plans.

- Communicate with the business units on strategy, timelines, products, and features to be delivered and those that are needed.

- Communicate with business clients and operational/implementation teams on experiences, lessons learned, must-have features, nice-to-have features, and functions.

- Attend all key product development and marketing briefings.

- Provide management timetable for assessment and deployment of technologies.

- Approve all technology pilots and production deployment policies, configurations, and designs.

- Verify and establish processes for installation, testing, integration, architecture, and design of technologies.

- Acquire, assess, and provide recommended implementation and operational support processes, methodologies, and tools.

- Assess tools, methodologies, and resources for implementation and support.

- Manage technology-specific AVVID budget, capital, expense, and resource allocations.

- Establish priorities and coordination requirements for technology integration and deployments.

AVVID Engineering

Expertise: Requires expertise in both voice and data as well as a solid foundation with PBX dial plans, infrastructure, trunking, traffic analysis, and an understanding of user requirements.

Roles and responsibilities:

- Manage the development of the network designs.

- Facilitate issues in the implementation phase.

- Assist with testing procedures.

- Monitor network reliability.

- Provide backup expertise to the support team.

- Set design standards and templates for all applications and hardware installations.

- Work closely with the business unit and attend all key product development and marketing briefings.

- Facilitate all software and hardware upgrades.

- Provide compatibility matrices for all applications, software, and hardware platforms.

LAN Team

Expertise: Understands current LAN infrastructure requirements and its effect on the new converged data/voice IPT network.

Roles and responsibilities:

- Order catalyst chassis, power supplies, and 10/100 cards for all buildings and sites in coordination with IT-Telecom project managers (PMs). (The IT-Telecom PMs will order all FXS cards for buildings and Digital Gateway Cards for NOCs.) Both teams will work together in the installation and configuration, although most of the configuration will be done from the CallManager interface.

- Order sufficient capacity slot space and 6509 chassis to accommodate Foreign Exchange Station (FXS) ports, analog ports to service polycoms, faxes, and modems in each building.

- Provide the forecast capacity plan and management of tie lines and digital circuits to service provider networks required in the NOCs.

- Order and install the Catalyst 6509 equipment (chassis, power, ports) necessary to support Digital Gateways. (The IT-Telecom team will order the Lennon Digital Gateway cards.) Both teams will be responsible for installation and configuration setup for the Digital Gateways.

Theater Implementation Managers—Corporate, Americas, Field Sales Offices, EMEA, Asia Pacific

Expertise: Requires an understanding of core business requirements for a specific theater.

Roles and responsibilities:

- Communicate global technology deployment objectives and policies.

- Implement global and theater-specific designs, implementation policies, and operational policies.

- Provide management reporting for implementation, operations, and design functions.

- Provide feedback on lessons learned, needs, and experiences for implementation, support, and design teams.

- Implement methodologies and processes across theater-specific teams.

- Attend weekly global program and technologies meetings.

- Assess integration and deployment practices and polices for technologies.

- Provide organization structures and process models within theaters.

- Highlight common and theater-specific resource requirements.

- Acquire assigned dedicated resources for AVVID technology deployments and assessments.

- Establish objectives, metrics, timelines, tasks, and deliverables for contributors within theaters.

- Provide MBO ratings, rewards, and assessments to assigned resources and individual contributors.

- Gather and organize business plans and user requirements from internal clients and in-region managers.

- Assess tools, methodologies, and resources for implementation and support within theater.

- Manage theater-specific AVVID budget, capital expense, and resource allocations.

- Establish priorities and coordination requirements for theaters.

- Track all feature gaps and product feedback attained from user clients.

Remote Field Office-Theater Implementation PM Responsibilities—Countdown to Cutover

Twelve to ten weeks before cutover:

- Submit telco room requirements to telco carrier.

- Place order to extend telco d-marc if required.

- Verify existing telco/PBX services.

- Gather user data from client.

- Review telco drawing and approve or return for revisions.

- Verify overhead paging need/status.

- Review final design received from design team.

- Provide kick-off documentation to implementation team.

- Place telco order and request customer service records (CSRs) and site survey.

- Substantially complete (75 percent) floor plans received.

- Complete cabling for secondary main point of entry (MPOE).

- Place equipment orders.

Nine to seven weeks before cutover:

- Installation team provides statement of work (SOW) to project manager.

- Confirm telco order and number assignments.

- Request voice mail purchase order.

- Research and confirm equipment orders that were approved.

- Sign off and return SOW to installation team.

- Forward floor plan (FP) and extension information to local contact (field sales administrative manager, or FSAM).

- Place voice mail order.

- Receive voice mail quote.

Six to four weeks before cutover:

- Issue voice mail purchase order.

- Order Sprint 8XX numbers.

- Order polycom (operations center phones).

- Submit cutsheets to installation partner.

- Provide cutsheets to voice mail vendor.

- Submit cutsheet to partner.

- Finalize cut date with entire project team.

Three to one week before cutover:

- Complete disconnections and referrals (if applicable).

- Complete BDF and IDFs.

- Confirm equipment that is delivered to the site.

- Provide partner with access to the extranet.

- Provide IP information to the support vendor/organization.

- Submit pre-cutover web viper dates to program manager.

- Submit pre-cutover operations package to the IT-telecom team.

- Notify the change management group of office downtime.

- Install CallManager and configure LAN.

Cutover weekend:

- Deploy AVVID solution.

- Test AVVID and UPS.

- Update voice mail bill groups (new sites only).

- Perform end-to-end testing.

Day two of operation (cutover weekend):

- Prepare and submit post-cutover operations package.

- Facilitate the inventory and shipping of old PBX.

- Provide customer satisfaction report (first day of service).

- Cancel old world PBX maintenance agreement.

- Submit LAN as-built and handoff documents to partner.

- Submit LAN as-built and handoff documents to IT operations.

One week after cutover:

- Forward results of customer satisfaction report to team.

Support Track Lead

Expertise: Must have technical expertise and experience in both the voice and data world, as well as in-depth familiarity with technologies such as CallManager, IP phones, Personal Assistant, SoftPhone, Unified Messaging, and so on. Must also be able to understand the overall implementation vision and have the ability to plan support requirements for future applications and technologies and how they would seamlessly integrate into the current AVVID infrastructure.

Roles and responsibilities:

- Develop and drive global support process and standards within IT and customer advocacy (CA).

- Establish metrics.

Finance Track Lead

Expertise: Must have a comprehensive understanding of the financial process, such as creation and maintenance of budgets, financial closing, project commit process, and performance of ad-hoc financial analyses, including ROIs and scenario analysis.

Roles and responsibilities:

- Track spending against budget and support the day-to-day finances of the AVVID rollout.

- Build financial models and prepare ad-hoc scenario analysis for members of the team.

- Prepare and consolidate standard reporting based on data from each theater, including headcount and capital expenses.

- Help the team build a lease scenario analysis for equipment returns.

- Work with PMs to ensure that proper procedures for PBX equipment returns are in place to avoid additional lease fines.

- Identify ROI factors and keep the team in alignment with key business drivers.

- Manage depreciation factors, upcoming lease renewals, headcount, outside services expenditures, and equipment orders.

- Ensure that budgetary spending stayed on track and that the goals of the deployment were in line with the goals of the company.

Appendix 2-B: Project Planning Flowchart

You can use this Excel spreadsheet to identify and describe the actions to be taken for the low- and medium-change risk areas. The Organizational Change Management questionnaire can offer some assistance in determining proper actions. Appendix 2-B is available at http://www.ciscopress.com/1587200880.

Appendix 2-C: Voice of the Client Survey

Please identify all phone features that are critical to how you conduct your business. This list of features in no way represents all the available phone features; however, it is important that you distinguish the following phone features as "must have" versus "nice to have" so that we can prioritize your user requirements for the new phone system. This appendix is also available at http://www.ciscopress.com/1587200880.

Feature	Must Have	Nice to Have	Optional
Answer/answer release			
Application sharing			
Attendant console			
Audio volume adjust			
Automated phone installation configuration			
Automatic phone moves			
Call detail records			
Call forwarding (off-premise)			
Call forwarding (ring or no answer)			
Call forwarding (self-directed)			
Call hold/release			
Call park/pickup			
Call transfer			
Call waiting			
Calling line ID line and name			
Chat			
Conference (unicast)			
Conference (multicast)			
Add-on conference			

continues

Feature	Must Have	Nice to Have	Optional
Company directory access via phone			
Intercom hands-free			
Hands-free answerback on intercom			
Hands-free dialing			
Speed dialing			
Overhead paging			
Speaker phone paging			
Distinctive ringing (internal versus external call)			
Do not disturb			
Place call on hold			
Distinctive station ringing pitch			
Last number redial			
Multiple calls per line appearance			
Multiple line appearances			
Multiple ring tone options			
Message waiting indicator			
Music on hold			
Mute functionality			
Night service			
Number portability			
Privacy (prevent barge in on bridged extension)			
Barge in (allow barge in on bridged extension)			
Special personal privacy lines			
Ringer pitch adjust			

Feature	Must Have	Nice to Have	Optional
Ringer volume adjust			
Shared extensions on multiple phones			
Single button collaborative computing/virtual meetings			
Speakerphone mute			
Speed dial (auto-dial)			
Saved number redial			
Station volume control			
Prerecorded messages			
Remote access to phone features			
Tone on hold			
Video			
Visual message displays (all digital telephones) (name, extension, and so on)			
Web administration			
Web documentation			
Web-based speed dial (auto-dial) directory			
Web-based access from phone			
Whiteboard			
Other: (write your answer in)			

Appendix 2-D: General Preimplementation Considerations Checklist

This appendix offers a baseline of core design requirements, outside of the phone features, that you should address in your network design. This appendix is also available at http://www.ciscopress.com/1587200880.

Design Considerations

In addition to phone features, be sure that your design represents all of the following mentioned considerations:

- LAN infrastructure

- WAN infrastructure

- Call processing

- Feature list

- Call admission control

- Gateway selection (MGCP/H.323)

- Fax support

- Modem support

- Transcoding and MTP

- Conferencing

- Dial plan

- Emergency services and backups

- Security

- Manageability

- Corporate directory integration

- Calling restrictions

- Billing/accounting

- NightService

- Operator console

- Other Cisco applications: IP IVR, Unity voice mail, Unity unified messaging, IP ICD, PA

- Third-party applications

If You Have Legacy PBXs

❑ Are there free analog or digital interfaces to which the Gateway can be connected?

❑ What is the make and model of the PBX?

❑ Does the PBX have any free interfaces?

❑ What are those interfaces? E&M; FXO; E1 Q.931 PRI?

❑ Do your digital interfaces support network-side ISDN Q.931?

❑ Do you have an operator/receptionist/hardware console on the PBX?

Call Flow

❑ Are all calls presented to the operator/receptionist?

❑ How many operators are there?

❑ If there are no operators, are incoming calls presented directly to phones?

❑ How many discard digits instructions (DDIs) exist?

❑ How many digits are presented to you from the PSTN on your DDI range?

❑ What is the average call volume through your receptionist/operator?

❑ Roughly, what is the total number of calls incoming and outgoing per day/week?

Sites

❑ How many sites exist?

❑ What design would best fit this situation?
- ❑ Single site
- ❑ Single site campus (that is, 100-Mbps LES links)
- ❑ Centralized CallManager design (WAN clustering)
- ❑ Centralized CallManager design (WAN)
- ❑ Distributed CallManager design

User Population

❑ What is the total number of users?

❑ What is the total number per site?

❑ What is the call flow from these sites to the PSTN?

❑ What is the call flow from the PSTN into these sites?

❑ Is conferencing a consideration?

❑ How much WAN bandwidth exists between the sites?

(Note: Data + (number of voice calls * bandwidth per call) = Should not exceed 75 percent of link capacity)

❑ Are these self-managed offices?

❑ Is there anyone else in your building?

❑ Do you lease office space to anyone else?

❑ Do these people need to use your phone system?

❑ Is there a need to connect fax machines to Gateways?

❑ How many potential ports? Check the MCEBU website for modem/fax.

❑ Have you considered your current IP addressing scheme? Public or private?

❑ What applications (such as video) are planned for the future?

_____

_____

_____

❑ Do you have an existing directory for users?

_____

❑ Is the directory standards-compliant, such as LDAP v3?

_____

❑ Are you planning to move to Active Directory, or do you use Active Directory today?

_____

LAN

❑ Provide a detailed network plan showing full LAN and WAN infrastructure.

_____

❑ Is your infrastructure LAN switched?

_____

❑ Is this 10/100? Gigabit?

_____

❑ Copper or fibre?

_____

❑ What type of wiring do you have? CAT 5? CAT 5e (mandatory)?

_____

❑ Are all pairs terminated at user desks?

_____

❑ Have you turned on QoS?

_____

❑ Is your infrastructure based on Cisco Catalyst?

_____

❑ Are your switches able to provide line power?

_____

❑ How many users are already connected to your switched network?

_____

❑ Is Layer 3 routing used?

_____

❑ Are VLANs with inter-VLAN routing using Layer 3?

_____

❑ Is redundancy and resiliency built into your LAN?

_____

❑ Have you used redundant power supplies?

_____

❑ Do you use UPSs for your LAN infrastructure?

_____

❑ What is the volume of data traffic currently on the LAN?

_____

❑ What applications are you using on the LAN?

_____

_____

❏ Does any site have Ethernet distance limitations?

❏ Do you utilize DHCP and DNS services on your network?

❏ Can additional options be provisioned?

WAN

❏ Please provide a detailed network plan showing full LAN and WAN infrastructure.

❑ What is the bandwidth going between the sites within the WAN?

❑ What is the total number of calls between sites, including MoH streams, conferencing streams, call transfers, and so on?

❑ Depending on the bandwidth in the WAN, which codec are you going to select for calls between remote sites and the central site?

❑ What Gateways are you using within your existing network?

❑ How much memory do you have in these routers?

❑ Are there free slots within your routers?

❑ Are your routers capable of voice?

❑ Has QoS been turned on?

❑ Are existing voice solutions running within the network that you could leverage?

❑ How many calls do you currently make between sites?

❑ Do you have data-on-call capacity and busy hour calls?

❑ Do you have call accounting information?

Analog Connectivity

❑ How many fax machines will be used at each site?

❑ How many analog conference phones do you need to connect? (Leverage 7935 if possible.)

❑ Is there a need to connect DECT (Digital Cordless) handsets for warehouses, for example?

❑ Do these DECT handsets want call pickup? (You might have to position VG200.)

❑ Are wireless phones an option, subject to site survey?

❑ How many modems are used and where? How many ports are used?

❑ Do you plan to use the ATA186 as a low-end Fax Gateway?

Digital Connectivity

❑ Are you going to allow users to break out from their local sites?

❑ Do you have existing Gateways at these sites that are capable of voice?

❑ Do you want to receive incoming calls at these remote sites locally as well?

❑ What do you envision the call volume in and out of that remote site would be?

_____

❑ Are you looking at BRI, fractional PRI, or full PRI? (This decision influences your choice of Gateway.)

_____

❑ If you are ordering a PRI, IOS Gateways support, full or fractional PRIs, how many digits do you want to deliver on the PRI? (DE30+ does not support fractional PRI.)

_____

❑ Have you ordered Euro ISDN? Digital Access Signaling System (DASS) is not supported natively on our Gateways. (You will need a converter if this is the case.)

_____

❑ Which does the PBX support?
   ❑ Q.SIG
   ❑ DPNSS

_____

Dial Plan

❑ How many digits is your dial plan?

_____

❑ Is there a unified dial plan across your sites?

_____

❑ Are there overlapping dial plans? How many digits?

_____

❑ What are the DDI ranges, and how many digits will the provider present?

_____

❏ Do users on the system have calling restrictions? (If yes, break these down per user groups.)

❏ Can callers break out from other remote sites?

NOTE   Cisco TAC does not officially support an NANP edited dial plan, such as the UK dial plan. (The UK dial plan can cause reporting issues to the Administration and Reporting Tool [ART].)

You can find an example of a simple table for a dial plan at http://www.cisco.com/warp/public/788/AVVID/dp_isdn_gateway.html.

Third-Party Special Features

❏ Do you need billing and call accounting?

❏ How advanced does the billing system need to be? (That is, do you want to bill by department, number of unanswered calls, and so on?)

❏ Do you need simple call accounting and billing?

❏ Do you need automatic call distributor (ACD) type functionality to route calls to skills-based people?

❏ Do you need advanced hunt groups?

❏ Do you need a hardware console?

❑ Do you need conferencing with a large number of people?

❑ How often is conferencing done between sites?

❑ How often does conferencing occur between users on a site?

❑ Is conferencing performed at remote sites?

❑ Do you think users use ad-hoc conferencing?

❑ What type of phones do you currently have? Manager handsets?

Features

Assess the features you need:

❑ Manager/secretary?
❑ Call forward per phone?
❑ Queuing of calls?
❑ Do users typically use speed dials? How many does each user typically have?

❑ How many system speed dials are in use?

❑ Do you need hotdesking today? Is this per site—extension mobility?

❑ Conferencing: Provide details of conferencing both between and internal to your sites.

_____

_____

_____

❑ Are you planning to use SoftPhones?

❑ Which users would typically use SoftPhones?

_____

❑ Is there a need for web services to phones (such as to access the intranet for company information)?

❑ Are users expecting music on hold?

❑ How many people do you envisage being on hold at any one time?

_____

❑ Do remote sites have music on hold or tone on hold capability?

_____

❑ Do you require an automated attendant?

_____

❑ Do you use IVR products?

_____

❑ Are you thinking about implementing IVR applications such as database queries for information retrieval?

_____

❑ Do you need overhead paging services?

_____

❑ How do you use night service?

_____

❑ Do you use night bell?

❑ Are call park and call pickup facilities used? Describe their use within the organization.

Voice Mail

❑ Are existing voice mail packages in use?

❑ Is this a PBX-included voice mail?

❑ Is this centralized or networked voice mail?

❑ What protocol/signaling does your voice mail package use to talk to your PBX?

❑ Do you plan to use unified messaging?

❑ How many line appearances will you require for each phone?

❑ Do you use Outlook?

❑ Do you use Exchange?

❏ Which version of Exchange do you use?

_____

❏ What is PBX Model, including software version?

_____

❏ Does PBX have analog or digital cards for voice mail connectivity?

_____

❏ What type of integration exists between customer's legacy voice mail and PBX?

_____

❏ What advanced features are supported?

_____

_____

❏ Is CallManager required to interoperate with legacy PBX?

_____

❏ Is legacy PBX or voice mail networked to other PBXs/voice mail systems?

_____

❏ How many users are on each PBX?

_____

❏ Other application details?

_____

_____

_____

❏ What is the customer's CallManager migration plan?

_____

_____

_____

❏ What is the customer's voice mail cutover date?

_____

THE MIGRATION STRATEGY

As you prepare for the implementation, the migration strategy should be well thought-out and documented. It should clarify the plan set by the design phase and confirm the expectations for the implementation. This chapter discusses the steps that the Cisco implementation team took and the processes that they put into place to set the stage for the migration.

Hold Planning Workshop

As discussed in Chapter 2, "Before You Begin," a successful project team includes representation from every group within the organization that is impacted by the initiative. With our IP Telephony Tiger Team members selected, it was time to prepare for the implementation, which we kicked off with a planning workshop that each member of the team attended. With 55 buildings on the Cisco San Jose campus, each consisting of up to four floors and housing up to 800 employees, our goal of converting one building per week would require everyone's complete participation and cooperation from the first day throughout the entire endeavor.

The workshop is essential to ensure that the initiative stays true to the specific business requirements of the organization and meets the objectives of the implementation. Project team members work together to plan the project deliverables, address solution capabilities, define hardware and software documentation, assign partner implementation services, identify the project-critical path, and agree on project milestones.

- **Define expectations**—Clearly define the goals and expected results and ensure that everyone understands exactly what is expected of him.

- **Prepare project plan**—As project manager (PM), I worked with team members to develop a project plan that would meet the specific business requirements and goals of the initiative and ensure the completion of deliverables. I communicated to each team member his deliverables and his role in accomplishing them, and ensured that each team member agreed and was on board right from the start.

- **Develop implementation budget**—The project manager works closely with the team's financial analyst to outline all the expenditures, order equipment, and time the equipment's arrival when needed. Each key member of the team outlines his expenses (that is, infrastructure equipment, tools, contract resources, training, PRIs, T1s, scanners, and so on) so that the budget for each building as well as the entire project can be developed. Breaking down the budget by building enables you to track your expenses so that you can easily identify the opportunities for cost reductions. Key stakeholders should then validate the proposed budget to ensure that they can track progress against expenditures feasibly.

TIP   Be sure to track all your PBX lease expenses in your overall budgetary plan to ensure that you do not incur additional fees for missing lease return deadlines.

- **Designate project management structure**—As the PM, I managed equipment, labor, project timelines, and other resource scheduling, as well as coordinated work activities. I also made sure that there was a consistent flow of information between the team members and from the team to our end users.

- **Establish project communication plan**—Defining the communication processes—both formal and informal—for routine status reporting, issue resolution, change control, quality assurance, and key milestone date validation was critical. (See the section "The Communication Plan" later in this chapter for more detail.)

- **Create an issues log and an action plan**—This enables you to track action items to be sure they have either been completed or will be completed on time to mitigate risk. The action plan is a short condensed version of the project plan. The action plan segments out the issue log in a single sheet that you can allocate to your team leads for resolution during staff meetings.

- **Develop a training strategy**—Determine the training needs and outline the various high-level approaches to meet the end user's needs. (See the section "User Training" within this chapter for more detail.)

- **Develop a support strategy**—Develop a high-level support strategy, including the benefits and responsibilities surrounding network monitoring and Day 1/Day 2 support. (See Chapter 5, "Day 2 Handoff and Support" for more detail on support issues.)

- **Conduct risk assessment**—Review the high-level approach and action plan developed during the workshop and identify any risks that might be associated with it. Develop contingency planning related to those items. (See Chapter 6, "Final Piece of the Conversion" for more detail on managing risk.)

- **Determine organizational change readiness**—After you identify change impacts, assess the organization's readiness for the change resulting from the IP Telephony implementation and integration. The Organizational Change Plan should cover the following four areas—sponsorship, resistance, cultural alignment/communications, and skills. (See Appendix 2-B for the Organizational Change Template).

- **Review project templates**—Ensure that adequate tools and templates exist to support the execution of activities in the planning, design, and implementation phases. Using templates saves time and creates efficiencies between the teams. Make sure you update the templates as process improvements are identified.

- **Obtain final acceptance**—Complete the workshop by validating the findings and direction with key stakeholders via either a formal or informal process. This final step ensures that all key stakeholders have agreed to the design, the migration strategy, and the implementation process. We accomplished this by asking each stakeholder during our "Go/No Go" meeting to give his verbal approval that the project and design were ready to proceed. To ensure accountability, you might want to have each person sign off on an approval sheet.

Use the Cisco Planning Workshop Template to begin your planning sessions. The Planning Workshop is intended to help articulate the customer requirements and expectations for the solution. It also allows the existing network to be clarified. The Planning Workshop is scheduled after all site surveys have been returned and analyzed. All information that is obtained during the Planning Workshop is utilized in the planning deliverable and ultimately in the design phase.

Appendix 3-A, "Planning Workshop Template," provides a checklist that outlines the topics and issues that must be discussed during the Planning Workshop. This appendix appears at the end of this chapter and is also available at http://www.ciscopress.com/1587200880.

A Phased Approach

The number of employees, complexity of the user requirements, size of the campus, and scope of dispersion all have an effect on the migration strategy and the ability to manage a constantly changing landscape. Like most organizations, Cisco employees are consistently on the move, with existing employees changing locations or new employees being added on a regular basis.

With a population of nearly 20,000 employees located throughout a large campus environment, the Tiger Team knew they were not dealing with a static environment. To accommodate this issue, we developed new processes and procedures that took into account all the variables that can change or otherwise affect the new converged voice and data network we were implementing.

We divided the migration into categories: new employees, existing employees who were moving to a new location, retrofitting existing buildings, and installing IP phones in new buildings (also known as *greenfields*).

New Employees

The Tiger Team began the conversion process by issuing all new employees an IP phone with an external power supply. Working with human resources, the Cisco new employee checklist was changed to reflect the allocation of an IP phone along with other standard equipment requirements, such as a new computer and the assignment of an office or cube location. Allocating an IP phone to all new employees right away helped introduce them to the Cisco technology culture and began the process of culture change from old-world PBX to IP Telephony.

When I first started my career at Cisco, the migration was in its early pilot stage. Because I had joined IT—one of the first few groups targeted to try out the new technology—I was given an IP phone. Most new employees (including me) took the new technology in stride because the new phone did not require much training. New employees were already in the mode of change, and being issued an IP phone did not really have a startling impact.

Basic training included a pamphlet that offered user instructions as well as a telephone number to call if additional assistance was required. Keep in mind that I was joining IT during the pilot phase, so if I had serious questions, I could ask my neighbor sitting next to me for assistance. I should also note that our training requirements did change after the migration was in full swing. Those requirements are outlined in the "User Training" section found later in this chapter.

Relocations (Adds, Moves, Changes)

Location changes occur often within Cisco. At any point in time, 300–600 employees are in the process of moving from one location to another. It is common around Cisco for the average employee to move from one building to another at least three times. This happens for a variety of reasons, including new positions within the company, business expansion, and organizational changes.

By the time the conversion process neared completion, a large percentage of employees already had an IP phone, and a policy change was instituted instructing employees on how to update the company directory with their new office or cube location.

The Tiger Team's migration policy required employees who were still using a PBX phone at the time of their relocation to be issued a new Cisco IP Phone. Employees were given instructions on how to disconnect and leave behind their old phones, and a "pick-up" procedure was incorporated as part of the new policy. The team worked with Cisco WorkPlace Resources (WPR) and Facilities Management (FM) to ensure compliance with the new policy.

Individuals who already had IP phones could move their phones themselves and found that their relocations were more efficient and easier for them and for operations. Their relocations were also less costly for Cisco.

Existing Buildings

The retrofit process stage of the migration included the infrastructure upgrade and user conversion of all locations building by building. During the retrofit, the team identified all users and phone lines within each building, and performed a weekend conversion in which all verified lines were steered to the CallManager and the allocation of IP phones. "We found that conducting the conversion in this way ensured that regardless of the diverse make-up of the user groups or the DID prefix assignment of an employee, everyone within the building was part of the conversion," said Bill Lowers, AVVID senior network engineer.

New Buildings

At the time of the IP Telephony implementation, Cisco was periodically adding new buildings to the San Jose campus and in certain branch locations as part of an ongoing organizational expansion. However, because these buildings were not yet occupied, there was no need to include them in the phased implementation approach because no users would be involved, requiring training, scheduling, and other factors necessary as part of the initiative. Therefore, IP Telephony infrastructure was implemented in these new buildings as a flash cut—a single event.

"A parallel deployment was integrated for new buildings at the same time as the retrofit for the rest of the campus that allowed those users to migrate slowly to the new system," said Lowers. "This was done typically on number ranges to reduce the translations between the two systems."

The San Jose campus included a phased migration (see Figure 3-1) for which 55 buildings and 50,000 direct inward dials (DIDs) were in existence. We created a plan ensuring that all users, buildings, and lines were included in the conversion.

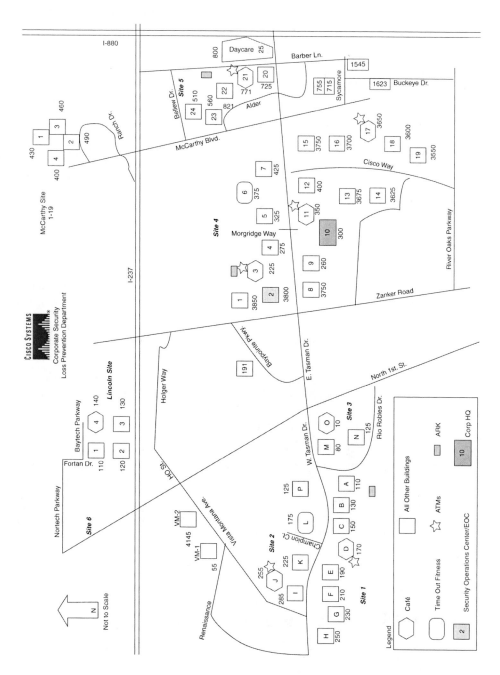

Figure 3-1 *Cisco Systems San Jose Campus Phased Migration*

Best Practices: A Phased Approach

Conducting a smooth migration takes forethought. Use the following tips to build your migration plan and set the stage for success:

- Conduct a pilot session with a smaller population and noncritical buildings to ensure that the plan is smooth, bugs are worked out, and a workable process is in place.

- Begin the conversion by issuing all new employees an IP phone.

- Whenever an employee moves his location, issue an IP phone rather than moving the old PBX phone to the new location.

- Ensure that your migration strategy covers potential schedule changes that might affect the conversion process.

- Incorporate policy changes that encourage the conversion to the new IP phone.

- Develop a strategy to convert all your PBX-leased-equipment buildings first so that when leases come up for renewal, there is more flexibility during the migration process.

- Work closely with the operations teams that are responsible for adds, moves, and changes to maintain a uniform policy on IP phone installation and configurations.

- Be sensitive to the company calendar; do not schedule a migration at the same time as a quarter end. Employees are extremely busy during this time, making the migration difficult.

Optimize Project Pace and Schedule

Most initiatives burst out of the gate with enthusiasm and good intentions, but many times things happen to slow down that momentum. To complete the initiative within the timeline, we created a schedule that established the project's pace, kept things on track, reduced risk, and identified and removed all major roadblocks.

Establish Milestones

A large-scale IP Telephony implementation is an evolving initiative. Keeping the migration team focused on the goal for more than a year would be a challenge. To address this, we identified specific short- and long-term milestones to guide the team and demonstrate to senior management that we were making progress. This helped to keep the momentum going and the motivation level high. These milestones can be instrumental in determining the project pace, but only if they are relevant, provide value, are achievable, and are aligned with company goals.

One of the milestones used in the Cisco deployment was the impending PBX leases that were coming up for renewal. The goals that senior management established required that no leases be renewed past the renewal deadline. Tying that goal to the deployment objectives was a great opportunity to drive the project team for measurable results.

In all, 22 PBX Expansion Port Network (EPN) leases were coming up for renewal within a six-month period. We massaged the schedule to accommodate the lease deadline, resulting in some buildings converted earlier and some later to coincide with the lease agreements.

That strategy enabled the implementation team to disconnect all relevant PBXs—except for the main PBX switch that supported call centers—in time to avoid extending any of the lease agreements. This satisfied the senior management directive of no lease renewals and helped us to meet a measurable and important milestone.

Work Closely with Technology Team

Joining forces and working closely with the LAN team helped ensure that the implementation schedule remained on track. The implementation team stayed at least two to three weeks behind the LAN upgrade team to allow time to put the appropriate infrastructure in place and to solve problems that could negatively impact the project.

For example, in the early stages of the implementation, the team had to install power supplies with each phone in those areas where the infrastructure was not yet in place. After the team had installed the desktop LAN switches and retrofitted the rest of the infrastructure, inline power was available for the phones, and the implementation team no longer had to spend precious time working around that critical need.

TIP	If IP phone power supplies are deployed because the LAN infrastructure is not yet in place, add the task of picking up these power supplies during the project cleanup phase, which is outlined in Chapter 6.

The engineering team helped to maintain the pace of the project as well. Due to the sheer volume of users impacted by the migration, the team had to accommodate several unique phone setups. The engineering team helped find workarounds for those situations and other special configurations that required additional assistance, time, and attention.

Once, we found that one of the lines we needed to convert was a "hot line" for customer-critical calls. The phone needed to ring on multiple desks so that several people could pick up that call. Engineering was able to jump in and help us work through that issue to keep us moving on schedule.

Remove Obstacles

Removing obstacles from the path of the implementation team not only kept the project on track, but also kept the team motivated because they were able to spend more time moving forward and less time fighting fires.

For example, the last thing we wanted was for the implementation team to find that the equipment was not delivered or the revolving operations staging room door was locked, causing a delay while we waited for security to come and open it. The implementation team members were Cisco IP Telephony partners; having them stand around idle while waiting for equipment to show up could have quickly caused the schedule to slip and costs to spiral out of control.

I spent a lot of time thinking about and preparing for project delays. One step I implemented to reduce some of the risk factors was to automate as much of the process as possible. Therefore, instead of having to remember a task each week, I made arrangements for the various cross-functional teams to complete a certain task automatically.

For example, it was necessary to identify a revolving operations staging room along with a locked door every week. I set up an automated process with facilities to align the allocation of a staging room with our room schedule. I also had a locksmith put a lock on every staging room door. I then asked the locksmith to create the same key for each room so that my team could have the same key every week, thus reducing delays and confusion as to getting access to a locked staging room.

Incorporating processes like this enabled the weekly change to stay consistent yet efficient.

Develop Vendor Relationships

Although some of the vendors and partners that Cisco worked with were not involved at the beginning of the initiative, the Tiger Team brought them in early enough to ensure that they knew the scope of the project and the process. This also made the vendors and partners understand that they were a vital part of the team.

"We found that because we had engaged the partners early, on more than one occasion they were willing and able to jump in and help us resolve issues that came up periodically," said Doug McQueen, manager of strategic program management.

Vendors included the cable vendor, locksmith, telco carrier, PBX vendor, security team, facility WPR team, change management controller, and so on. All were critical to the success of the project. Creating relationships with these vendors ensured that if a problem arose, they would be much more willing to jump in and offer the needed assistance to get an issue resolved.

Identify an Operations Center

At the heart of the implementation was the operations center (also known as the "war room"), a room in each building that was designated as the implementation team's center of operations. Because the schedule called for converting one building per week over a period of 12 months, it was imperative that when the implementation team arrived, everything was ready to roll.

Equipment used in the installation process was delivered to the operations center the Wednesday before the team arrived, along with all necessary tools, diagrams, reports, and other incidentals that they required to perform the retrofit.

To make updates quick and easy, the issue log was posted on whiteboards in the operations center so that as team members entered the room, they could immediately see the outstanding issues of the day and what they needed to do. (Obtain a copy of the Cisco Steps to Success Issues Log at http://www.cisco.com/go/stepstosuccess. A Cisco.com login is required.)

Taking full advantage of our own new technology, we issued designated IP phones to the operations center team members to take with them as they traveled from one building to another. This strategy enabled the support team to receive calls from users in the current building—as well as users from the building just completed—no matter where they were.

The calls followed the implementation team as they moved between buildings and ensured that someone was always available to answer the phone, even if that person was not actually in the operations center. The phones were also programmed to page the implementation team any time a user left a voice mail, ensuring timely response to calls 24 hours a day.

Finally, the operations center served as a centralized location where users could come to ask questions, see a demo, get training, and pick up accessories. The operations center was open and staffed from 7 a.m.–5 p.m. For before or after hours, users had access to the implementation team's voice mail and e-mail alias.

Best Practices: Optimize Project Pace and Schedule

Maintaining the project pace and schedule are critical components of a phased migration. The following best practices will help keep the team on track and surprises at a minimum:

- An experienced implementation team and support team who intimately know the history of the telecommunications system can identify nonstandard phone setups and any other "gotchas."

- Consistent review of all processes, procedures, and routine requests ensure that little issues do not become big problems, such as the following:

  - Post deployment status and schedule on the IP Telephony website. (See the next section.)

  - Automate all routine procedures, such as equipment deliveries, pickup, storage, and operations center reservations for each building.

- Conduct PBX dumps early to identify all business-critical lines and unique setups, and perform continuous traffic studies.

- Ensure prolific communication among the following teams: operations, implementation, engineering, support, security, WPR, call center, LAN infrastructure, and security operations.

- Assign a room in each building to be used as the operations center, and issue an IP phone that can travel with the team.

- Users are not the only ones who can take advantage of the newly installed IP Telephony solution. Take advantage of the power and flexibility of the IP Telephony solution to help you provide consistent and cost-effective support during the transition.

- Minimize disruption by planning the IP transition to follow the LAN infrastructure upgrades by a few weeks. This allows LAN infrastructure deployment, testing, and stabilization before cutover to the new voice infrastructure.

The Communication Plan

Chapter 2 identified the importance of a well thought-out and comprehensive communication plan. No change initiative can be successful unless all the stakeholders — the implementation team as well as the end users — know what to expect. Users need to know what the change is, why the change is being implemented, how the change will impact them, what behavior modifications are expected, and when the change is coming. The implementation team must work toward shared goals, implementing the initiative in an effective manner and maintaining consistency throughout the initiative.

The executive sponsor also played a key role in the communication plan, broadcasting messages and conducting hands-on meetings to share information concerning the impending rollout. The Cisco sponsor, John Chambers, shared the reasons behind the deployment in his messaging so that all employees knew how the change would benefit them.

As the project team lead, I was responsible for developing and managing the communication plan. To maintain consistency, all communication was filtered through me. A variety of communication vehicles ensured that the message was consistent, accurate, and highly relevant to each user. We utilized tools that made the support process easy for both the team and for the user. These tools included e-mail, web postings, Video on Demand (VoD), e-alerts (targeted e-mails) pointing to news on the website, and e-communities (online discussion boards).

Develop the Communication Strategy

Developing a specific communication plan helped us to achieve the communications objectives of the project, which included ownership, development and delivery timeframes, ordering all equipment, and proposed communication vehicles. The plan sought to discover who the stakeholders were, what they needed to know, how to identify resistance, and how to respond.

The first step we undertook was to decide what our communication approach would be for the change initiative and create a strategy around how we planned to achieve it. We identified the following four elements and used them throughout the deployment to measure and provide an objective for the overall communication plan.

- **Content and information**—Provide people with the right information so they can continue to be effective in their jobs and contribute to the success of the deployment. Make sure the content is relevant to users and post only useful or interesting information that will encourage use of the communication vehicles.

- **Strategic context**—Ensure that the information is relevant to the user's situation and help him understand how it fits into the organization's strategic direction.

- **Leadership alignment**—Align the team's actions with leaders' words, ensuring consistency in messaging.

- **Listening and feedback**—Ensure that a process for two-way communication has been enabled and translate the feedback into a timely action.

Other strategies we developed that enabled us to ensure a smooth and consistent flow of communication included web-based tools that made our jobs easier and allowed users to access the information they needed when they needed it. These strategies included developing a project website and creating e-mail aliases.

Initiate a Project Website

We created a project website on Cisco Employee Connection (CEC), the Cisco internal employee intranet. The website served as a central source for anyone who wanted information on the project. As the initiative unfolded, the information posted was available for the entire company and served as an effective way to relay summary information quickly and provide a map to the more detailed information. We put our project's web address in our .sig (e-mail signatures) file so that every e-mail we sent pointed people directly to the address.

The project website was the most effective way for the end users to see when their buildings were scheduled to be converted and identify the cross-functional team members who would be conducting the implementation and providing assistance. The site provided status information, including which buildings had already been converted, how many remained on the schedule, as well as a link to the PBX return status so that users could see which PBX would be disconnected, where it was, and what time it would happen. The website communicated access to the online user guide, tutorial, and supplemental documentation in lieu of physical training. Employees could even use the website to order accessories, such as headsets, for their new IP phone.

The project website also served as a consolidated place for all communication that was relative to the project team members. Many templates were posted on the website, such as the IP Phone Test Procedure and templates for signage and box labels. The project team list was available to identify the design lead, install lead, WPR representative, and a full team roster with roles and responsibilities. In addition, I posted a progress report of the rollout and updated the website on a weekly basis.

The following list shows the files most accessed on the project website:

- Deployment status report, which provided the percentage of users currently on the system, with a rising graph indicating the conversion rate

- "IP Phone Tip of the Week" and answers to frequently asked questions (FAQs)

- General information, such as environmental diagrams, timelines, project scope, special access project information folders, and project goals

- Online IP phone tutorials, user guides, demos, and documentation on advanced IP phone features

Create E-Mail Aliases

To develop communication outlets that enabled users to voice concerns, ask questions, and request specialized training, the communications team developed e-mail aliases to make the process as easy as possible for both users and Tiger Team members. An e-mail alias creates a distribution list of recipients so that relevant information can be targeted to specific individuals and groups. This was useful in distributing building notifications only to those users who were impacted during that week.

- **Customer case alias**—The customer case alias was developed to enable users to send questions and comments directly to the implementation and support team. Two weeks before the conversion, an announcement was distributed detailing the deployment and how users could communicate with the retrofit team. We received great feedback from the user community on this tool. Our policy mandated that every e-mail be reviewed and a response sent within 24 hours. All members of the implementation team were added to the customer case alias distribution list to provide them with frontline visibility to the issues, concerns, and questions that were being raised. My assigned backup and I handled all responses to ensure consistency and adherence to protocol. Some of the questions were repetitive, but we were able to point those to the FAQs site on our website, which helped to keep the number of responses manageable.

- **Project team e-mail alias**—The project team e-mail alias was a vehicle for all members of the project team to receive timely updates on the conversion, such as which buildings were coming online and when, and highlighting any special configurations or issues that they needed to be aware of. During the weekly status meetings, all cross-functional team members were invited to discuss issues that might cause the project to slow. For those members who were unable to attend a meeting, the project team alias was a way for them to catch up on what they missed, provide critical information to the rest of the team, and prevent unnecessary two-way information gaps.

- **Implementation team alias**—The implementation team alias enabled those individuals to receive specific and focused communications that the rest of the team did not need to receive. It prevented an overload of information to everyone else and kept the installers up to speed on special setups, unique situations, or other relevant issues.

- **Building notifications alias**—Even before the IP Telephony initiative began, WPR routinely used a building e-mail alias to communicate with residents of each particular building. Residents included those who telecommuted from home but were a part of a workgroup located in that particular building. The Tiger Team capitalized on that alias to send an announcement two weeks before each building conversion, providing in-depth information about the schedule, what to expect, how to inform the team about special configurations or business-critical phone lines, and how they could request additional information. Because the migration strategy involved a phased approach, deploying IP Telephony one building at a time, the building alias enabled the team to focus their communication on the needs of the individuals in that building for the seven days it took to convert it.

Refer to Appendix 3-B, "Sample Users Conversion Notice." The Users Conversion Notice is an example of a communication medium that was sent to users about the impending cutover to their new IP phone. Use this sample to create your own communication message.

This appendix is available at the end of this chapter and is also available at http://www.ciscopress.com/1587200880.

Best Practices: Communication Plan

Developing a communication plan is one of the most important components of a project. Use the following best practices to develop a plan that will lessen anxiety, encourage change, and create excitement for the migration to IP Telephony.

- State the project benefits in terms that employees can understand, describing the change from their frame of reference, and articulating the impact on behaviors and tasks.

- Communicate the reasons for the change, make a strong case for why that change is necessary, and explain how the organization will differ as a result.

- Ensure that communication is behavioral as well as verbal. Management must demonstrate sponsorship behaviors that reinforce the verbal communication of change.

- Communicate how the change is grounded in the organization's existing values and commitments. If a change in culture is required to implement the change, make a strong case and begin the process of culture change with the IP Telephony initiative.

- Consistently communicate the vision statement down through the organizational hierarchy to ensure a cascading network of communication and sponsorship.

- Enable opportunities for two-way communication. Enlist employee ideas and suggestions for how to make the vision a reality, and then act on those ideas.

- Develop a project website that users can go to for more information concerning the schedule, FAQs, training, and so on.

- Develop an e-mail alias that is targeted for each specific group so that people are not overloaded with information that is not relevant to them. Also, limit communication to important messages only. Most employees are bombarded with e-mails, and you do not want your message to get lost.

Identify Business-Critical Phone Users

People use their phones differently. Although some might require only occasional use for two-way voice conversations, others need high-speed fax capability. Administrative assistants might support multiple managers and need separate lines for each. Eliminating buyers' remorse and meeting the expectations of your clients relies heavily on the ability to understand the usage pattern and the business requirements of each department and group before scheduling the migration.

Reports generated from the existing PBX switch, the voice mail system, and the directory listing provided Cisco with critical information about its existing phone population. "These consolidated lists helped us to determine which users were working from home and which users would need a phone set in the office," said Mary Tsang, service and support manager. The lists are available from the PBX and should be obtained as early as possible to avoid unnecessary changes at the last minute or, even worse, on the first day of production. "Those kinds of changes make it extremely painful for both the project manager and the end user," Tsang said.

We took extreme care when deploying the phones to business-critical users to ensure that no disruption in service occurred and that specific configuration solutions were identified and resolved in advance.

TIP	Review your existing PBX contract to ensure that you have ownership of your PBX configuration report. Some PBX vendors might challenge the release of this information when the decision has been made to migrate to a new technology. Access to this data becomes critical when you are duplicating the configurations of all your users to your new Voice over IP (VoIP) solution.

Business-Critical Phone Users

The Cisco business-critical phone users include the following:

- Call center agents and their backups

- Modem lines that call center agents use

- Lobby receptionist who is configured with a call center setup

- Call center agents who support callers over the weekend and require uninterrupted service

- Call center agents who are tied to the leased PBX and scheduled for disconnect

- Modem lines used for high-speed financial transmissions or for other critical and timely transactions

- Support teams who troubleshoot live customer calls

- Senior management private lines where sensitive information is shared

- 1-MB lines tied directly to the telephone company (telco) carrier rather than the production network

- TV studio where live feeds are broadcast

- Administrative assistant who has unique configurations

- Administrative assistants who support more than one manager

- Hotlines that are designated "drop everything and answer"

- Engineering labs with special modem lines

- Test labs that tie directly into the PBX

- Emergency phones, such as those located in the elevators or parking lots

Call Center Agents

Call center agents are the most business-critical phone users at Cisco. These individuals act as the front line to the customer on a variety of issues—from the routine to priority-one urgency. As part of our effort to implement a phased migration, the Tiger Team made the decision that the call centers would not be cut over to IP until Internet Protocol Contact Center (IPCC) features that provide customers with equal or better service than PBX became available. (Cisco has since made the transition to its IPCC solution. See Chapter 7, "Moving Forward: Continuing to Be Cisco's First and Best Customer," for more information.)

IPCC features combine voice and data technologies and facilitate customer interaction that originates from multiple sources, such as IP voice, time-division multiplexing (TDM) voice, web, e-mail, and fax to empower a true multimedia customer contact center. Because IPCC was not yet available at the time of the Cisco IP Telephony deployment, the implementation team conducted only a partial retrofit of all protected buildings — those areas where call center agents, backup agents, and analog devices requiring special consideration were located. This type of partial retrofit enabled voice services to place approximately 5000 lines on the IP network and eliminate those lines off the PBX.

"This was a big win and huge cost savings for Cisco," said Shelby Roshan, IT financial analyst. "The partial retrofit of our ten protected buildings allowed us to complete the campus conversion and leave the nonleased PBX EPNs until the Cisco IPCC solution became available."

The implementation team worked closely with the contact center team to ensure that all call center lines were flagged as "Do Not Touch" and removed from the retrofit cut sheets. The teams then continued to work together to investigate the IPCC solution, which provides call center agents with the IP functionality but without the use of a PBX EPN.

The Cisco contact centers handle more than 100,000 calls per week in addition to a multitude of e-mails and web requests. Global Call Center (GCC), the most complex call center at Cisco, acts as the "frontline" for the Technical Assistance Center (TAC), answering calls, creating TAC cases, and dispatching the technical response teams. The GCC will be the first to use this solution to manage the more than 20,000 calls that it will receive monthly. At the time of this writing, IPCC was successfully being implemented into the GCC.

Best Practices: Business-Critical Phone Users

All phone users are important and tolerate little room for error. However, for specific users, failure is not an option. Use these tips to keep critical phone user issues from halting the project:

- Know who your business-critical phone line users are, and have a solution in place in advance of the conversion.

- Do not rely on users to tell you their configurations. Verify their understanding of their configuration with a PBX dump.

- Configuration mistakes are serious. Do the homework, and use the operations team to help flush out "special configurations."

- If critical features are not available, conduct a partial retrofit of everyone except for users who depend on those features so that you can still convert the building.

- Call center agents are critical. Ensure that you have a strong check and balance policy to ensure 100-percent voice access.

- Customer service is key to a smooth transition. Ensure that the implementation team abides by a 24-hour or less response time to all user inquiries.

- Use the communication vehicles thoughtfully. Users are already bombarded with e-mails, so you want your message to be relevant, timely, and useful.

- Eliminate buyers' remorse by meeting user expectation. Do your homework—if you spend 80 percent of your time planning, you should only spend 20 percent of your time implementing.

Converting "Executive Row"

Executive row is the nickname that Cisco employees use to describe the building and the floors where the organization's senior staff resides. Although the needs of all the organization's users are important and receive the team's undivided attention, executive row is one of the most publicly visible and is another example of a business-critical user group. This group has the highest use of administrative assistant staff, the highest need for special configuration, and a greater sensitivity for getting it right the first time.

Executive row consists of the Cisco CEO and senior executives who routinely speak to government officials, customers, the media, and other highly visible organizations. The availability of their phones and the phones of the admin staff who support them is critical. Their jobs often revolve around the availability, flexibility, and quality of their phones. The team soon learned that if it could get the admin staff through the conversion, migrating the executive staff to the IP phones would be a much smoother process.

Simple courtesies and exceptions to policies whenever necessary proved to be effective here, just as they were when we were working with our business-critical users. "The dynamics of executive row is fast paced and process driven. Being sensitive to their needs and maintaining some flexibility in operational policy to get issues resolved quickly for them was necessary," said Marisa Chancellor, director of voice services.

Engage Your Sponsor

When executive row was scheduled for conversion, the first thing the team's executive sponsor, CEO John Chambers, did was to send a private message to his staff about the impending conversion, requesting their cooperation. Because of heavy workload and total dependency on phone availability, this group was understandably apprehensive about the conversion. However, Chambers' message eliminated potential pushback from both the executives and the admin staff because they understood how critical this initiative was to the organization.

For starters, the team prepared a list from the Cisco Directory of all those who were identified with an admin title. After the team identified a reliable list, it met personally with employees on the list to understand their current phone setup, how they used their phone, and which features were most important to them.

The team anticipated, however, that most users would not be well versed on their phone setup. Therefore, they also took the time to pre-identify all private lines, emergency phone lines, and unique configurations. Identifying key phone users and cross referencing their understanding of the setup with that of the data dumped from the PBX ensured that there would be no surprises after the cutover. The team also reviewed the senior executives' existing configurations culled from the PBX review to ensure that their new setup would be the same.

Visual Confirmation of Phone Configuration

After the team completed the interviews, it provided the admin staff with a visual confirmation template of their new phone configuration. Because most admins support multiple managers and multiple phone lines, missing a single phone line configuration would be detrimental. The team took special care to avoid that possibility.

To ensure that expectations were met from the admin's perspective as well as from the implementation team, I created a picture of the front of the IP phone with its buttons visible and arrows drawn to indicate the new button setup. Presenting this confirmation document before the conversion provided the users and implementation team time to agree to the setup or make changes.

Refer to Appendix 3-C, "Phone Configuration Template."

In instances where a specific configuration is required, it is important that both the end user and the installer be in agreement as to the setup requirements. Use the IP Phone Configuration Template as a visual confirmation of how the new phone will be configured. Because most users will not understand CallManager jargon, this confirmation template will go a long way in helping users understand what their new IP phone settings will look like.

This appendix is available at http://www.ciscopres.com/1587200880.

Plan the Schedule

The implementation team then identified the heavy call volume phone users to migrate on the Thursday night before the weekend conversion so that they could get comfortable with their phones on Friday, which is typically a lighter call volume day. This early conversion lessened the impact of the senior admin personnel having to manage typically heavy Monday call volume on a new phone system. The team also facilitated additional training sessions, carefully walking the admin staff through the conversion.

Because admins use their phones differently from standard users, these special training opportunities ensure their understanding of the IP phone features that are most frequently used by support personnel, such as transfer, conference calls, hold, release, and so on.

After the team completed the weekend conversion, they updated voice mail distribution lists and directories and communicated all new phone number changes to the entire admin staff. "This was an important point," said Doug McQueen, manager of strategic program management. "These individuals use distribution lists heavily and special directories daily. Forgetting to update this list will cause a major snag in their distribution system. The last thing you want is someone missing an important message because the distribution list wasn't updated with a new phone number."

Provide Additional Support

Because of the sensitivity of executive row and the larger number of special configurations, the team reserved a conference room nearby for the entire first week to provide additional support to the staff. Floor monitors were assigned to walk the floors and offer proactive and immediate resolution to problems or questions. Learning speed was critical for this particular segment of our audience; therefore, the more support that was available to them, the smoother the conversion would be. In about ten days, the support hotline stopped ringing with questions and concerns, and at that point, the team felt confident that they could close that building's operations center.

The final step to converting executive row was to incorporate a "red carpet" system, which gave the executive admins an immediate vehicle to resolve issues. Executive row houses the most highly visible people in the organization and requires the extra attention to detail to ensure that the transition is smooth and problems are resolved quickly.

"I was a little nervous about the impending conversion and really didn't want my existing phone to leave my desk," said Debbie Gross, chief executive assistant to the president. "But I knew I had to jump in with both feet. The IT project team was absolutely fantastic in terms of being 'on call' and available, helping us learn how to use the phones, solving problems, and in general holding our hands."

Gross admitted that it was difficult at first to get used to the phone. "We had to pay attention to things like pictures of 'off-hook' phones that told us we had a call coming in and envelopes flashing telling us we had voice mail. But it really didn't take that long to train the ear and the eye in terms of what to watch for, and after I got used to it, I really began to like the phone," Gross continued.

Refer to Appendix 3-D, "Executive Row Checklist."

Converting senior management to their new IP phone system is a different process from converting your standard IP phone user. Use the Executive Row Checklist as a reminder of the specific consideration or task these users might require.

This appendix is available at the end of this chapter and at http://www.ciscopress.com/1587200880.

Best Practices: Converting Executive Row

Converting the senior management team requires a certain level of patience and understanding of their unique phone needs. Use these best practices to make the transition easier for all those involved.

- Take extra care to prepare and prioritize the cutover effort for executive row.

- Provide a secondary IP phone to accommodate multiple offices, private phone lines, and private conference rooms. Allocate multiple phone numbers to the same user only when a private line is imperative. However, treat this as an exception to the rule and not a standard option.

- To lessen the anxiety of having to change one's phone number, whenever possible let the user select his own phone number from the available list.

- Install the Cisco 7914 expansion modules to accommodate additional line appearances, heavy speed-dial users, and administrative assistants who support more than one manager.

- Never disconnect unidentified modem lines in executive row until you find the owner to provide authorization.

- Continue to use 1-Mbps lines for critical transmissions (that is, Live TV studio phone lines, fast-speed financial transactions, emergency lines, and so on).

- Provide adequate support staff to man the operations center, and assign floor monitors to offer quick response for user questions and problems.

- Request the onsite assistance of an operations senior staff manager to remain in the operations center to approve requests that fall outside the normal procedure.

- Incorporate a "red carpet" support team for the executive row Day 2 handoff to manage IP phone support issues for senior management and their admin staff. Try allocating a special phone number for this purpose, and be prepared to keep the building's operations center open if a longer transition time is needed.

- Define a boss/admin configuration that optimally supports the objectives of the administrative assistants, and work with engineering to define a boss/admin shared line appearance template so that all setups from both the operations and implementation teams are standardized.

- Interview the administrative assistants to identify their special needs, and create a visual confirmation document that confirms your understanding of their setup. Then conduct a PBX dump to verify each admin configuration.

- Give the administrative assistants prototypes of the phone setup so that they can provide feedback and acclimate to their new phones before the cutover.

- Design a training program that provides individual or small group training sessions.

- Create a simple "cheat sheet" of IP phone symbols so that the admin staff can use it to quickly decipher the new symbols.

- Work with the senior executive admin to identify all the heavy phone users and individuals who might require special assistance, and then convert them on Thursday to lessen anxiety and give them time to learn the new phone setup.

User Training

In a large campus environment such as at Cisco, it was important that a training method was selected that was scalable yet effective for the various levels of experience. Selecting a method that is not scalable slows the pace of the project and might cause unnecessary delays. Basic phone users require little or no training, whereas others might take longer to achieve an acceptable level of comfort. A good rule of thumb is to use a baseline from an existing training initiative that resulted in a favorable outcome. Leverage existing best practices to build the right training strategy for your organization.

The most effective tool for training a large campus environment is the IP Telephony communication website. Utilizing website links, online tutorials, streaming video, and Video on Demand (VoD) allows users to select their own training tools and—more importantly—allows users to decide when it is convenient for them to obtain training.

Every organization learns and trains differently and is usually driven by its own cultural standards. Users might find a structured classroom-type training session useful in the beginning. However, expect to have attendance taper off as the IP phone becomes more familiar. Being flexible and offering several training options is the key to addressing the training needs of all your users.

For those "techies" who want more in-depth information, such as product release notes or advanced product features, provide web link access to that information.

As part of the communication plan, the Tiger Team distributed an announcement to all users (see Appendix 3-A) outlining the changes that users should expect as well as the various links to training tools.

"We did have a couple of instances where users requested a special training session," said Del Hays, AVVID support lead. "So we put together a 10–15 minute overview of key phone features followed by a Q and A session. And, of course, it's always a good idea to have a working phone on display to show real-world examples of how to use the phone."

Early in the conversion process, the IP phone was an anomaly, and users wanted to spend more time understanding the features. We held town hall meetings early on to introduce the phone, share advanced features, and give users an opportunity to ask questions. We distributed copies of the user guide, directed users to the online tutorial link and FAQs, and had several working phones on display to encourage users to play with them. The team also reassured users that in most cases they would not have to change their phone number and that no existing or archived voice mail would be lost.

 Refer to Appendix 3-E, "User Frequently Asked Questions."

A FAQ list is quite useful when the IP phone conversion begins. This FAQ list is beneficial when you begin to capture and build your own FAQ document.

This appendix is provided at the end of this chapter and also at http://www.ciscopress.com/1587200880.

After the IP phone became part of the culture, user training was no longer necessary. However, for those who did request training, a 10-minute IP phone overview was usually sufficient. The implementation/support team used the operations center as a training room and set it up on the Monday and Tuesday after each weekend conversion so that users could drop by and obtain hands-on training.

Use the Operations Center

The operations center added a level of comfort for users because users knew that support was readily available if they needed it. Interestingly, though, the team found that only a small percentage of users actually stopped in for training support or assistance.

"Most of the users' frequently asked questions included information about the headset, phone cords, and how to use the more advanced features of the phone," Hays said. The operations center offered user training and demos and gave users the flexibility of contacting the team using the medium that was most convenient to them—physically coming to the operations center, calling on the phone, or sending an e-mail.

The Cisco culture conducted training at the individual's pace. Figure 3-2 demonstrates survey results indicating that although various training options were provided, the most optimal training solution for learning to use an IP phone was to use online documentation rather than a structured classroom-type session.

Figure 3-2 *Cisco IP Phone User Learning Preferences*

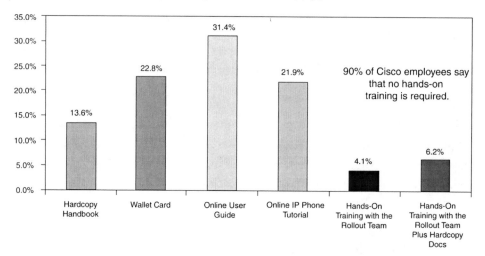

Which methods would you prefer with
learning how to use your Cisco IP
phone? (Choose all that apply.)

Best Practices: User Training

Be sensitive to the needs of your users by offering various training options. The following best practices should serve useful as you design your training strategy:

- Develop a support FAQ document for the support team to ensure uniformity within operational policy. (See Chapter 5.)

- Provide a variety of training methods so that users can choose the ones that best fit their needs, and make those options available via the web.

- Hold town hall meetings early to introduce the phone to your users and help reduce the fear factor. Communicate with your users so that they know the timeline of their migration, expected behavior changes, and places for training.

- Communicate the support team "hotline" phone number, location of the training room, and e-mail alias.

- Allocate an IP phone with the same phone number to the support team so that they can take the phone with them and answer questions wherever they are in the building.

- Use the operations center as a training room so that users have one place to go for answers to questions and for training.

- Set up the building e-mail distribution lists or alias as a communications vehicle to introduce the various training options.

- In the beginning, users will want more training because the IP phone is unfamiliar. After the IP phone becomes part of the culture, five to ten minutes of training per user will suffice for those who want it.

- Admin personnel use the phone differently from other users. Expect to provide additional training for them. After they become familiar with it, they will serve as advocates for the phone. They will also serve as additional outlets that users can go to for answers on IP phone features and functionality.

- Be flexible in your training options because most people will want alternatives to hands-on user training.

Identify Operational Policy Changes

IP Telephony is not just a new technology; it is also a new way of communicating. As such, it requires that new operational support be designed and instituted throughout the organization. Because IP Telephony provides a level of flexibility that was not available before, the team found that it was necessary to institute new operational policies. Although operational policies and other standards are sometimes unpopular, failure to set standards typically results in higher operation costs due to reduced levels of integration, reduced productivity, and increased time to deploy new technologies.

Modem/Analog Policy

The Cisco Information Security Group (InfoSec) already had an established policy on the use of modem lines—who was authorized to have one and how to get authorized if an employee needed one. As part of the building notification process, the Tiger Team sent a web link to all users in that facility that pointed them to InfoSec's modem policy.

The modem/analog policy was something we took very seriously. Since the success of the initiative depended upon following the appropriate security guidelines developed by InfoSec, we wanted to make sure we followed it closely.

Users were asked to respond within one week if they were authorized to use a modem/analog line so that the implementation team could make arrangements to migrate those lines to the CallManager. If the existing lines were not identified within that timeframe, the team disconnected them so that unused or rogue analog lines were not part of the implementation.

With the number of lines we were dealing with—up to 600 lines at a time—it made more sense for us to disconnect those unidentified or unclaimed noncritical modem lines. We could then easily reconnect them if someone came to us later claiming ownership.

Bill's "Clean Network" Theory

The modem/analog policy tied in neatly with Bill's "Clean Network" theory. Bill Lowers, senior network engineer at Cisco, had convinced the team that migrating from PBX systems to a converged voice and data network was the perfect time to clean house. With up to 3000 analog lines located throughout the Cisco San Jose Campus buildings, it was likely that many of those lines were unused, forgotten, or unassigned. Rather than blindly moving those unnecessary lines over to the CallManager, the team took that opportunity to trace and disconnect all noncritical lines that were unidentified or unassigned.

"Obviously, you have to take care when you're in a building with critical phone users, such as our call center agents who troubleshoot problems for customers," said Lowers. "But building as much integrity into the system as possible prevents having to purchase additional infrastructure to support lines you don't even use."

See Chapter 6 for more information on retrofit cleanup.

Operational Security Policy

Security involves technology and practice. Cisco technologies such as Virtual Private Network (VPN), firewalls, and access control lists need to be matched with strong security policies. Therefore, the first step in any security implementation is to establish a security policy. Common security practices include physically restricting access to wiring closets and data centers to authorized staff only, using keyed or electronic locks on doors, installing IP video surveillance equipment, and setting up alarm capabilities.

An IP phone is a direct connection into your network. Lobby phones or phones made available to visitors in other public areas of the organization can create a security breach if they are not managed properly.

"If a visitor chooses to plug his or her laptop into the public IP phone, it can be a direct connection into the organization's data network," said Paul Molyski, IT LAN project manager. "We had to make certain policy changes when deploying these phones in order to ensure security." After each building conversion, Molyski was given a list of all public phones that required LAN network restrictions.

You can find additional information on securing an IP Telephony network in the IP Telephony Solutions Guide. In addition, an online seminar titled "How to Make Your Network SAFE for E-Business" is available at Cisco.com. The seminar describes the essentials of Cisco security and VPN solutions. See http://www.cisco.com/warp/public/779/largeent/issues/security/safebprint.html.

Emergency Phone Lines

Emergency phones were set up on analog Foreign Exchange Station (FXS) boards with separate partitions within the calling search space that were set up to route the call to the correct destination. The implementation team added these lines to the CallManager, just as they did any analog circuit. Then the team changed the calling search space for the correct routing.

"The calling search space tells the call where to go on an outbound call," said Bill Lowers, senior network design engineer. "In this case, all calls were directed to go straight to security. These partitions were set up by the design engineers prior to the line being installed." Analog installation is a manual task requiring that all information for each line be added individually.

"Emergency phones can be configured to place the call," Hays said. "Some of the emergency phones on the San Jose campus were configured to route to security instead of the CallManager. In this case, we only supplied a normal analog line to the phone. Then we did the programming on the phone for the routing to security."

Best Practices: Operational Security Policies

Network security requirements will change with your new VoIP network. The following best practices outline a few key areas of consideration.

- **Protect the network elements**—Routers, Ethernet switches, and VoIP Gateways define network boundaries and act as Gateway interfaces to all networks. Securing these vital pieces of voice and data networks is a requirement for securing the data, voice, and video applications running across the infrastructure.

- **Design the IP network**—Understanding and following sound IP network design principles not only allows the network to scale and perform, but also increases the security of all attached devices.

- **Secure the CallManager server**—Securing the voice call processing platform and installed applications is the most vital step in providing security to IP Telephony networks.

Best Practices: Operational Policy Changes

Your new IP network offers added flexibility that requires new or different operational policies. Use the following best practices to begin designing appropriate operational policies to support your new network.

- Because users can take their phones from location to location, the Cisco policy stated that one phone should be issued per employee.

- Put in place a standard naming convention for identifying all the types of phones in your network (that is, lobby phones, break room phones, emergency phones, and so on). This extra step of consistency will be helpful when you want to query a specific group of phones to make changes or disable certain features.

- Incorporate the auto numbering tool to automatically disperse numbers for multiple clusters. Doing so prevents one cluster from being top heavy and requires the use of additional infrastructure. Ensure that all DID numbers are equally distributed among all clusters to adequately manage traffic.

- Review all circuit IDs to ensure that tags and owners are identified. Clearly labeling the owner's building and cube or office location identifies the line as a critical user or regular use line.

The Good, the Bad, and the Ugly

Managing a change as large in scope as an enterprise-wide IP Telephony deployment takes special care, attention to detail, and adherence to policy. A lot could go wrong if the project is not managed properly; however, with the appropriate planning, the initiative can go smoothly and successfully. The following sections list the top ten things to watch out for and the top ten things that a smooth implementation will enable.

Top Ten Things That Can Go Wrong During the Retrofit

1 Disconnection and removal of critical phones that are unidentified or unassigned can backfire. Announce the impending removal of analog lines so that users who rely on these lines have the opportunity to come forward and prove ownership. If unassigned modem lines are located in a building that houses the call center team, it is better to just leave these lines. Adherence to corporate policy on the use of modem lines for non-contact center buildings helps with the cleanup. 1-MB (measured business) lines are assigned when users want an additional level of redundancy; removal could cause a major problem during an emergency. Identify the owner and building location on all circuit orders and termination points and conduct a periodic audit of these lines to continually assess their viability.

2 The Cisco contact center product was not yet available at the time of Cisco conversion. Removing a call center agent from the PBX too soon could have been a critical mistake. Obtain a resource from the call center team to attend project status meetings and to provide a list of all center agents who are located in the scheduled building as well as backup support agents. Provide the list to the contact center deployment team that will convert the call center agents to the call center application later.

3 If a virus can affect the data network, it can also affect the new converged IP network. Ensure that systems are in place to address viruses and protect the network.

4   IP phones carry the same potential for abuse as PBX phones, including enabling call forwarding to a secondary number and unauthorized long-distance charges. Take steps to ensure that all lobby phones and other courtesy phones have restricted features.

5   Because IP phones run off the data network, they can create a security breach if access is unrestricted on public phones, allowing visitors to download sensitive data from the corporate intranet. Ensure that public phones are secured against fraud.

6   If resistance to change is not properly anticipated, it creates havoc. Gain acceptance by taking away the mystery. Demonstrate the phone at town hall meetings and put a working IP phone on display in public areas. Ask your executive sponsor to help you manage the change and encourage acceptance.

7   Eliminate buyer's remorse by developing a comprehensive communication plan, identify must-have business critical phone features, and set the right expectations up front. Understand how your culture manages change, and use proven methods for accepting change as part of your migration strategy. Use the PBX configuration report to understand your users and check your existing PBX contract to ensure that you have access to this data during the migration.

8   If you do not plan software upgrades carefully, the conversion could result in delays and unnecessary issues. Cross-functional communication is critical. Make sure that a thorough test procedure is in place, and use the engineering lab to test all CallManager software upgrades to prevent painful problems later.

9   Incorporate new policies and processes that support and improve current organizational procedures. For example, giving users more than one phone could distort network and CallManager capacity planning. Emphasize the benefits of CallManager and IP Telephony that eliminate almost any need for a second line, supporting the organization's need for multiple extensions per person but with only one phone per employee.

10 Cross-train and combine the LAN teams with the data teams so that network troubleshooting is easier and adverse network changes are not made. Do not forget that a change made to one environment now affects all environments.

Top Ten Things That Will Improve as a Result of the Retrofit

1   After the implementation team has successfully converted several buildings, it will have developed a level of confidence, knowledge, and experience to tackle almost every building configuration for future technology deployments. Continue to remove obstacles to help keep the team on track.

2   After the team has converted the first few buildings, the process has been proven, and word begins to spread, users will change from dreading the move to anticipating it eagerly.

3   The convergence of teams and processes is now possible. The ability to manage a single infrastructure for both voice and data offers more flexibility, enhanced functionality, and a more efficient use of resources.

4   Users will find the mobility of the phone useful. For example, lab technicians who have both a primary desk and a lab cube will find it useful to be able to take their phones with them to either location. They will also find the IP phone Received Calls Logs effective in identifying callers, prioritizing phone calls, and enabling them to decide whether to check voice mail immediately or wait until a more convenient time.

5   User training will be easier than you think. A combination of web-based training and hands-on training will be likely, but let your organization's culture dictate which methods are most effective. Soon you will find a paradigm change in your users in which their demand for more flexible communication will become the norm. Users will become efficient at using the IP phone and will begin to offer suggestions on how to make the new IP phone system better. They will offer more creative and efficient suggestions on how to increase employee productivity and even suggestions for XML applications. For example, as a result of user input, Cisco has deployed various enterprise information services (such as company directory and current stock price lookups) to the Cisco 7960 phone sets.

6   The new infrastructure sets the groundwork for new applications that will follow (that is, call center applications, personal assistant, conference connection, SoftPhone, XML applications, and unified messaging). Therefore, plan your network for the future, not just for today.

7   Adds, moves, and changes will be conducted with ease, simplicity, and less cost. Operations will be able to close cases more quickly and accommodate the numerous changes that a large campus experiences. In addition, you will be able to troubleshoot your satellite offices remotely and with less resource allocation. Collaborate with your workplace/facility team to take advantage of your new IP solution to identify process improvements that streamline the add, move, and change process.

8   New buildings can take advantage of the installation of a single cable, eliminating the necessity for both network cables and telecommunications cables. This saves time and reduces the cost of bringing your new buildings online.

9 With some preplanning, the conversion to a "clean network" is easily achievable. Do not simply dump your entire roster of phone lines onto the new network. Use this opportunity instead to migrate only those lines that are identified as viable, and install your infrastructure accordingly. The value proposition with IP Telephony becomes even more apparent as you begin to disconnect the hundreds of analog, modem, 1-MBs, and other lines that are no longer being used but are still being billed. It also streamlines the campus numbering system by adding numbers to the recycled number availability list. By instituting this new policy change that converts only viable phone lines, you ensure that no unverified lines are placed onto the CallManager.

10 With the migration of IP Telephony comes the option for flexibility. PBXs that are up for renewal now have an additional option. They can be removed and converted to a more flexible VoIP solution, or they can coexist with TDM and IP Telephony.

Resources

Throughout this chapter, you have seen references to utilities made available for download at http://www.ciscopress.com/1587200880. You are encouraged to use these utilities for your own purposes during the premigration strategy phase. Following is a list of the resources:

- Appendix 3-A: Planning Workshop Template

- Appendix 3-B: Sample Users Conversion Notice

- Appendix 3-C: Phone Configuration Template

- Appendix 3-D: Executive Row Checklist

- Appendix 3-E: User Frequently Asked Questions

Summary

Planning the plan will result in a smoother migration with fewer bumps and surprises. This chapter focused on the various elements that prepare the initiative for success—from pulling together the right team to communicating with users to identifying necessary operational changes. The list that follows describes the preparation tasks for building an effective plan.

- **Hold a planning workshop**—Ensure that the initiative meets the specific business requirements of the organization. Plan the project deliverables, address solution capabilities, define hardware and software documentation, assign partner implementation services, identify the project-critical path, and agree on project milestones. Finally, obtain a Go/No Go decision from each stakeholder to ensure his readiness.

- **A phased approach**—Dividing the retrofit into logical segments and manageable chunks ensures that the retrofit will be easier to implement. The phased migration was segmented by new employees, adds/moves/changes, and then completed building by building.

- **Optimize project pace and schedule**—Set goals and establish milestones to keep the project moving and show progress. Create a schedule so that the LAN team stays two to three weeks ahead of the implementation team to ensure that the infrastructure is in place. Set up an operations center in each building being converted to act as ground zero for both users and the implementation team.

- **The communication plan**—Determine who your users are, how you can best facilitate two-way communication with them, and what they need to know. Use e-mail, a project website, e-mail alias, and other media to keep communication consistent, relevant, and useful.

- **Identify critical users**—Identify users who have special configurations and ensure that their new phone setup exceeds their needs. From high-speed fax capability to separate lines for admin personnel to call centers and help desks, people use their phones differently.

- **Converting executive row**—Develop a plan that provides the extra time to make the transition for executive row personnel easy and problem free. Executive row, including senior executives and their admin staffs, is populated with high-volume phone users who cannot afford to be without communication—even for a short time—and cannot take much time to learn how to use the IP phone's new features.

- **User training**—Provide different training options, and let your users choose what best fits their needs. Options can include web-based training, demos, user guides, and hands-on sessions, among others.

- **Identify operational changes**—Revisit operational policies to ensure a smooth migration and keep the new system clean. New support models, attention to operational security issues, handling of modem lines, and restrictions on migrating unused lines are considerations of the new converged voice and data network.

- **The good, the bad, and the ugly**—List the top ten things that will improve as a result of the new IP Telephony network and the top ten things that could go wrong without proper planning.

Chapter 4, "Implementation," addresses implementation topics such as network management, power backup, monitoring and troubleshooting, serviceability, and the importance of a backup support plan.

Appendix 3-A: Planning Workshop Template

The Planning Workshop is intended to help articulate the customer requirements and expectations for the solution. It also allows you to clarify the existing network. You schedule the Planning Workshop after all the site surveys have been returned and analyzed. You can use all information that you obtain during the Planning Workshop in the planning deliverable and ultimately in the design phase.

The sections that follow provide checklists that outline the topics and issues that you must discuss during the Planning Workshop. As the facilitator of the workshop, it is your responsibility to drive the conversation to these topics and ensure that they are documented correctly. This appendix is also available at http://www.ciscopress.com/1587200880.

Executive Requirements and Expectations

Intent: To allow the executive sponsor to articulate the company's goals and vision for the next 3 to 5 years. Also allows the executive to define requirements for the new solution.

- ❑ Overview of company vision—Proposed goals and growth of the company
- ❑ 3- to 5-year plan—3- to 5-year plan for both the voice and data networks
- ❑ Solution expectations—Executive expectations and requirements for the completed solution, including features and functionality
- ❑ Project expectations—Executive expectations and requirements surrounding the project (such as timetables, site priority, and success criteria)

Technical Requirements and Expectations

Intent: To discuss and document the current and future requirements for the network.

❏ General solution expectations

    ❏ What does the client ultimately need the network to accomplish to best serve his users? (Actual applications will be discussed later.)

___

    ❏ Why is a new system required?

___

    ❏ What is missing from the old system (features, scalability, integration, and so on)?

___

❏ Deployment and timing expectations

    ❏ What expectations does the client have for the deployment of the solution?

___

    ❏ What timeline does the client have for the deployment of the solution?

___

    ❏ Should particular sites/departments/users be given priority for deployment?

___

❏ Network availability/redundancy requirements

    ❏ What is the required up-time for the network?

___

    ❏ Redundancy versus cost discussion—How much redundancy is required?

___

❏ Network management requirements

    ❏ Does the client want to upgrade/integrate a network management system?

___

    ❏ If so, what are the expectations for the management system (monitoring requirements, scalability, alarms)?

___

❑ Security requirements

    ❑ What requirements does the client have for security?

_____

    ❑ What requirements does the client have for virus protection?

_____

Existing Network Review

Intent: This discussion topic assumes that you have completed, documented, and reviewed all the site surveys. After you are familiar with the environment, the time you spend on the Existing Network Review section allows you, as the partner, to confirm site survey data and assumptions with the customer. It also allows you to probe deeper into configurations and ask specific voice and data questions to the appropriate personnel.

❑ LAN network topology

    ❑ Naming convention.

    ❑ Server location and purpose.

    ❑ DNS (domain, parent, child).

    ❑ Domains and trust relationships.

    ❑ Client configuration—Is there a standard client image for the operating system and mail client (Windows 2000/Outlook 2000, Windows NT 4.0/Outlook 98, and so on)? If not, is the client moving to a standard? What is the timeline?

_____

❑ IP addressing scheme

❑ WAN network topology

    ❑ WAN circuits (network analysis)

    ❑ PVCs

    ❑ Mesh networks

    ❑ Protocols, policies, and quality of service (QoS)

❑ Legacy Telephony infrastructure (trunking, signaling, and analog)

    ❑ PBX or KSU vendor and model (from site survey)

_____

❑ Quantity and locations of PBX/key service unit (KSU) systems (from site survey)

❑ Release of software running on PBX or KSU (from site survey)

❑ Quantity and location of PBXs with which IP Telephony might interface (from site survey)

❑ Hardware models and revisions of installed cards (from site survey)

❑ Number of existing digital connections for each PBX/KSU (from site survey)

❑ Number and capacity of ISDN trunks connected to each PBX (from site survey)

❑ Number of existing analog connections for each PBX or KSU and three expected to remain following deployment

❑ Toll by pass applications

❑ Legacy dial plan/DID configurations

    ❑ Will the organization use existing or distributed dial plans among multiple sites?

    ❑ Are there number ranges to be reserved for PBXs? If so, what are they?

    ❑ Are there number ranges to be reserved for analog phones? If so, what are they?

❑ Redundant or backup paths (transparent to the user)

_____

❑ Emergency dialing call patterns

_____

❑ Automatic call distribution

_____

❑ Call blocking where individual groups or numbers have limited offnet access

_____

❑ Legacy voice mail
  ❑ Voice mail system models and vendor (from site survey)

_____

  ❑ Quantity and locations of voice mail systems (from site survey)

_____

  ❑ Hardware model and revision cards of voice mail systems (from site survey)

_____

  ❑ Software features currently deployed with voice mail system

_____

  ❑ Does the voice mail system have a Station Message Desk Interface (SMDI)?

_____

  ❑ Does the voice mail system support AMIS?

_____

  ❑ How is the voice mail system connected to the PBX?

_____

  ❑ Is the message waiting indicator integrated into the voice mail solution?

_____

❑ Legacy Exchange environment (where applicable)
  ❑ Version of Exchange (from site survey)

_____

❑ Upgrade plans for Exchange?

_____

❑ Is LDAP enabled in Exchange?

_____

❑ Do all users currently have Exchange accounts?

_____

❑ Virus protection

Applications and Features

Intent: Discuss the current applications and features and define which applications and features are required for the proposed solution.

❑ Existing phone applications—Which applications are they currently using with their existing solution (per site if necessary)?

    ❑ Automatic call distributors (ACDs)—Please define all ACDs in terms of the number of users

    ❑ Contact center applications

    ❑ Interactive voice responses (IVRs)

    ❑ Auto attendant

    ❑ Music on hold

    ❑ Call accounting

    ❑ Time of day routing

    ❑ Voice mail/unified messaging

    ❑ Fax software

    ❑ Conferencing

    ❑ Call transfer

    ❑ Call hold

    ❑ Call park

    ❑ Calling line identity

    ❑ Calling party name

- ❑ New solution applications—Discuss which applications the new solution must have to be successful:

    - ❑ ACDs

    - ❑ Contact center applications—IP Contact Center (IPCC)/International Code Designators (ICDs)

    - ❑ Integration with existing IVRs

    - ❑ IP interactive voice responses (IPIVRs)

    - ❑ SoftPhones

    - ❑ Auto attendant

    - ❑ Personal assistant

    - ❑ Call accounting

    - ❑ Time of day routing

    - ❑ E911

    - ❑ Call setup

    - ❑ Conferencing

    - ❑ Call transfer

    - ❑ Call hold

    - ❑ Call park

    - ❑ Calling line identity

    - ❑ Calling party name

- ❑ Voice mail/unified messaging—Discuss voice mail/unified messaging requirements for new solution.

    - ❑ Text to speech—Real Speak/TT3300

    - ❑ Fax integration

- ❑ Collaboration

    - ❑ What are the current voice collaboration devices and uses (such as voice bridges and third-party conferencing)?

    _____

    - ❑ Any there applications for voice collaboration devices that users frequently use (such as e-learning, Placeware, and NetMeeting)?

    _____

❑ Are future requirements for voice collaboration devices in the proposed solution? Is a voice bridge in the client's 3- to 5-year plan? If so, discuss call flow and sizing network correctly.

❑ What are the current video collaboration devices and uses (such as Vtel, PictureTel, and webcams)?

❑ Which applications does the client currently utilize for video collaboration devices?

❑ What are the future requirements for video collaboration devices in the proposed solution? Is video in the client's 3- to 5-year plan? If so, discuss sizing network correctly.

❑ Existing data applications—Discuss the following applications, and clearly understand and document where the application is used, how often, by whom, and what the estimated bandwidth utilization is.

  ❑ CRM
  ❑ Client server databases
  ❑ Imaging software
  ❑ User transactions
  ❑ XML applications
  ❑ E-mail server transaction
  ❑ Directory/Lightweight Directory Access Protocol (LDAP) transactions
  ❑ Unified messaging transaction
  ❑ Toll bypass application

❑ Proposed data applications—Discuss the client's 3- to 5-year plan for applications.

  ❑ CRM
  ❑ Client server databases
  ❑ Imaging software
  ❑ User transactions
  ❑ XML applications

Planning and Strategy

Intent: Understand the client's requirements for the future of the network and the deployment of the new solutions.

❏ Company growth estimates

    ❏ Number of users

    _____

    ❏ Number of sites—Where are the sites located?

    _____

❏ PBX migration/integration

    ❏ Will PBX be displaced right away, or will the solution coexist with the legacy PBX?

    _____

    ❏ When will the PBX be displaced? Will the users be migrated on a schedule, or will some users stay on the legacy environment?

    _____

❏ Country-specific considerations (any regulations)

    _____

    _____

    _____

❏ Client's change management process—Clearly understand the client's change management process.

    ❏ What is the process for reviewing a change management request?

    _____

    ❏ How are change management requests submitted?

    _____

    ❏ What is the average turnaround time for approval?

    _____

Support

Intent: Clearly understand and articulate the client's current support strategy and the support requirements for the new IP Telephony solution.

❏ Existing data and voice support services

    ❏ Is the voice network supported by a third party, and if so, who? If the voice network is supported internally, which resources support it?

    _____

    _____

    _____

    ❏ Is the data network supported by a third party, and if so, who? If the data network is supported internally, which resources support it?

    _____

    _____

    _____

❏ Day 2 support expectations for the IP Telephony solution—Is the new solution going to be supported by a third party or internally?

    _____

    _____

    _____

❏ Internal support training program

    ❏ What are the client's training expectations from you, the partner?

    _____

    _____

    ❏ Is there a budget to train the administrators for supporting this environment?

    _____

    _____

    _____

❑ End user training requirements

    ❑ What are the client's expectations for training the end users?

_____

_____

_____

    ❑ How has training been done in the past?

_____

_____

_____

Appendix 3-B: Sample Users Conversion Notice

This appendix provides an example of a communication that was sent out to users about the impending cutover to their new IP phone. Use this sample to create your own communication message. You can also find this appendix at http://www.ciscopress.com/ 1587200880.

To: All Building Employees

From: Cisco IT AVVID Tiger Team

Our plan is to convert all users on the San Jose campus to the Cisco IP Phone. Your location is scheduled for conversion on Saturday _____. Exceptions to this include all call center agents and lobby receptionists who are part of the contact center operators group. There are three areas of sensitivity for us: modems, boss admin support, and Oryx System users.

Modems—The Cisco corporate security policy states that modems are not approved or supported for use. The exceptions would include those areas where customer-facing support is provided. To ensure that your approved modem has been identified, please send an e-mail to open_a_case@cisco.com. If you would like to obtain the necessary approval for a modem, you can find the procedures at *(insert internal URL here)*.

Office analog/ISDN line security policy—*(insert internal URL here)*.

Modem access and authentication policy—*(insert internal URL here)*.

Dial-out modems for customer network access from a centralized access server—*(insert internal URL here)*.

Oryx priority call management system—Oryx is not a supported feature with the Cisco IP Phone and will eventually be replaced with the Cisco personal assistant product. Other options to consider in managing your priority calls include configuring your IP phone to forward your calls to your cell phone or alternate phone number, or utilizing the pager notification system available on your voice mail system to alert you when you have received an urgent, private, or regular voice mail.

Boss admin support—The Cisco IP Phone has a six-line admin share support feature. Users who have other extensions appear or ring on their phone might face a challenge transitioning from the legacy PBX system to the AVVID CallManager phone system. AVVID presently supports the feature; however, the primary user's number and any additional number must have the same prefix. Example: If an admin user has a 525 prefix and wants to have a manager's line appear/ring on the same phone, the manager's number must also have a 525 prefix. Mixing prefix numbers such as 525 and 526/527 or 853 prefixes will not function at this time within the AVVID CallManager. If you and your manager have a different prefix or would like your IP phone provisioned to manage the calls of your manager, please e-mail us at *(insert internal URL here)*.

Facsimile machines—Cutover support for faxing should not be an issue. However, we encourage all admin and support centers to inform us of any special applications by sending an e-mail to *(insert internal URL here)*.

During this transition, we understand that you might have questions and concerns. We ask that you reference our FAQ site at *(insert internal URL here)*.

Following are some additional useful links designed to answer your questions:

- **Using Your Cisco IP Phone 7960**—(*insert internal URL here*)

- **Cisco IP Phone Tutorial**—(*insert internal URL here*)

- **Release Notes for the Cisco IP Phone 7960**—(*insert internal URL here*)

- **Cisco IP Phone 7960 Quick Start**—(*insert internal URL here*)

- **Ordering an IP Phone Compatible Headset**—(*insert internal URL here*)

- **How to Use the Voice Mail System**—(*insert internal URL here*)

Thank you for your support.

Cisco IT AVVID Tiger Team

Appendix 3-C: Phone Configuration Template

This appendix provides an IP phone configuration template as a visual confirmation of how the new phone will be configured. Because most users will not understand CallManager jargon, this confirmation template will go a long way toward helping users understand what their new IP phone settings will look like. This appendix is available at http://www.ciscopress.com/1587200880.

Appendix 3-D: Executive Row Checklist

Converting senior management to their new IP phone system will be a different process than converting your standard IP phone user. Use the executive row checklist as a reminder of the specific consideration or task these users might require. This appendix is also available at http://www.ciscopress.com/1587200880.

- ❏ Spell check by name on all number changes within voice mail and in the local and global directory.

- ❏ Ask senior managers which phones they want to keep and which ones you can remove.

- ❏ Verify with PBX dump so that you know which numbers are already assigned to users.

❏ Remind users to update their voice mail distribution list when number changes occur.

❏ Identify users who have more than one number, and ask if they prefer a separate voice mail for each or if they want multiple lines to roll into one voice mail.

❏ Submit global directory updates.

❏ Follow up with engineering to ensure that global directory is updated for all CallManagers.

❏ Ask whether additional phones are required in public areas where there were none previously.

❏ Identify how many admins will require the 7914 expansion modules, and preorder them to accommodate each one's needs.

❏ Verify that all voice mailboxes for shared line appearance confirm that voice mails are being directed to the right user. Press the Messages button to conduct a quick test.

❏ Identify the number of rings preferred by each admin and his manager. (Preferences will vary.)

❏ For all senior executive conference rooms, ask if the silent ring option is required. Some vice presidents do not want the disruption of a second phone ringing while they are in a meeting.

❏ Senior executive offices often have heavy call volume and might have ACD functionality that will route callers to a secondary office or number (that is, a prompt to allow callers to press 1 for shareholder info, press 2 for media questions, and so on). If this is the case, work with Telecom to route these calls appropriately on the IP phone. A simple phone swap-out does not automatically continue this feature.

❏ Test for understanding, and make sure that all admins know how to transfer calls directly into voice mail. This is a common function, but it is conducted differently on an IP phone.

❏ Provide a visual confirmation of all phone changes so that both the implementation team and the administrative staff agree to the new phone configuration.

❏ Confirm that the standard numbers of shared line appearances are enough; users with heavy call volume might require additional line appearances. Forgetting this step could result in numerous full voice mailboxes from missing incoming calls.

❏ Use the conversion as an opportunity to clean up unused phone lines (including analog) and remove any phones that are no longer being utilized.

Appendix 3-E: User Frequently Asked Questions

A FAQs list will become useful as the IP phone conversion begins. This FAQ list will serve useful as you begin to capture and build your own FAQ document. This appendix is also available at http://www.ciscopress.com/1587200880.

IP Phone Support Information

- General questions

- Using IP Phones

- Troubleshooting general questions

Cisco IP Phones

- What is an IP Phone?

- When will I get an IP Phone?

- Why are we using the Cisco IP Phone?

- How can I get an IP Phone for my house?

- How can I order the appropriate headset/cord for my IP Phone?

- How do I request or suggest features for IP Phones?

- How do I drop or end a call?

- How do I forward all my calls?

- How do I program my speed dial?

- How do I use the directories?

- How do I adjust the ringer volume?

- How do I change the ring sound?

- How do I connect two IP Phones with only one phone jack?

- How do I adjust/save speaker volume levels?

- How do I transfer a call?

- How do I place a conference call?

Troubleshooting

- How do I report problems with my IP Phone?

- My message waiting indicator (MWI) is not working. What's wrong?

- What do I do if my IP Phone appears "dead"?

- What do I do if my IP Phone appears to be in configuration mode or registering mode?

- What do I do if my IP Phone is stuck in configuring mode?

- IT Internal Technical Support Library FAQs—*(insert internal URL here)*.

CHAPTER 4

IMPLEMENTATION

Chapter 4 is where the pedal meets the metal. All the planning and preparations discussed in previous chapters have paved the way for a smooth transition from PBX-based phones to IP phones, but this stage pulls it all together. In this chapter, you will learn how the LAN and WAN were prepared for the convergence of voice and data; the importance of conducting a thorough site survey of each building; and the implementation steps and techniques that the retrofit team uses. The appendixes included at the end of this chapter and at http://www.ciscopress.com/1587200880 will provide you with templates, samples, checklists, and other tools that the retrofit team used to make the process more efficient and consistent.

Planning the Implementation: Steps to Success

The implementation phase is all about proper planning, consistent communication, doing the prep work up front, having a solid process, paying attention to detail, and automating as much of the process as possible. I believe the winning formula for the success of the Cisco migration consisted of 80 percent prep and 20 percent installation, which means that if you focus on the plan first, the implementation will go a lot more smoothly.

As a result of the implementation, Cisco created a knowledge management portal titled Steps to Success—IP Engagement Guide. This guide outlines the various steps that are necessary during the implementation planning stage and is summarized next. These guidelines were created as a baseline to enable our customers and partners to create their own implementation plan. The following sections are summaries of steps you should consider when beginning and completing the implementation phase.

NOTE	You can find the templates referenced in this section on the Cisco Steps to Success website at http://www.cisco.com/go/stepstosuccess. (Access requires a partner Cisco.com login.)

Step 1: Implementation Planning Phase

As you prepare for implementation, this step should clarify the plan set forth in the design phase and confirm the expectations for the installation.

Hold Implementation Planning Meeting

Conduct a meeting with the implementation team regarding the deployment effort. In general, the customer should reconfirm the network design requirements (including features), the deployment timeframes, and the Go/No Go decision-making process. Also, this meeting should allow discussion and creation of a plan for completion of the following implementation considerations:

1 Design confirmation

2 Implementation plan, including feature considerations

3 Migration/integration strategy, including system and acceptance testing

4 Proposed installation dates and caveats

5 Customer to-do list

6 Roles and responsibilities, including issue resolution strategy, escalation procedures, and management briefing

Refer to Appendix 4-A, "Steps to Success Project Management Process." This appendix is available at http://www.ciscopress.com/1587200880.

The Steps to Success Project Management Process document is a visual reminder of the various steps required to complete the entire planning, design, implementation, operations, and optimization (PDIOO) lifecycle of steps and tasks required for each IP Telephony engagement. Print this process flowchart at poster size as a guide through each step and a visual reminder of the remaining steps within the process.

Refer to Appendix 4-B, "Implementation Planning Template," at http://www.ciscopress.com/1587200880.

You can use the Implementation Planning Template document to gather all the information you need to complete the implementation phase. This document identifies the necessary components for an IP Telephony engagement that the customer and the partner must complete.

Develop Response and Escalation Plan

To ensure resolution of potential problems during the implementation, the team and customer should define the plan for trouble response, including escalation procedures based on severity. This should address dedicated plans for customer response, team response, and Cisco response, and should be communicated prior to installation.

Verify Customer To-Do List and Action Plan

The project manager and the customer task owner(s) must ensure that the action items from the customer's to-do list have been completed or will be completed on time to mitigate risk around the implementation.

Prepare Installation Documentation

Document the detailed installation information needed to carry out the implementation of network equipment and software at the customer site. The documentation should also include the tests required to verify basic operation. This serves as a guide for an implementation engineer to follow the installation guidelines. Separate documents typically exist for each customer site.

Keep the customer-specific network implementation plan produced from the template as brief as possible, with minimal unnecessary text. It should detail the "what" with pointers to other references for the "how to." This information is typically available in Cisco product documentation.

User Training

Create the training class outline/content, proposed class schedule, and team and customer responsibilities. Based on findings in the plan phase, a team might have the opportunity to propose additional training for newly discovered considerations.

TIP	Reference the best practices for conducting a user training section previously outlined in Chapter 3, "The Migration Strategy," when you are preparing the training documentation.

Order Equipment/Software

After you have established the design, identify the customer's equipment/software considerations. After placing your order, keep track of your customer by taking inventory of all equipment and software as it arrives, and add a tab label to every box identifying the location (building/floor/cube) where the equipment and software will reside.

Secure a staging area that you can lock to keep out everyone except members of the implementation team. Finally, ask the project manger to schedule outages when the equipment/software will be installed.

TIP	Reference http://www.cisco.com/go/stepstosuccess (required Cisco.com partner login) to access the Low Level Implementation Plan Template that supports the implementation planning stage.

Step 2: Project Monitor and Control

Safeguard the health of the project by establishing processes, such as status reporting, change management, issue resolution, and quality assurance, to monitor progress and mitigate risk.

Status Reporting

The team and customer should designate a status reporting structure and frequency to ensure stakeholders' awareness. If needed, you can establish status meetings with core team members.

Change Management

During this early stage of the implementation phase, the team should help the customer develop a change control process to mitigate deviations from the intended design. This process should accommodate implementation-critical changes. Change control forms might facilitate this process, as well as document opportunities for post-implementation enhancements.

Issue/Risk Management

Establish lines of communication to highlight risk surrounding the implementation and the proper channels for issue resolution. This task can be critical to maintaining project health.

Quality Control

Build in mechanisms for quality control throughout the implementation. These mechanisms can take many forms, including internal team, cross-functional team, and external third-party quality assurance. You can perform quality control while conducting milestone checkpoint meetings with the customer stakeholders.

TIP	Capture all support issues during the implementation so that you can add their resolution procedures to the support FAQ document.

Step 3: Site Preparation

In previous phases, the team assisted the customer in completing a survey of the infrastructure that would affect installation and began to take steps to address deficiencies. Prior to installation, the team must conduct a thorough site survey and assess the state of readiness of all infrastructure components. Considerations should be given to the following:

- Equipment room readiness

- Power; grounding; and heating, ventilation, and air conditioning (HVAC)

- Conduit, cabling, patch panels, and racks

- Demarcation of telephone company (telco) services

TIP	Many times the site survey introduces things that were not considered previously during the design. However, this does not mean that you should refrain from doing another site survey prior to installation. A proper physical visit ensures that the right equipment is budgeted prior to ordering. This might include additional cables, patch panels, racks, and so on.

 Refer to Appendix 4-C, "Site Survey Form," which is available at http://www.ciscopress.com/1587200880.

TIP	With existing buildings, ensure that there is a plan to transition from the existing system to the new system because the process and procedures are different for a new building conversion.

Validate Site Specification

At this point, refer to the Site Requirements Specification developed in the plan phase and address any gaps. This task should generate a site verification to-do list and outline required actions for resolution.

Complete Site Survey

Using the implementation plan, develop a complete floor plan showing the location of all components, including set and jack locations. For an IP Telephony installation, the project manager should obtain a customer signoff regarding the floor and cutover plans. You can use the floor plan for E911 emergency response location (ERL) layouts.

Prepare Site

After the customer and team have completed the site survey, prepare the site to receive the solution equipment for installation. This might include ensuring that the staging area is clear and scheduling the delivery of equipment to the customer site. The project manager should finalize the scheduled outages for when the equipment will be installed.

Site Verification

The implementation manager should validate that site surveys completed in earlier phases are still valid and that the site confirms scheduled receipt of the equipment. In addition, he must resolve any gaps in the site specification to ensure successful installation.

TIP	When the site surveys are complete, the facility manager should hold all adds, moves, and changes to maintain the integrity of the gathered data.

Step 4: Install and Configure

The engineer should stage the equipment/software and, after confirming operability, install/configure the equipment/software at the customer site. In general, this step entails equipment/software staging, installation, testing, resolution of installation issues, retesting, user migration, and acceptance.

Stage Hardware/Software

The need for staging depends on the size and complexity of the engagement. Having a team available to stage the hardware/software to ensure that components are ready for operation makes things go more smoothly. The staging should incorporate all the major design features that exist in the network design document. The main purpose of staging the network in this way is to maximize the efficiency of the implementation process, to identify faulty components, and to test the network configuration prior to rollout.

Staging tests should demonstrate that the network hardware/software has been correctly configured and operates in a manner that will enable the customer to accept that the network can be rolled out as a working system. Tests should include basic hardware/software testing, network-level connectivity testing, software configuration, and network service-type functionality testing.

The staging test results are typically used as a benchmark for similar acceptance testing during site installation. After the staging test results have been confirmed, the hardware should be asset tagged, repacked in the staging area, and then deployed to the landing site for installation.

TIP　　Be sure to include the customer's acceptance criteria in the staging process because the customer will have specific requirements regarding how the hardware/software should be operational. The team should have a list of items to test and validate per the customer's requirements.

Install Server Software

After successful staging of the server software, receive the hardware for installation at the final landing site and place it according to the deployment plan detail.

1　**Ensure that the LAN infrastructure is in place and that it is ready for the IP Telephony deployment**—Verify that the IP addressing scheme, voice VLAN configuration, and quality of service (QoS) have been configured and tested in accordance with the approved design.

2　**Install the Voice Gateway**—Install, configure, and test the Voice Gateway. Ensure that both the local exchange carrier (LEC) and inter-exchange carrier (IXC) facilities have been tested.

3　**Install convergence server(s)/integrated communication**—This task includes configuring and testing the Cisco CallManager server hardware and operating systems, as well as ensuring the proper configuration of clusters.

4　**Install telephony software**—In this technology-specific task, the team installs the core software, including configuration, building of databases (such as dial plans), and testing of the IP Telephony solution.

5　**Deploy/place the Cisco IP Phone**—The customer can choose certain Cisco IP Phones for solution deployment. Cisco provides guides and considerations for the type of phone specific to the solution.

Load, Configure, Integrate, and Test Client Software

This baseline task refers to the installation of software that supports the application portion of the solution. The specific details of this task vary among technologies. In general, however, any loaded software should be configured according to the requirements, integrated with any other applications, and tested in the implementation environment.

1 **Load and configure third-party telephony software**—Although third-party software is not provided by Cisco, it can provide a valuable part of the system's ability to deliver functions that the customer requires. A team can obtain installation and integration procedures from the third-party vendor.

2 **Configure the E911 solution**—Cisco provides several solutions for dealing with 911 and E911 calls, as well as configurations and implementation processes for these solutions. Cisco is also in the process of developing a solution for automatically tracking phones when they move as well as providing location information in compliance with some states' E911 legislation.

3 **Integrate with voice mail**—Cisco offers customers the ability to utilize their investment in legacy voice mail systems. The Cisco product line includes a series of digital PBX adapters (DPAs) and analog telephone adapters (ATAs) that integrate CallManager with the most common voice mail systems. The adapters need to be installed, configured, and tested prior to the IP Telephony deployment. Customers might want to implement Cisco Unity voice messaging at the same time they move to CallManager. Cisco Unity voice messaging integrates with CallManager via the IP network. You can find additional information on Cisco Unity at http://www.cisco.com.

4 **Integrate with other Cisco applications**—Cisco has several applications (Personal Assistant, Conference Connection, SoftPhone, and so on) that integrate with the Cisco CallManager. The team might need to integrate with these applications if the customer selected these features as part of the overall solution.

Network Implementation Plan Acceptance

The installation and configuration step is completed when the customer provides confirmation of the voice network implementation according to plan. This can be a formal or informal acceptance that confirms satisfaction of the equipment installation, installation testing and issue fixes, and retesting of the installation to ensure that all issues have been resolved.

Step 5: Test and Acceptance

The engineer should stage the equipment and, after confirming operability, install/configure the equipment at the customer site. In general, this step entails continued equipment staging, installation, testing, resolution of installation issues, retesting, user migration, and acceptance.

Test the Solution

Per the requirements set forth in the solution acceptance criteria, the field engineer should test and document the solution. As with any new system, issues might arise; therefore, the team must provide resources onsite or online to monitor the systems as well as take and resolve trouble calls. The customer, project manager, and implementation lead should review the agreed-upon deliverables and assess the system.

The team can use the Test Plan Template for installation tests to prove that each piece of equipment is operational for commissioning tests. This ensures that each site is operational and ready to be brought online and, for a set of network ready-for-use tests, to prove that the network as a single entity is operational and manageable. You can find the test plan template at http://www.cisco.com/go/stepstosuccess. (Access requires partner Cisco.com login.)

Conduct a Prelaunch Test

The team might want to select a site (with noncritical users) where it can benchmark execution against the system design in a low-risk environment. The team can increase the rollout pace after the environment variables stabilize and the implementation rollout process is solid. Using this "crawl-walk-run" approach, the team can move to the next phase of the migration with minimal risk.

Network Ready-for-Use Acceptance

After the testing of the implemented solution yields satisfactory results in the production environment, the customer should provide a network ready-for-use acceptance letter to the team. This letter should address the physical and logical acceptance of the solution into the production environment and confirm satisfaction of limited production testing and issue resolution. A signed acceptance should allow the team to begin transition of the network to the customer's operations team.

TIP	Be sure to capture all the issues during the test or pilot phase, including process changes and implementation procedures. Monitor the stability and performance of the network, and determine your threshold for a successful pilot. Offering written feedback to the design/engineering team and outlining your success factors in advance are essential for measuring your success.

TIP	Gather a consensus from the design, engineering, operations, implementation, and support teams that the site is now ready to move from pilot or test phase into production. Reaching an agreement helps you manage expectations.

TIP	Be sure to obtain a network-ready acceptance letter before moving into the production phase. This extra step helps ensure that the customer and partner have an agreement on the performance and design of the new network.

Step 6: Knowledge Handoff

The team should prepare to complete the implementation phase by ensuring that the customer's system administration team and end users obtain the knowledge to realize the benefits of the solution.

Train the Administrator

Per the training strategy outlined in the design phase, the team ensures that voice network administrators are trained to support the solution. The team schedules a solution knowledge transfer for the customer administrators. Cisco offers many options for training the administrator. Go to http://www.Cisco.com to find these options.

Perform End-User Training

Making sure that the customer's employees (especially the administrative assistant staff) know how to use the phones and the features of the new systems has a big impact on how well these employees accept the new system and what their ongoing satisfaction will be. Documents are available with the sets that explain their use. Cisco also provides a video-on-demand training session. You can find these documents and more at http://www.cisco.com/go/stepstosuccess. (A Cisco.com login is required.)

Hold Cisco TAC or Day 2 Handoff Meeting

The project manager should lead a meeting that explains the following:

- Day 2 Technical Assistance Center (TAC) benefits and limitations

- How, when, and who should engage Day 2 support

- Tasks to perform prior to calling the Day 2 provider (Day 1 onsite support activities)

- Any unique design considerations that are specific to the customer's solution

- What documentation to have available (that is, as built)

TIP	A great tip for maximizing user productivity is to send regular updates to the end users on how to better use their IP Phones and increase awareness on the phones' various features. An "IP Phone tip of the week" is a great way to share methods to optimize your new IP voice network.

Step 7: Closeout

The team should complete the implementation phase by assisting in the customer's transition to operations, including the lessons learned documentation; highlighting the customer's unique design considerations; introducing Cisco TAC; and obtaining the customer's letter of acceptance.

Perform an Internal Review to Determine Lessons Learned

The project team should review with the team the lessons learned and modify any templates or processes to help improve the next installation.

Create TAC Transition Documentation

The team should create documentation for the customer that highlights features of the Day 2 support and familiarizes the customer's system administrator with the ways to interact with the TAC. This documentation should reflect as-built information—indicating customer-specific design requirements and configuration.

Project Acceptance

The project manager should lead a final meeting with the customer that completes the implementation phase.

With the completion of the solution in production, the team should present a letter of understanding to the customer. The letter of understanding serves the following functions:

- A customer acknowledgement that the solution has been implemented per the customer acceptance criteria

- A customer acknowledgement that the team has fulfilled the engagement obligations and completed the implementation phase

TIP In 30 days, the project manager should schedule a meeting with the customer (or key users) to ensure customer satisfaction and discuss options for network optimization.

The Cisco LAN Infrastructure

A successful implementation of Cisco IP Telephony requires the LAN infrastructure to provide a stable, voice-capable platform. Before the Cisco LAN team added voice to the network, it took great care to ensure that the data network was configured properly.

"To prepare for the Cisco IP Telephony retrofit, we reviewed the desktop LAN infrastructure and retrofitted the areas that needed upgrading," says Paul Molyski, IT LAN project manager. Although a LAN upgrade was already in the planning stages, the decision to deploy IP Telephony throughout Cisco accelerated the upgrade deployment.

At the time, part of the existing Cisco LAN infrastructure was still running on older technology. Some of our buildings had the same network equipment that was installed when the buildings were constructed several years before. Because the timing for some of the network upgrade happened to coincide with the IP Telephony deployment, Cisco decided to avoid deploying IP Telephony with a mix of new LAN infrastructure equipment (inline power) and old LAN infrastructure equipment (no inline power). It decided to complete the LAN upgrade for each building prior to the IP Telephony deployment in the building.

Standardization

The Cisco LAN was constructed over several years, growing as Cisco grew. The result was a nonhomogeneous architecture that facilitated product development but was difficult to support.

In 2000, Cisco developed a new LAN architecture standard for the San Jose campus and implemented it as part of the IP Telephony rollout. The first step toward integrating the new standard was upgrading the various campus sites and intersite backbone portions of the LAN for the new converged network.

This all happened during a time of rapid growth for Cisco. To keep the LAN upgrade consistent throughout the organization, all new buildings that came online during this process were fitted with the new LAN architecture.

As part of the IP Telephony deployment, a new LAN segment was created, which was similar in design to a data center LAN segment. Meant to contain the CallManagers as well as the Catalyst 6000 switches that terminated the public switched telephone network (PSTN) connections, this segment would also contain future telephony servers, such as those for interactive voice response (IVR), Unity, and Personal Assistant applications.

After the site and backbone portions were rebuilt, the retrofit of the desktop LAN began later that same year.

"The goal was to maintain consistency by strictly adhering to the new LAN architecture," Molyski says. "Since we would end up with over 500 CAT 6500 switches and 100 smaller switches in the desktop LAN, ongoing support and the higher availability requirement would be a problem if consistency [were] not maintained."

Before the deployment of IP Telephony, LAN availability and QoS were less of an issue. Three-9s (99.9 percent) availability was acceptable for most services on a data-only network. Now, however, five 9s(99.999 percent) is the standard for telephony.

"Today, the LAN has an uptime of 99.999 percent," Molyski says. "The side effect of installing a high-availability LAN is that we ended up with a much better LAN for all the services that rely on it. In a nutshell, installing a LAN that was suitable for [IP Telephony] resulted in better service for all LAN applications."

| NOTE | Refer to Chapter 6, "Final Piece of the Conversion," for the current Cisco performance rating on the converged network. You can also reference a Cisco white paper titled "IT-LAN High Availability" at http://www.cisco.com/application/pdf/en/us/guest/tech/tk769/c1550/cdccont_0900aecd800b29ac.pdf. |

QoS on the Cisco IT Network

The implementation of IP Telephony throughout Cisco was the driving factor in the development of a QoS strategy on the Cisco IT global network. "Cisco's QoS solution had to provide the necessary special handling requirements by certain traffic types," says Craig Huegen, chief network architect. "Cisco's desire was to build QoS end to end across the entire global network, with predefined classes of service that [would] permit any application to ride over the network with appropriate quality of service levels."

Cisco IT had been using QoS features of IOS for several years, leveraging priority queuing (PQ), custom queuing (CQ), and weighted fair queuing (WFQ) features in IOS to give some priority to business-critical applications across the WAN. However, Cisco typically only applied these features to WAN links on an ad-hoc basis, usually when utilization was running high. These features were not part of a global QoS strategy. The introduction of the Voice over IP (VoIP) modules for the 3600 series routers spurred the first Cisco requirements for a more consistent, global QoS policy.

"At this time, Cisco was beta-testing a new QoS mechanism called class-based weighted fair queuing (CBWFQ), and Cisco IT participated in the test," recalls Huegen. CBWFQ allowed us to lump types of traffic together into classes, and then give certain amounts of bandwidth to each particular class.

The addition of priority queuing to CBWFQ allowed for low-latency queuing (LLQ), which was necessary for carrying real-time applications across the IT network. LAN switches like the Catalyst 6500 series were introduced with multiple queues and thresholds, enabling us to extend QoS into the LAN for IP Telephony.

"Now that we had the functionality in IOS allowing us to give priority service to real-time applications such as voice, we wanted to put together an end-to-end QoS strategy," Huegen says.

The process was outlined in three significant steps. "First, we elected to use a Diffserv-based QoS strategy. We established our five major classes of service that we were to use for the global networks' voice, video, signaling and high-priority data, normal/default data, and batch traffic. We also identified the requirement for a "trusted edge"—that is, we wanted the edge of the network controlled by IT to ensure traffic was marked at the appropriate Diffserv levels."

"Next, a classification and marking strategy was built," Huegen says. "We leveraged the auxiliary VLAN feature of the IP Telephony solution to identify voice traffic from IP telephones. The Catalyst switches' capabilities to remark traffic to appropriate Diffserv levels were also used. And finally, the necessary configurations to the LAN switches and WAN routers were enabled globally, giving us the appropriate level of service to the traffic that had been marked at the edge."

In summary, Cisco took advantage of the QoS features that were inherent within its products to implement an effective end-to-end QoS solution not only for voice but also for other types of real-time traffic.

NOTE   Following are some QoS reference sites:

- http://www.cisco.com/univercd/cc/td/doc/product/voice/ip_tele/qoslink.htm

- http://www.cisco.com/univercd/cc/td/doc/product/voice/ip_tele/qoslink.htm

- http://www.cisco.com/univercd/cc/td/doc/product/voice/ip_tele/qoslink.htm

You can find more information on the Cisco Architecture for Voice, Video and Integrated Data (AVVID) IP Telephony solutions (including AVVID infrastructure, deployment models, dial plans, and so on) at the following sites:

- http://www.cisco.com/en/US/netsol/netwarch/ns19/ns24/networking_solutions_packages_list.html

- http://www.cisco.com/en/US/netsol/netwarch/ns19/ns24/networking_solutions_packages_list.html

- http://www.cisco.com/partner/WWChannels/technologies/IPT/index.html

Inline Power

Integrating IP Telephony support added some requirements to the overall LAN design. "Most noteworthy was the use of inline power for the desktop Ethernet connections," Molyski says. "This required us to configure the Catalyst 6500s (CAT 6Ks) with 2500 watt (W) power supplies, and the wiring closets (IDFs) — where the CAT 6500s were installed — with 208 volt (V), 20-amp UPS power."

Although not every installation required the use of 2500W power supplies, the LAN team used that standard throughout the network. "The CAT 6Ks provide excellent real-time power consumption information that can be used to determine the exact power requirements on a switch-by-switch basis," Molyski adds. "With Cisco's ever-changing requirements, standardizing on 2500W power supplies was the way to go for us."

The LAN team installed CAT 3524-PWR switches in locations where IP phones were deployed, but where desktop network services were not provided. The standard for desktop Ethernet service was to provide two 10/100 patches to each Category 5 wall plate.

"The intent was that the IP phone would use one live jack, and a PC would then be connected to the IP phone," Molyski says. This left the second live jack available for another device and resulted in a noticeable decrease in the number of requests for additional connections, reducing overall support costs.

We then deployed CAT 6Ks with Foreign Exchange Station (FXS) blades to support analog telephone connections, including modems, faxes, and polycoms. These CAT 6K FXS switches were part of the desktop LAN, installed where the Category 3 cabling system terminated in each building's main wiring closet. We then reconnected analog devices that had been connected to the PBX to the FXS CAT 6Ks via this Category 3 cable plant.

"In cubes, offices, and conference rooms, converting PBX phones to IP phones was not a problem because CAT 5 cabling was readily available in those locations for use by the IP phones," Molyski adds. "However, in locations where wall phones were implemented with a single CAT 3 jack, we were stuck with using the CAT 3 cable."

We rewired the Category 3 runs that went to the PBX to the CAT 6500s, and then configured the IP Phones to operate at 10 Mbps. In locations where the Category 3 cable run was too long to support the IP phones (that is, out of spec for 10 Mbps Ethernet), we replaced the Category 3 cabling with Category 5 cabling, enabling us to operate the IP Phones at 10 Mbps for much longer distances.

Security

In some instances—such as lobby phones and other public access areas—the team needed to provide IP phone service but was restricted to voice-only to prevent unauthorized access to the desktop network. The IP phone is designed so that a computer can be connected to it, allowing the computer to access the network as well. The voice-only restriction was accomplished by allowing only the voice VLAN to be active on the CAT 6500 port to which the IP phone was connected.

"This was simple to do because auxiliary VLANs were used to carry voice traffic," Molyski recalls. As a result, any PC that was connected to that phone was unable to gain access to the internal Cisco network.

Many of the cable paths from the desktop wiring closets (IDFs) to the phone locations in the labs far exceeded the 100 meter (m) Category 5 cable spec. The solution was to place 3524-PWR switches in secondary wiring closets (SDFs) within the lab areas and connect these back to the desktop network.

"Even after implementing this practice, we still had some cable runs which exceeded the 100m spec," Molyski says. Because running at 10 Mbit over Category 5 allows that to happen, the team configured the 3524s for 10 Mbps Ethernet with the data VLAN blocked, knowing that if the IP phone were able to power up using the inline power, it would operate satisfactorily.

The Results

"I can't say enough about the advantages of inline power," Molyski remarks. "The convenience of not having to use an external power adapter should not be underestimated. During the installation, our test phones went through hundreds of power cycles with no problems." The inline power feature was later used to power the access points for the wireless network, which provided an added bonus of having implemented inline power.

"Adding voice traffic to our LAN demanded a higher availability standard than what [was] acceptable for data only," Molyski concludes. "The additional cost for this was not that great, and we ended up with a better LAN not only for voice, but for data and video as well. The net result was that we had a LAN that was more reliable and required less effort to support."

The concepts and implementation techniques that the Cisco LAN team used are valid regardless of whether the retrofit involves a headquarters with tens of thousands of users or a small branch with fewer than 100 users. However, the size of the network determines the actual components, platforms, and details that account for the scalability, availability, and functionality of the network.

 Refer to Appendix 4-D, "LAN Upgrade Test Procedures." The LAN Upgrade Test Procedure checklist is a list of best practices that you should consider when conducting a LAN upgrade. You can find this appendix at the end of this chapter, or you can download and modify it to suit your needs at http://www.ciscopress.com/1587200880.

Best Practices: LAN

Preparing for your LAN infrastructure includes a review of your existing architecture. If your new IP network requires a LAN upgrade, the following best practices will help to alleviate known pain points:

- Standardize on the LAN architecture to maintain consistency, and reduce support costs.

- Integrate inline power for the desktop Ethernet connections, and remove IP phone power adapters.

- Allow only the voice VLAN to pass traffic on public access phones to prevent security breaches.

- Do not connect devices that produce heavy data traffic—such as Network File System (NFS) workstations—to IP phones. The internal switch in the phone might drop packets in this situation.

- Implement change management practices that encourage processes for the data infrastructure to complement those for voice services.

- Define the operational turnover and production/support of the LAN prior to bringing the system online so that the team can verify that all systems are "go," make sure that support personnel are trained, and check that all new support processes are approved and in place.

Preparing the WAN

IP Telephony WAN deployments require significant planning. Multiservice traffic that travels across a converged WAN requires the network to support and supply the prerequisite QoS features. The design and dimensioning of the WAN must also be compatible with traffic profiles, business requirements, and circuit tariffs.

The Cisco WAN uses a hierarchical model that enables the most cost-effective platforms to be provisioned at the edge. This model's tiered architecture provides several layers of network devices from the edge to the core, strategically moving certain "work" functions to those devices, and enabling routing decisions to be made closer to the core.

"Due to the high amount of processing and memory power required in the core for routing decisions, firewalls, etc., the devices in the core tend to be higher-end devices, such as Catalyst 6500s," says Amy Rogers, IT engineer. "That process allows us to put more cost-effective devices near the edge because routing decision overhead is saved for the non-edge devices. Edge devices essentially forward packets and reside on the access layer of the Cisco hierarchical model."

Bandwidth

In addition to adhering to the design philosophy, the team must provision the WAN bandwidth requirements adequately. Because the requirements for data traffic outstrip those of voice, the percentage of the wide area bandwidth required for voice decreases, lowering costs at the same time. The team must provision the WAN links to support the minimum requirements for data, as well as the bandwidth required for voice and video traffic. When other applications are inactive, the bandwidth is then available for data.

"Originally, when we first began to put VoIP on the WAN, we had some areas of bandwidth constraints that wouldn't allow us to put a large amount of voice traffic on the link," Rogers says. "For instance, the WAN links to Europe and Asia Pacific were quite saturated just with data on them. When we implemented VoIP using the AS5300 platforms, we then used a QoS feature called rate limiting, which enabled us to carve out some bandwidth for a limited number of calls."

Equally important to bandwidth is latency, which is as critical to VoIP traffic quality as bandwidth constraints. Cisco documentation on the limitations of VoIP traffic states that the acceptable limit of roundtrip response time for packets is 300 milliseconds (ms).

Approaching that type of latency over long WAN links—such as from the United States to Australia—could easily cause so much latency that VoIP traffic would be rendered useless.

The Cisco WAN backbone then went through a large upgrade, replacing the existing backbone circuits with greater bandwidth and more redundancy. "In some cases, we pulled off a 999 percent increase in bandwidth—almost 1000 times the bandwidth we originally had," Rogers says. "So, once the new backbone was in place, the issues of bandwidth constraint disappeared. Today, we have no bandwidth constraint issues in our AVVID deployment over the WAN."

Software and Hardware Upgrades

In the days of the AS5300 when the PBXs were still in place, hardware, firmware, and software upgrades were needed often. However, this was the result of a still-developing technology.

"Being on the bleeding edge of this technology often resulted in using prereleased hardware and engineering code on our production network," Rogers says. "Prereleased components and code are not yet available on Cisco.com and typically [are] unavailable to anyone outside of Cisco."

Using special engineering builds is a practice rarely recommended for an external customer. "But, as Cisco IT, we share the common goal with the business units in developing the best product possible. By implementing these types of new technologies in our production networks, we've uncovered many bugs, made major feature enhancements, and improved the quality of the products before making them available to our customers," Rogers notes.

The testing and troubleshooting procedures for this technology followed the same methodologies of any network troubleshooting scenario, as defined in the *Cisco Network Troubleshooting* book. The real critical piece became less of working through technical issues, and more of becoming skilled at collaborating across cross-functional teams.

"A typical troubleshooting scenario meant involving engineers from the legacy Telecom group, NT administrators from the CallManager group, [and] network engineers capable of capturing and interpreting debug output on network end points," Rogers says. "And, of course, end users [who] could place bidirectional calls and provide feedback on voice quality and characteristics of test calls."

Best Practices: WAN

Preparing for your WAN infrastructure includes a review of your existing architecture. If your new IP network requires a WAN upgrade, the following best practices will help to alleviate known pain points:

- To analyze the gaps between existing bandwidth and device requirements, collect several categories of information, including the existing WAN topology, device information, and resource utilization.

- Voice bandwidth requirements depend on a number of parameters, such as the sampling rate, codec, link type, header compression techniques, and number of simultaneous voice calls.

- Analyze upgrade requirements for hardware, software, and WAN connectivity. Hardware upgrades ensure adequate processing power; software upgrades support IP Telephony features; and WAN upgrades support the additional traffic load.

- Prior to voice deployment, perform all upgrades on centralized call processing, WAN, and LAN, enabling the solution to be tested prior to live voice traffic.

- Use a combination of assessment methods, including live testing, Internet Performance Manager, and Cisco VoIP Readiness Net Audit.

- Define the operational turnover and production/support of the WAN prior to bringing the system online so that the team can verify that all systems are "go," that support personnel have been trained, and that all new support processes are approved and in place.

NOTE   For more information on WAN requirements, see "IP Telephony Solution Guide" at http://www.cisco.com/univercd/cc/td/doc/product/voice/ip_tele/sol_up11.pdf.

Category 5/Category 3 Wiring, Cabling Requirements

At the time of the IP Telephony rollout, the Cisco San Jose campus cabling configuration consisted of four Category 5 and two Category 3 cables per standard wall plate. Several new buildings were going up on campus. To prepare those new buildings for the IP Telephony deployment, the team decided to eliminate the Category 3 cables. Those old cables would not be needed for the IP phones.

Because Internet telephony runs on existing IT data network infrastructure, the user's PC plugs directly into the IP phone, requiring only one port to support both the phone and the PC, eliminating the need for additional cable. At Cisco, this had the added advantage of leaving three Category 5 cables open in each office.

"This configuration helped us attain significant cost savings," says Al Valcour, RCCD, construction planning project manager. "It meant that we didn't need to install extra cables to each office."

The next area of business addressed the riser cable within each building. The riser cable ran from the Building Distribution Frame (BDF) to the Intermediate Distribution Frame (IDF). "We have one BDF per building and at least one IDF per floor, although in most cases, there are two IDFs," Valcour continues.

Because there was no longer a PBX in the BDF, it reduced the amount of riser cabling in each building from 900 pairs of copper running to each IDF, down to just 100 pairs. "Although we still have the extra cable in our existing buildings, we have substantially reduced its usage," Valcour says.

Cable Distance and Wall Phones

The primary challenge that the team experienced during the retrofit was cable distance on existing wall phone installations. Although PBX phones can be run close to 3000 feet on Category 3, IP Phones are limited to 330 feet (100 m).

"We knew that distance might be a problem in some locations, but we found that it made more sense to use the existing cable that was there and then replace it if there was a problem," Valcour says. "We ran into a few situations where CAT 3 cable went beyond the 100 m and wouldn't retain the connection, so in those cases we had to install new cable to a new, closer location. And since we were replacing cable anyway, we upgraded to CAT 5, which is a voice and data grade cable."

When distance was a factor and Cisco upgraded to Category 5, Valcour retained a Cisco vendor/partner to do the installation. "We also used the cabling vendor to install all of the wall mounts required for the wall phones," Valcour says. The cabling vendor tested all wall phones for connectivity to ensure full functionality and to give Valcour and his team at least three to five days in case they needed to upgrade the cabling before the retrofit.

Valcour added that in most cases today, and with the new industry standards in place calling for Category 5E, new cabling will be maintained at the 90 m wiring closet to wall plate Category 5 standard. Category 3 cabling is limited to 10 Mb, whereas Category 5 provides up to 100 Mb. Although both maintain the same distance limitations, they have vastly different data rate capabilities.

"As long as the total CAT 3 cable length is within 100 m, it will function properly," Valcour says. "But the new industry standard minimum is CAT 5E, which is what we're currently installing here at Cisco. The advantage is that regardless of the service (voice, data, video), CAT 5E will support the service and enable scalability and growth potential."

Wall phones are also considerations, and depending on routing and where the cabling is running, they might require an extended length of cabling. To enable the required access from the wall field to the racks where the new IP phone connectivity is mounted on the wall, Valcour and his team ran tie cables from the wall to the racks within each IDF.

A Simplified Process

IP Telephony has made life simpler for Valcour. "In the past, we'd have large riser cables that we had to design to distribute voice, separate wall fields, and a separate voice component," Valcour recalls. "With integration, we now design the cabling to support the network, and it supports whatever applications ride on it."

Currently, Cisco is in the process of installing Category 5E. The next migration will be to Category 6, which is under review for certification and provides a higher bandwidth—up to Gigabit Ethernet.

Power, Rack Space, and Ordering Circuits

Because Cisco implemented a large IP Telephony deployment, an important component of the migration was to ensure adequate rack space to fit all the servers that would be needed and adequate power requirements to keep them running. After Cisco verified or adjusted that to meet the requirements of the new converged network, the implementation progressed smoothly, and Cisco also gained the flexibility to scale in the future.

"We walked every building [and] entered each BDF or the locations chosen to house the FXS switches and the DPAs [Digital PBX Adapters] to make sure there was adequate rack space for the different switches and the circuit installation," says Anthony Garcia, network engineer. "We reserved rack space and verified that the necessary power was in place. If it wasn't, then we worked with facility WorkPlace Resources to get power installed there."

"Every business has unique networking needs," says Dennis Silva, senior network engineer. For the T1 CAT 6Ks, Cisco used the ten network operations centers (NOCs—central campus wiring closets) located throughout the San Jose campus because of their UPS power and generator capability as well as multiple SONET rings to multiple vendors.

"What that means is that your single point of failure is eliminated. If we lost one NOC, it would be just a blip on the screen. Nobody would even know the difference," Silva notes.

This strategy afforded the greatest protection to the network. "The buildings all have multiple entrances," Silva continues. "So, for instance, if someone on the facility grounds staff is out there with a backhoe and digs up one of our cables coming in from PacBel, Sprint, AT&T, or MCI, it won't affect the service because it's on a ring. The other entrance, which is on the other side of the building, will activate and take over."

All the Cisco NOCs have multiple entrances and SONETs and adequate UPS and generators for power backup. "They're pretty bullet proof," Silva says. "And because we're located on a flood plain, they're never on the ground floor."

Best Practices: Network Provisioning

- Like Cisco, most organizations do not have in-house expertise for cable installation. Ensure that the partner you choose is certified in the equipment that is being installed.

- Have a full understanding of the existing infrastructure before you start the retrofit. Know how your current cabling system is set up, whether there are wall fields or patch panels, and whether the existing cabling is Category 3 or Category 5.

- Make sure there is appropriate rack space to fit all the additional servers and that the existing power configuration is adequate.

Provisioning the VLAN

The Cisco converged network architecture uses one set of IP addresses (VLAN) for data and another set (VVLAN or Auxiliary VLAN) for voice. Both coexist on each desktop switch port, enabling the connection of an IP phone to the switch port and a PC connection to the phone while using different VLANs.

Each IP phone requires an IP address, along with associated information such as subnet mask, default gateway, and so on. This means that the need for IP addresses will double as IP phones are assigned to users. The information can be configured statically on the IP phone or provided by a Dynamic Host Configuration Protocol (DHCP) server.

You can assign IP addresses to IP phones in three ways:

- Assigning IP addresses using the same subnet as the data devices

- Modifying the IP addressing plan

- Creating a separate IP subnet for IP phones

"We used the method that enabled us to create a separate IP subnet for IP phones," says Paul Molyski, IT LAN project manager. The new subnet was positioned in a private address space—network 10.0.0.0. Using this scheme, the PC was placed on a subnet that was reserved for data devices, and the phone was on a subnet reserved for voice.

"Having the phone learn its IP configuration dynamically eliminated our having to manually configure the IP phone," Molyski says. "So when the IP phone powers up, it gets its voice VLAN number automatically, [and] then sends a DHCP request on that subnet for an IP address."

The automated mechanism by which the IP phone gets its voice subnet was provided through enhancements to the Cisco Discovery Protocol (CDP). "IP addresses are a valuable commodity," Molyski says. "Using private IP addresses for the IP phone system avoids 'burning up' any valuable registered IP addresses."

Best Practices: Provisioning the VLAN

- Use the IP Telephony deployment as an opportunity to review your entire IP address space allocation scheme, making reassignments and readdressing changes that benefit the organization.

- Align the data and voice address block assignments so that they are the same size. This makes the network design easier to follow and aids in troubleshooting.

- For large installations, take advantage of the auxiliary VLAN feature of Cisco switches because it preserves registered IP address space.

Connecting to Voice Mail

Depending on needs, an organization might integrate CallManager to its existing voice mail system or install a new voice mail system.

"At the time of the installation, we still had our extensive legacy voice mail system, and we ended up using both digital and analog port adapters to integrate to it," Garcia says. "It was critical that we performed the traffic analysis up front in order to identify how many ports were actually being utilized."

NOTE   Since the IP Telephony rollout, Cisco has begun to replace its legacy voice mail system with the Cisco Unity product.

Site Survey

Site readiness is crucial to rapid deployment because site deficiencies will most likely delay the implementation. The implementation team used the site survey to ensure readiness by collecting key information highlighting the gap between what currently existed at the site and what would be required to implement the solution. "The survey team was probably the most important piece of the entire retrofit process and the reason why it went so smoothly," says Del Hays, AVVID support team lead.

The survey team was responsible for surveying every telecom service in the building, including fax machines, modems, regular phones, and those users who needed special configurations, such as the boss/admin feature.

"They identified every service that was in the building and verified whether that service was currently working," says Chad Ormondroyd, implementation team lead. This saved the team hundreds of hours when it performed the weekend uploads because it identified and corrected problems ahead of time.

The survey team consisted of up to four Tier 1 technicians, depending on the size and population of the building. On Monday and Tuesday of the week prior to the weekend conversion, the survey team walked through the building, verified the information, and then created a spreadsheet with the updated data. On Wednesday, the spreadsheet was given to the retrofit team, who then used it as the final cutsheet for the upload.

The site survey was instrumental in helping to clean up the network as well. "If there was a modem or a fax line that was supposed to be in a particular location, the survey team would find it and test it to see if it was working," Ormondroyd says. "If it wasn't, then we didn't include it in the retrofit. That helped us clean out the old data at the same time we were installing the new system."

NOTE   You can find Cisco site survey tables at http://www.cisco.com/go/
stepstosuccess. (A Cisco.com login is required.)

Best Practices: Site Survey

- Identify every service in each building to ensure a complete database upload to the CallManager.

- Conduct the survey on the Monday and Tuesday of the week prior to the conversion to give the retrofit team time to prepare the cutsheet and create solutions for unique configurations.

- Delete nonworking and unidentified modems and fax lines from the spreadsheet to ensure a clean network. (The exceptions are those buildings with business mission-critical users.)

- Use an experienced survey team composed of Tier 1 technicians who are already familiar with the existing setups.

 Refer to Appendix 4-E, "Implementation Checklist." The implementation team used the Implementation Checklist as a quick reminder of the various tasks required for each site. Each site requires specific requirements; therefore, you should alter the checklist for each site. You can find Appendix 4-E at the end of this chapter or download it from http://www.ciscopress.com/1587200880.

 Refer to Appendix 4-F, "Retrofit Implementation Guide." The Retrofit Implementation Guide was created as a cookbook for the entire project team to use as a reference for all standards required for the installation team. You can find Appendix 4-F at the end of this chapter or download it from http://www.ciscopress.com/1587200880.

The Implementation

The implementation phase is perhaps the most critical time in the project and, if you have properly prepared, it will progress much more smoothly. During the implementation, the team will stage, install, configure, test, and verify the solution. In addition, the team will finalize all operations, conduct user training, and hand off to operations (Day 2 support).

Properly preparing for the implementation was crucial to the success of the Cisco IP Telephony deployment. Each building that was scheduled for migration was readied for equipment installation prior to the implementation team's arrival. This process included checking power rails, air conditioning, and circuit installation. In addition, the live circuits that connected to the equipment were fully tested to ensure that they were suitable to carry network traffic.

After those steps were in place and the survey team had conducted the walkthrough, it was time to begin the retrofit and cutover to the new system.

"We gave ourselves two to three days to prep the cutsheet and identify those who needed the boss/admin configuration, who needed number changes, where phones might be missing, etc.," Hays says. "Then we contacted each group to get number changes set up, voice mailboxes built, and make any other necessary preparations."

The next step was to set up the Bulk Administration Tool (BAT), scan the phones, and label the boxes with the locations, separating everything by floors. After the team scanned the phones, it waited until after hours—typically after 5 p.m. on weekdays—to upload them into the system.

After the team finished the upload, it began to install the new phones and remove the old PBX translations. Then the implementation team went back and tested the phones to make sure that everything was in agreement with the worksheet and to address any discrepancies. Although testing was a manual process, as the team gained experience, the process became more efficient and required less time to complete.

Boss/Admin Phone Configurations

The IP Telephony boss/admin feature enables admin personnel to answer other users' phone lines, such as a manager or anyone else in the administrative team's call group. To configure the appropriate phones, the survey team needed to identify which users required that feature.

NOTE   See Chapter 3, "The Migration Strategy," for templates that will help you collect this information, as well as user training tips on how to train the administrative assistant community.

After we completed the retrofit for a specific building, we interviewed all administrative assistants to ensure that they were comfortable with the IP Phones and to address any problems. We used the following script during the interviews:

- Does your phone work appropriately? Is the configuration correct?

- If you could change anything about the phone, what would it be?

- Have you found any IP phone feature gaps?

- Describe your call volume. Do the number of line appearances you now have support the way you manage your incoming calls? Do you require more or less line appearances to effectively manage the number of incoming calls you manage?

- Do you know how to transfer a call directly into voice mail without making the phone ring? (If no, provide instructions.)

Provide telecom help desk information and make sure everyone is familiar with the Day 2 support process.

TIP	Do not assume that all administrative assistants require the same number of line appearances. Plan ahead and discuss call volume with them to avoid making a mistake, and then set up the phone line appearances that complement their call volume.

System Admin Tools

Preparing for the implementation required a concise combination of planning, procedures, processes, and tools. To aid the process and ensure this smooth transition from the PBX environment to the new IP Telephony application, we used system admin tools and procedures throughout each stage of the implementation. Following is a description of each tool. At the end of this chapter are several templates, samples, and other helpful tools that the implementation team used during the retrofit process.

Exporting Existing Phones

Telecommuting is a large part of the Cisco organizational culture. Enabling users to work and maintain productivity from remote locations was a critical "must-have" feature.

Export stations allow users to access voice mail and other features remotely—from home or other locations. Simple Network Management Protocol (SNMP) features for the CallManager enable network management applications to retrieve data from the server in a standard fashion.

Following are examples of the exported data:

- Cisco CallManager group tables

- Region tables

- Time zone group tables

- Device pool tables

- Phone detail tables

- Gateway information tables and status traps

- Call detail record (CDR) host log table and performance counters

Although export stations are typically easy to enable, the team did run into a challenge that caused an otherwise avoidable delay. "One of the problems that we had in the very early stages of the implementation was an errant comma in the exported data file," Hays says. "Because someone had entered an extra comma at the end of the script, it wouldn't upload."

Hays cautions that when you enter information into the hardware address that identifies the user's phone, you must enter the information in a specific sequence. "If you just scatter or throw in any kind of MAC address, it will be rejected, saying it's already in use."

TIP   The Media Access Control (MAC) address must be a 12-digit number using characters 0 through 9 or A through F. For people who had no phones (that is, 1 VM only), we set up a MAC address of '000000000001', '000000000002', and so on to ensure that the MAC addresses didn't conflict.

Bulk Administrative Tool/Scanner

Collecting the data and entering it manually into the new system could have been a long and cumbersome process, fraught with human error. To save time, reduce errors, and simplify the process of entering all the data into the exported data file, the implementation team used an automated collection process. Scanning the phone's UPC bar code—located on the outside of the box—into an Excel spreadsheet and converting it with a BAT, the team was able to populate the template in batches of 250 phones. The team then segmented the data according to which phones were going to be uploaded into which CallManager.

"Utilizing the BAT tool took us only about three hours versus the two days it would have taken had we entered the data manually. It also saved us from having to troubleshoot manual errors," Ormondroyd says.

NOTE	You can find a sample of the BAT at http://www.cisco.com/univercd/cc/td/doc/product/voice/c_callmg/3_3/bulk_adm/index.htm.

Phone Installation Test Procedures

After the team installed the phones, it tested them to ensure that calls were routed accurately for inbound calls, outbound calls, and voice mail. The test procedure for IP phones was similar to the test procedure for PBX phones.

"To double check that everything worked correctly, we used a manual procedure in addition to the software reports that indicated whether the calls were being steered correctly," Hays said. "Basically, we picked up each phone and dialed out to test outbound calls, performed inbound dialing to ensure that it rang to the right phone, and then tested it to see if it went to voice mail appropriately."

The team also tested the handset, speaker, and accessories and checked other external devices and parts visually to ensure that none were missing or broken. "The goal was to have 100 percent of the phones up and working by the time the user came in to try it out," Ormondroyd says.

On average, only about two to three percent of phones experienced problems steering or experienced bad LAN connection during the install. The typical causes ranged from incorrect MAC address to misspelled names. Because of our thorough test procedures, when the users arrived, we had a less than one percent failure rate on the phones—a record we are quite proud of.

 Refer to Appendix 4-G, "Cisco IP Phone Test Procedure." Each phone installer uses the Cisco IP Phone test procedure template as a guide on how to manually test each phone to ensure it meets the operational standards set by the project manager, design engineering, and the customer. You can find this appendix at the end of this chapter or download it from http://www.ciscopress.com/1587200880.

You can review the Cisco Solution Acceptance Test site for additional testing material at http://www.cisco.com/cpropart/salestools/cc/so/neso/vvda/iptl/iptna_dg.htm.

Removal of Stations from PBX

After the implementation team had downloaded all the data onto the CallManager, the team needed to delete the data from the PBX. After retrofitting those lines into the new system using the BAT and scanner, the team removed phone numbers from the PBX database and steered them onto the uniform dialing plan on the CallManager.

"The most important point of this step is that in order for the phone to ring in one system, it must be completely removed from the other," Hays says. The team verified that this step was complete by running a script in the PBX to test that all extensions had been removed properly, followed by a manual test in the UDP tables to correct any problems found with individual extensions.

Postponing Adds, Moves, and Changes

All adds, moves, and changes in the building scheduled to be retrofitted were halted at least a week before the implementation team arrived. The team worked closely with WorkPlace Resources (WPR) and Facilities Management (FM) to ensure that this process was followed.

This alignment proved useful in locking down all add, move, and change requests until after the migration. WPR also provided a list of all users, their cube locations, and the phone numbers of everyone in the building, which the team used to build the final cutsheet. This also enabled WPR to conduct an accurate dump of the PBX database to identify which lines were on that PBX switch, who they belonged to, and how they were configured.

"The survey team went in ahead of us and surveyed the entire building to make sure everybody was in the location they were supposed to be in and that the PBX dump was current and accurate," Hayes recalls. After the implementation team compiled and verified the information, it was able to upload the data into the CallManager.

Retrofit Implementation Guide

The Retrofit Implementation Guide details the process that the implementation team used to ensure consistency and standardization of the retrofit. This guide provides comprehensive information relative to each step in the process and includes the following topics:

- General phone information, including main prefixes, associated CallManager server names, and voice mail numbers

- Cutsheet requirements, such as naming standards and call restriction standards for common area phones

- Operations retrofit process

- Procedures for adding IP Phones and analog phones

- Procedures for IP Phone testing

- Procedures for IP Phone spreadsheet creation

- Procedures for BAT import

- Procedures for restricted phone configuration

- Miscellaneous phone installation notes

- Floor walk-through checklist

- Wall phone and wiring punchdown

- Headset support

- Boss/admin configurations and voice-mail-only configurations for telecommuters

- Information on troubleshooting phones

- Operations room FAQ

 Refer to Appendix 4-F. You can find this appendix at the end of this chapter or download it from http://www.ciscopress.com/1587200880.

Staffing Required for Retrofit Team

The team outsourced the plug-and-play part of the retrofit to a Cisco partner who was already familiar with the internal Cisco telephony network and did not have to learn everything from the ground up. I designed a matrix to help ensure that the implementation team was becoming progressively more efficient after each building's retrofit.

We multiplied the number of phones being converted by how long the retrofit took to ensure that our partner was becoming faster and more efficient. As the project moved forward and the process became more streamlined, fewer people were needed to maintain the momentum of the installation.

 Refer to Appendix 4-H, "IP Telephony Retrofit Efficiency Report." The project manager uses the IP Telephony Retrofit Efficiency Report to track the progress and pace of the phone installation team. Creating a metric assists the project manager in determining whether the installation process is becoming more efficient and also helps to maintain a consistent momentum. You can find this appendix at the end of this chapter or download it from http://www.ciscopress.com/1587200880 .

TIP	Have a member of the design team on call during the weekend cutovers. This extra layer of support might come in handy if a unique design issue surfaces.

Move Team

All weekly moves required the changeout of a PBX phone to an IP phone. Weekly moves were estimated at 250 per week, 75 percent of which were PBX phones. Moves due to levitations (cube resizing) averaged 120 per week. During the period of September through May, one new building opened each month, resulting in an additional 500 to 1000 moves per month. Staffing requirements included a project manager and six field technical engineers (FTEs).

Following is a list of the work this team was responsible for:

- Manage inventory control

- Identify phones to be converted

- Prepare the master spreadsheet

- Notify users of change

- Program IP phones

- Program PBX changes into batch loading tool, including removal of stations and steering changes

- Secure phones; assign moves, adds, and changes to individuals/locations listed; and write move/add/change address and name on box

- Deliver the equipment to the appropriate IDF, if required

- Install and test phones

- Collect and package the old PBX phones for return

Retrofit Team

The retrofit team uplifted one building per week and averaged 500 to 600 phones per building, requiring three telecom representatives consisting of one team lead and two FTEs.

The following presents the day-to-day responsibilities of this team:

- **Day 1**—Secure floor plans for buildings to be converted that week. Conduct PBX dump for the building to be converted. Secure spreadsheets from call centers outlining all agents and extensions to be exempt from the conversion. (The Cisco IP customer contact solution was not available at that time.) Provide communication to the building (that is, e-mails, posting notices, and so on) regarding work to be performed that week. Clean up from prior week. Begin identifying all building analog lines.

- **Day 2**—Perform walkthrough of the building during business hours to collect the following: extension and type of PBX phone, username, building number, floor, and cube. Identify and record information for conference rooms, lobbies, break rooms, and so on. Continue identifying analog lines.

- **Day 3**—Consolidate written information gathered by walkthrough into master spreadsheet and floor plan. Compile move information for that week. Consolidate call center information with walkthrough information. Complete all analog line information.

- **Day 4**—Send e-mail to users advising that telephone services will be unavailable Friday after 5:30 p.m. Consolidate written information outlining move/add/change assignments into master spreadsheet. Deliver the spreadsheet to the implementation team to perform a batch upload of information into the CallManager database and provide a copy to the project manager for archiving and for the operations/support team.

Early in the retrofit process, while the implementation team was still getting comfortable with the process, staffing consisted of up to 15 technicians. However, that number was reduced to 8 technicians by the end of the retrofit, installing up to 500 phones per weekend.

 Refer to Appendix 4-I, "IP Telephony Retrofit Project Gantt Chart." You can find it at the end of this chapter or download it from http://www.ciscopress.com/1587200880.

Implementation Schedule

A typical implementation schedule is as follows:

- **Monday–Tuesday**—Answer conversion questions and provide user training.
- **Wednesday**—No activity—team's day off.
- **Thursday**—Scan equipment.
- **Friday**—After 5 p.m., steer all phones to the CallManager. Prepare equipment and move it to identified locations. Configure special setups. Load phone information with BAT into CallManager.
- **Saturday**—Phone placement "plug and play." Begin installation.
- **Sunday**—Fallback day if the previous day's conversion requires extra time to execute.

 Refer to Appendix 4-J, "Sample Project Plan." You can find this appendix at http://www.ciscopress.com/1587200880.

 Refer to Appendix 4-K, "Sample Project Schedule." You can find this appendix at the end of this chapter or download it from http://www.ciscopress.com/1587200880.

Project Risk Assessment

Because of the rapid pace of the implementation, the team needed to put processes into place to get it done quickly and efficiently. To effect a smooth, risk-free conversion, the implementation team worked with design/engineering, the support team, and the business unit to identify the project's severity points.

Project risk factors put a stake in the ground that identified thresholds in which a decision had to be made whether to stop and take a step back or continue to move forward. The implementation team needed to understand where those hot zones were that could potentially affect the project and how to react to them.

We identified the risk factors by talking to the engineering and support teams and identified vulnerable areas that could cause problems to our users, to the network, and to the overall serviceability of the system.

TIP	Identify your risk factors early, and prepare a backout process in case something goes wrong.

Without this level of planning, the implementation would have been like a row of dominos—one misstep could have caused everything behind it to fall as well. A risk assessment provides an instruction manual that identifies what could happen, what you can do to prevent it, what to do if it does happen, and then what action to take.

 Refer to Appendix 4-L, "Project Risk Assessment Table." The Project Risk Assessment Table is a tool that the project manager uses to determine rules of engagement for the various possible risk triggers. The project team was asked to identify a list of possible risk factors and preventive action during the installation phase. The project manager was then responsible for determining a Go/No Go decision. Identifying these potential problems early helps to maintain momentum and efficiency. You can find Appendix 4-L at the end of this chapter or download it from http://www.ciscopress.com/1587200880.

Best Practices: Implementation

- The implementation should start off slowly and build momentum. A crawl-walk-run approach offers you time to work out the kinks and develop a process that works. Define the schedule according to the experience of the implementation team rather than by dates. Going too fast or too slow can have disastrous consequences. Ensure that the weekly schedule outlines key tasks, deliverables, and expectations for success.

- Be sensitive to potential burnout. Because the implementation team needs to work every weekend, ensure that one day off during the week is enforced. Schedule time off or retrofit cleanup time for the implementation team during slowdown phases such as software upgrades to provide additional breaks or lighter workloads.

- Maintaining momentum is critical; therefore, make sure that all equipment is in place before the weekend.

- Do a find and replace for any commas with spaces in the BAT phone description to prevent problems in the script.

- Use the BAT/Scanner to create the exported data file to save time and reduce human error.

- Conduct manual and visual phone tests in addition to software reports. Use the IP Phone test procedure to ensure that all phones are operational before the users arrive. This extra step saves you time and builds confidence within the user community.

- Cease all adds, moves, and changes a week before the retrofit, and involve your facilities team to help.

- Design an installation schedule that outlines all tasks for each day. Keep Sunday free as Plan B if you need more time because of something going wrong.

- Use experienced teams to conduct the site surveys, preferably technicians who know the current setups.

- Consider beginning the retrofit with a larger implementation team until the team becomes more efficient. After your process is well streamlined, consider scaling back the number of installation team members required to conduct the plug-and-play function.

- Design a performance matrix to determine how well and how quickly the team is conducting the conversion, and use this information to maintain the pace of the weekend conversion so that the installation phase continues to become faster rather than slower. Inform the team whether the previous weekend's pace was faster or slower than the current one; in this way, the team learns that performance, as well as error-free phone configurations, are accomplishments.

Customer Service

After six months, the Tiger Team was midway through the Cisco campus conversion. Things had gone relatively smoothly. After the team had converted a significant number of buildings without incident, the process was no longer a big deal. It had transitioned to an expectation that things would continue in that mode.

"After the twentieth building, our process had become very smooth," said Cisco director of IT strategic program management. "We had not experienced any escalations, problems, or issues, and the project had become a non-event. If we continued to maintain our commitment to customer service, we knew the rest of it would proceed equally as uneventfully."

However, although the implementation team had become comfortable and familiar with the technology, the conversion still loomed over the heads of those users who had yet to be converted. The implementation team had to remain sensitized to the apprehension experienced by those individuals and remember that this experience was brand new to those users. Maintaining the consistency of customer service was just as critical to the project at that point as it was in the beginning when the team retrofitted the first building.

We found that unhappy users typically had no problem escalating their concerns, so we constantly reinforced the importance of customer service to the project team—specifically, the implementation and support teams, because at that point, they were the most visible.

I found it helpful to design customer service rules that the team should follow as a benchmark. For example, we mandated that all questions from users must be answered within 24 hours. The team also maintained a log of user requests and concerns so that those requests did not get lost in the shuffle.

Solid IP Phone test procedures ensured that the phone was working correctly and helped us maintain a less than one percent failure rate throughout the 55 building conversion. We also added the entire implementation team to the customer care alias to ensure that everyone knew what was going well and what needed attention.

As the initiative's project manager, I handled all initial escalations with the Tiger Team lead, who acted as the point of contact for all next-level escalations. The team lead handled these escalations by applying the same rules followed by the installation team and myself. Flip-flopping the rules and making exceptions were rare. Consistency not only made my job easier, but it also enabled the team to maintain credibility when dealing with users who wanted us to bend the rules.

The team knew that complacency was not their friend. "Completing the campus conversion within one year had become the gold star we used to continue the momentum after the midway point," says James Robshaw, Tiger Team program manager. "Raising the expectation that we needed to complete the campus and convert all 20,000 users within that timeframe became an incredible motivation."

Even though the first six months of the implementation had gone well, the Tiger Team did not make the mistake of resting on its laurels. Consistent review of the PBX dumps enabled the team to anticipate potential problems and to keep the project moving forward.

Nothing stops a project more quickly than finding a special phone configuration at the last minute that has no timely solution in place. Process reviews were conducted every quarter to analyze what was working well and what improvements needed to be made. With the rapid pace of the schedule, it would have been easy to make the same mistake repeatedly.

A good rule of thumb to measure user satisfaction is when user phone calls switch from callers complaining about the impending change to callers wanting to influence the schedule to get their new IP phones sooner. That swing in customer acceptance was a critical measurement for us that the conversion was going well.

TIP Little things can easily turn into big things. Small considerations, such as placing the new IP Phone in the same location as the old phone, go a long way toward helping users accept the new phone.

Best Practices: Customer Service

- WPR or FM should be a member of the implementation team because they are familiar with the building, its layout, the various users, and their special needs.

- A survey team provides the additional checks and balances that make the retrofit proceed much more smoothly. Verification with the site survey along with the PBX dump ensures additional checks and balances and integrity of data.

- Involving a representative from the company's telecom group adds another level of expertise because they know the setups and unique configurations of the users.

- During the midpoint of the project, customer service can get harder to maintain consistently. Instill the importance of customer service to the implementation team, and be mindful of the little things that are important to users. You might find posting the rules for customer service around the team's work areas useful.

Resources

Throughout this chapter, you have seen references to a number of utilities made available for download at http://www.ciscopress.com/1587200880. You are encouraged to use these utilities to create your own implementation templates to build your process for managing the installation.

- Appendix 4-A: Steps to Success Project Management Process

- Appendix 4-B: Implementation Planning Template

- Appendix 4-C: Site Survey Form

- Appendix 4-D: LAN Upgrade Test Procedures

- Appendix 4-E: Implementation Checklist

- Appendix 4-F: Retrofit Implementation Guide

- Appendix 4-G: Cisco IP Phone Test Procedure

- Appendix 4-H: IP Telephony Retrofit Efficiency Report

- Appendix 4-I: IP Telephony Retrofit Project Gantt Chart

- Appendix 4-J: Sample Project Plan

- Appendix 4-K: Sample Project Schedule

- Appendix 4-L: Project Risk Assessment Table

- Site Survey Tables: http://www.cisco.com/warp/public/788/solution_guide/forms/index.html#ss

- Cisco IP Telephony Network Design Guide: http://www.cisco.com/univercd/cc/td/doc/product/voice/ip_tele/network/index.htm

- Cisco VoIP Readiness Net Audit: http://www.cisco.com/warp/public/cc/serv/mkt/sup/ent/avvid/nadit_ds.htm

- "Improving Security on Cisco Routers" technical notes: http://www.cisco.com/warp/public/707/21.html

Summary

With the right processes, procedures, and tools, the implementation phase can roll out smoothly, efficiently, and on schedule. Preparing the LAN and WAN for a converged voice and data network is a critical first step, followed by provisioning the network for proper cabling, providing access to inline power, and enabling the appropriate class of service. The cutover can be expedited with system admin tools and a thorough site survey that provides critical user information. Following is a short summary from each section:

- **LAN infrastructure requirements**—Standardizing on the organization's LAN maintains consistency, increases network stability, and reduces support costs.

- **WAN infrastructure requirements**—You must provision WAN links to support the minimum requirements for data, plus the additional bandwidth required for converged voice and data traffic.

- **Network provisioning**—IP Telephony greatly reduces the number of riser cables required at each site. However, you must address cable distance to ensure proper functionality.

- **Provisioning the VLAN**—In a converged network architecture, one set of IP addresses (VLAN) is used for data, whereas another set (VVLAN or auxiliary VLAN) is used for voice. Cisco created a separate private IP subnet for IP phones.

- **Connecting to voice mail**—By performing a careful and comprehensive traffic analysis up front, Cisco was able to integrate with its existing voice mail system.

- **The implementation**—Steps to Success ensure that you have a process for managing the implementation phase. Your process should include steps for managing the implementation planning phase to correct tools for transitioning to the Day 2 support team. An important step within the implementation phase is the collection of data for the site surveys. The site survey collects key information about every user, service, and special configuration in the building. System admin tools increase productivity and reduce errors by automating the data gathering process. Outsourced staffing requirements should decrease during the course of the implementation, as the staff becomes more efficient with experience.

- **Customer service**—Continue to address sensitivity to user apprehension about the new technology, even in later stages of the implementation when things have been proceeding without incident for the implementation team. Reinforce the importance of customer service to reduce escalations and offer users a sense of comfort with their new phones.

Chapter 5, "Day 2 Handoff and Support," addresses the Day 2 handoff to the operations and support team. Topics addressed include network management, power backup, monitoring and troubleshooting, serviceability, and the importance of backup support.

Appendix 4-A: Project Planning Flowchart

Appendix 4-A is available at http://www.ciscopress.com/1587200880.

Appendix 4-B: Implementation Planning Template

Appendix 4-B is available at http://www.ciscopress.com/1587200880.

Appendix 4-C: Site Survey Template

Appendix 4-C is available at http://www.ciscopress.com/1587200880.

Appendix 4-D: LAN Upgrade Test Procedures

The LAN Upgrade Test Procedure checklist is a list of best practices that you should consider when conducting a LAN upgrade.

This appendix is also available at http://www.ciscopress.com/1587200880.

1 Test at least one port in each CAT 6K 10/100 blade for data and voice traffic. Connect an IP phone and make sure it powers up and registers with the CallManager. Connect a laptop to the IP phone and make sure the laptop can access the network.

2 You can display the configuration of the IP phone by pressing **Settings_3** and scrolling through the various configuration parameters. The parameter settings, or lack of settings, indicate how far the phone registration has progressed.

3 Even if the phone does not register, the Ethernet switch portion of the phone will be operational, allowing data from an attached PC to pass through the IP phone.

4 After you disconnect an IP phone from an inline power source, wait 10 seconds before connecting another device. The inline power does not drop to zero immediately after a disconnect and could possibly damage another device.

5 After you put the CAT 6K in production and deploy the IP phones, verify available power in the CAT 6Ks by issuing the **show env power** command.

Appendix 4-E: Implementation Checklist

The implementation team uses the Implementation Checklist as a quick reminder of the various tasks required for each site. Each site has its own specific requirements; therefore, you must alter the checklist for each site.

This appendix is also available at http://www.ciscopress.com/1587200880.

❏ Unpack the equipment.

❏ Verify cabinet power feeds, rails, and earthing.

❏ Physically install the equipment in the cabinet.

❏ Record equipment serial numbers.

❏ Verify equipment slot allocations.

❏ Install intra-cabinet power cables.

❏ Install intra- and inter-cabinet communications cables.

❏ Verify circuit termination in customer patch panel.

❏ Power up Cisco equipment.

❏ Verify and load system software and firmware.

❏ Configure the equipment.

❏ Implement the dial plan.

❏ Deploy the dial plan architecture.

❏ Configure the dial plan.

❏ Configure E-911.

❏ Devise a dial plan.

❏ Select the Gateway.

❏ Configure Gateway interfaces.

❏ Make critical E-911 considerations for all IP Telephony deployment models.

❏ Make critical E-911 considerations for single-site deployment models.

❏ Conduct installation tests.

❏ Add equipment to the network.

❏ Conduct solution acceptance tests.

Appendix 4-F: Retrofit Implementation Guide

This appendix is also available at http://www.ciscopress.com/1587200880.

The Retrofit Implementation Guide details the process, or the "cookbook of standards," that the implementation team used to ensure consistency and standardization of the retrofit process. Review your process with the implementation team to ensure that the same standards and procedures apply. Use the Cisco.com website to access the latest documentation on the processes and procedures noted in this section.

This guide should serve useful because it provides a comprehensive outline of topics that are relative to each step of the process, including the following:

- General phone information, including main prefixes, associated CallManager server names, and voice mail numbers

- Cutsheet requirements, such as naming standards and call restriction standards for common area phones

- Operations retrofit process

- Instructions on how to add an IP Phone and an analog device phone test procedure

- IP Phone spreadsheet creation procedures

- Bulk Administration Tool (BAT) import procedures

- Restricted phone configuration procedures

- Miscellaneous phone installation notes

- Floor walkthrough checklist

- Wall phone and wiring punchdown

- Headset support

- Boss/admin configurations; voice mail only configurations for telecommuters

- Troubleshooting of phones

- Operations room FAQ

General Phone Information

Keep it simple for the project team by providing useful information, such as the following CallManager cluster and voice mail information:

- sjclstr1a – 853 Voice Mail: 36555

- sjclstr2a – 525 Voice Mail: 52222

- sjclstr3a – 526 Voice Mail: 68800

- sjclstr4a – 527 Voice Mail: 74800

If you are enabling the speed dial option, provide the project team with the website address for the CallManager administration configuration page and the help desk number that is given to the user group:

- Speed dial: http://sjclstr?a/ccmuser.

- Log in to server with username cisco_main\username and your NT password.

- Telecom help desk xxxxx option 3.

Cutsheet Requirements

The information in the following sections is required from IT Telecom.

Analog Phones

The retrofit team requires the following for all analog phones:

- Extension

- Floor

- Location/cube number

- Type: Polycom or fax (Modem information is provided by the approved modem user list)

- Description as per naming standards

- Intermediate Distribution Frame (IDF)

- Jack number and color (white or gray)

IP Phones

The retrofit team requires the following for all user IP Phones:

- Extension
- Floor
- Location/cube number
- Employee last name
- Employee first name
- Employee user ID

For all wall phone and lobby IP Phones (Jack #99x), the retrofit team requires the following:

- IDF
- Jack number

For all IP Phones, the retrofit team requires that the following be specified:

- The identify of all wall phones
- The identify of all phones requiring restricted access (such as public areas and break rooms)

IP Phone Naming Standards

Following are the IP Phone naming standards that are used for the installation team. A consistent naming standard for each type of phone makes it easier for the support team and when conducting phone query reports.

Type of IP Phone	Description Example	Display Example
Standard user phone	NAME: SJC10/5/537	Joe Smith
Conference room phone	Cf Hang Ten SJC16/2/252	Cf Hang Ten
IDF/BDF phone	IDF SJC XVI SJC16/2/217	IDF SJC XVI
Break room phone	Break Room SJC XVI 16/1/118	Break Room SJC XVI
Copy room phone	Copy Room SJC XVI SJC16/3/318	Copy Room SJC XVI
Lobby phone	Lobby SJC XVI SJC16/1/100	Lobby SJC XVI
Reception phone	Reception SJC XVI SJC16/1/100	Reception SJC XVI

Analog Phone Naming Standards

The following are the analog phone naming standards that appear to be used.

	Display Example
Polycoms	Py, Light House SJC16/4/401
Faxes	Fx, RAPD 53936 SJC16/4/G5-11
Modems	Md, Chambers SJC16/4/G5-11

Call Restriction Standards

Restrict the following types of phones for local-only access, which allows calling within the campus, local, and toll-free numbers.

- Lobby phones

- Break room phones

- Copy room phones

Operations Retrofit Process

Documents Prior to Walkthrough

1 Request document with all building occupants and locations from WPR.

   a. Remove all occupants that are currently assigned IP Phones with an 853 extension.

   b. Format list into the order requested by Professional Services.

2 Download all the extensions residing in the PBX EPN.

   a. Separate all analog lines from the list.

   b. Separate all common area phones from the list.

   c. Separate all lab phones from the list.

Walkthrough

1 Walk through all common areas.

   a. Verify room name or number.

   b. Verify extensions.

   c. Obtain jack numbers.

2 Walk through all conference rooms.

   a. Verify room name or number.

   b. Verify extension of digital phone. If wall phone, obtain or verify jack number.

   c. Verify whether room has Polycom.

   d. Verify extension.

   e. Obtain jack number.

3 Check the viability of all fax machines.

   a. Obtain correct locations for fax machines.

   b. Verify extensions.

   c. Obtain jack numbers.

   d. Verify all fax numbers. If you do not find the fax in the building, verify through your numbering management system to whom the fax belongs. If the fax is not in the database, send a fax to the machine asking the client to respond and call for verification. If no response is given, consider removing the fax line.

4 Walk through all cubes and offices.

   a. Verify whether each cube has a PBX phone. Also verify the client from the list. Finally, verify that the extension belongs to the client by pressing the voice mail button.

   b. If a cube has only a phone and is not on the client list, verify the PBX extension by calling a display phone.

      – Verify whether this is a guest phone in the switch, or through the numbering management system.

      – If the phone is dead or has a fast busy tone, bring it back to the operations center for reclaim.

   c. If there are two phones in a cube, do this:

      – Verify which has voice mail.

      – Reclaim second number, phone, and send to operations.

5 Verify the use of all lab phones.

    a. Gain access to the lab through security.

    b. Walk through the lab, and capture all extensions and jack numbers.

    c. Obtain the room and card reader numbers, and report them to professional services.

Spreadsheet Cleanup

1 Common area phones

    a. Insert correct room numbers.

    b. Insert jack numbers for wall phones.

2 Analog lines (faxes and Polycoms)

    a. Insert locations.

    b. Insert jack numbers.

3 Client phones

    a. Insert correct locations.

    b. Insert correct extensions.

4 Lab phones

    a. Create list from walkthrough.

    b. Insert extensions.

    c. Insert jack numbers.

Friday Switch Work

1 Tasman switch: Change the UDP table to EPN 6 for all extensions to be uplifted

2 Zanker switch

    a. Remove all extensions to be uplifted from the switch.

    b. Change the UDP to correct AAR code for each extension.

PBX Cleanup

1 List stations that still reside on EPN.

    a. Remove all stations.

    b. Change UDP tables in the switch to reflect removal.

2 Create a spreadsheet with all remaining extensions and send data to operations.

Add IP Phone

You might have to manually add IP Phones to the system. Use the following procedures:

1 Enter a MAC Address column on the spreadsheet.

2 Enter **Description** as per the naming standards.

3 Select **Device Pool** as per the spreadsheet.

4 Enter **Calling Search Space** = Unlimited Access (853=CSS_SJAllServices).

5 Select button template **Default 7960**.

6 Select **Insert**.

7 Select **Line 1**.

8 Enter **Directory Number** as per the Emptel column on the spreadsheet.

9 Select **Partition** = San Jose Campus (853=Cisco).

10 Enter **Calling Search Space** = Unlimited Access (853=CSS_SJAllServices).

11 Select **Call Waiting** = ON.

12 Enter **Forward Busy Destination** = Voice Mail Numbers, as per Section 1.

13 Enter **Calling Search Space** = Unlimited Access (853=CSS_SJAllServices).

14 Enter **Forward No Answer Destination** = Voice Mail Numbers, as per Section 1.

15 Enter **Calling Search Space** = Unlimited Access (853=CSS_SJAllServices).

16 Enter **Display as per Naming Standards** in Section 2.

17 Select **Insert and Close**.

18 Reset the phone.

To add User Directory information, do the following:

1 Enter **First Name**, as per the spreadsheet.

2 Enter **Last Name**, as per the spreadsheet.

3 Enter **User ID**, as per the spreadsheet.

4 Enter **abcd** for Password.

5 Enter **abcd** for Confirm Password.

6 Enter the directory number as per the Emptel column found within the spreadsheet. Select **Associate Devices**.

7 Search for the associated phone.

8 Select **Check Box** and **Radio Button** as primary extensions. Select **Insert**.

Add Analog Phone

1 Select the proper Gateway card.

2 Choose the next available port, and select **Add DN**.

3 Enter **Ext.** for Directory Number on the spreadsheet.

4 Enter **Partition** = San Jose Campus (853=Cisco).

5 Enter **Calling Search Space** = Unlimited Access without VM (853=CSS_SJAllServicesNoVoiceMail).

6 Enter **Display** in the Display column on the spreadsheet.

7 Select **Insert and Close**.

8 After you've added all ports, perform a reset; then restart on the Gateway for changes to take effect.

Phone Tests

Outgoing Call Tests

1 Test dialing voice mail numbers: xXXXX, xXXXX, xXXXX, xXXXX

2 Test calling PacBell 1000 Hz test number: 9-727-xxxx

Incoming Call Tests

1 Test call the new phone from another phone by dialing the 5-digit extension, and let the phone ring to ensure that voice mail picks up. (Enable voice mail on all IP Phones except for analog and guest phones.) (See Appendix 4-G, "Cisco IP Phone Test Procedure.")

2 Test call the new phone from another phone (9-xxx-xxxx) to ensure that the steering is correct.

IP Phone Spreadsheet Creation Procedures

Cutsheet Cleanup

1 Start with the template IP Phones spreadsheet.

2 Set the column to do a =PROPER function on the first and last names to set Users case properly.

3 Select **Copy > Paste Special** when inputting users, labs, common areas, and guest phones into a single IP Phone spreadsheet.

4 Spot-check the BAT Phones worksheet, and ensure it is displaying correct data.

5 Do a find and replace for any commas with spaces in the BAT phones description.

6 Ensure that the reception phone has a generic name and not the username of the receptionist.

BAT Users Worksheet Creation

1 Sort IP Phones by user ID.

2 Copy individual columns using Paste Special > Values of EMPFIRST, EMPLAST, USERID, MAC ADDRESS, and EXT. to the BAT Users worksheet.

3 Delete excess rows in the BAT Users worksheet for phones that do not have user IDs.

4 Re-sort the main IP Phones worksheet by FLR and SPID.

BAT Phones Worksheet Creation

The BAT Phones worksheet is created automatically as it is referencing the IP Phones worksheet.

NOTE Never sort on the BAT Phones worksheet. If you need to conduct a sort, use the IP Phones worksheet instead because it automatically sorts the BAT Phones worksheet for you. Performing a sort using the IP Phone worksheet ensures that you can re-sort the BAT Users worksheet without problems.

BAT Import Procedures

Create BAT Phone Import Files

1 BAT tools are constantly changing. Check with your Cisco engineering team for a list of vendors or software applications that can perform the BAT functionality. At the time of this book release, Unimax was a preferred vendor in the area of bulk admin, template creation, batch scheduling, audit trials, ad-hoc reporting, and automatic database synchronization.

2 Load the IP Phone spreadsheet and BAT.XLT spreadsheet into Excel.

3 Sort the IP Phones worksheet by the EMPTEL column.

NOTE Be sure to select all columns when sorting!

4 Switch to the BAT Phones worksheet and select from Column A to G a group of phones for a single device pool. Then select **Copy**.

5 Switch to the BAT.XLT Excel spreadsheet, Phones worksheet. Select **Paste Special**; then select **Values** within the Paste Special option.

6 Click the **Export to BAT** button; then enter a filename to save the .txt files.

    Example Name: c:\bat\ph525bdh.txt

7 Delete data that was copied to the BAT.XLT spreadsheet.

8 Repeat Steps 3–6 for all device pools in all clusters.

9 When you are finished creating all text files, check the beginning and end users in the text file against the spreadsheet that you used to scan the MAC addresses to ensure that the files are correct.

User BAT Phone Import Files

1 Sort the BAT Users worksheet by the EXT column.

2 Select from Columns A to F all the phones for a given cluster; then select **Copy**.

3 Switch to the BAT.XLT spreadsheet, Users worksheet. Do a Paste Special; then select **Values** within the Paste Special option.

4 Click the **Export to BAT** button. Then enter a filename to save the .txt files.

    Example name: c:\bat\users525.txt

5 Delete data that was copied to the BAT.XLT spreadsheet.

6 Repeat Steps 2–5 for all users in all four clusters.

7 When you are finished creating all the text files, check the beginning and end users in the text file against the spreadsheet that was used to scan the MAC addresses to ensure that the files are correct.

Running BAT

1 Select **Application > BAT** from Call Manager.

2 Select **Configure > Phones**.

3 Enter the filename, such as c:\bat\ph525bdh.txt.

4 Select the correct template; then double-check it against the filename entered.

5 Select **Insert**; then view the resulting log file.

6 Record any errors or conflicts.

7 Repeat Steps 3–6 for all device pools in a cluster.

8 Select **Configure > Users**.

9 Enter the filename, such as c:\bat\users525.txt.

10 Select **Insert**; then view the resulting log file.

11 Record any errors or conflicts.

12 Repeat steps 1–11 for all clusters.

Restricted Phone Configuration Procedures

1 Select the phone to be configured.

2 Change the Calling Search Space to Local without VM (853=Local).

3 Select line 1.

4 Change the Calling Search Space to Local without VM (853=Local).

5 Select **Update and Close**.

6 Reset the phone.

Miscellaneous Phone Installation Notes

1 Plug the IP Phone into an available yellow or green jack.

2 If both the yellow and green jacks are in use, connect the phone to the PC, and ensure that the cable is plugged in properly and you hear a click.

3 Leave documentation only at user desks, not in common areas.

4 For wall phones, loosely screw the bottom black screw into the wall plate to secure the phone.

5 Identify any rogue (extensions with 4xxxx) phone extensions and location information.

6 Identify any locations in which a phone was swapped for someone who appears to already have an IP Phone.

7 Identify any locations with headsets.

8 Place the new phone in the same location as the old phone. If necessary, use a longer patch cable.

Floor Walkthrough Checklist

1 Identify the cube and phone number for any remaining PBX phones that give a test tone when dialing 9-727-0020.

2 Identify the cube and phone number for any rogue phones—that is, phones that have extension 4xxxx.

3 Pick up any remaining PBX phones.

4 Ensure that all office doors are locked and that all IDFs/BDFs are closed.

5 Clean up any garbage that might have been missed.

Wall Phone Wiring Punchdown

Punch down the 110 block in the following manner:

White 110 Block (to RJ-45 Patch Panel)

```
3   4   5   6

|   |   |   |

3   4   5   6
```

Wall Phone 99x 110 Block

Headset Support

Use the following sample procedures with the different models of headsets.

Headset Model	Procedure
Plantronics	1. Remove the existing headset block and leave at the desk; it is no longer required.
	2. Plug the headset directly into the 7960 headset jack, and test it to ensure that it is functioning properly.
Telelink–SoftTalk Communications	Highlight the web address on the user project page, and inform the user that this model does not work with the Cisco IP Phone.

Boss/Admin Phone Configurations

Examples: Boss Ext.: xxxxx

Following is a sample template used to collect boss/admin information.

Use the Administrative Assistant ID form to identify and verify all admins by floor and their call coverage requirements.

Retrofit Administrative Assistant Identification Form					
No.	Name	Ext.	Cube Location	Supporting Manager(s)	Supports Call Coverage/ Name and Ext.

To ensure uniformity and consistency between the various support groups, the implementation team used the following template to standardize all the boss/admin configurations.

Table 4-1   *Boss Admin Configuration Template*

Boss X79551			Admin X75339		
Line 1 79551	Partition	Fourth line	Line 1 75339	Partition	San Jose campus
	CSS	Unlimited		CSS	Second line
	FWDB	74800 unlimited		FWDB	75339 second line
	FWDNA	74800 unlimited		FWDNA	74800 unlimited
	Call Wait	On		Call Wait	On
Line 2 79551	Partition	Third line	Line 2 75339	Partition	Second line
	CSS	Fourth line		CSS	Third line
	FWDB	79551 fourth line		FWDB	75339 third line
	FWDNA	74800 unlimited		FWDNA	74800 unlimited
	Call Wait	Off		Call Wait	Off
Line 3 79551	Partition	Second line	Line 3 75339	Partition	Third line
	CSS	Third line		CSS	Unlimited Access
	FWDB	79551 third line		FWDB	74800 unlimited
	FWDNA	74800 unlimited		FWDNA	74800 unlimited
	Call Wait	Off		Call Wait	Off
Line 4 79551	Partition	San Jose campus	Line 4 75339	Partition	Third line
	CSS	Second line		CSS	Fourth line
	FWDB	79551 second line		FWDB	79551 fourth line
	FWDNA	79551 second line		FWDNA	74800 unlimited

continues

Table 4-1   *Boss Admin Configuration Template (Continued)*

Boss X79551			Admin X75339		
	Call Wait	Off		Call Wait	Off
			Line 5 75339	Partition	Second line
				CSS	Third line
				FWDB	79551 Third line
				FWDNA	74800 unlimited
				Call Wait	Off
			Line 6 75339	Partition	San Jose campus
				CSS	Second line
				FWDB	Second line
				FWDNA	79551 Second line

Standard Boss/Admin: Two Phones with One Line Ringing on Both Phones

Use the following procedures to configure a standard boss/admin setup:

1 On the boss phone, make the following changes:

    a. Type on Line 1: (user's extension) in Partition=2nd Line

    b. Within Calling Search Space: select **Unlimited**

    c. Within Forward Busy: input extension in Calling Search Space Unlimited

    d. Within Forward No Answer: input extension in Calling Search Space Unlimited

    e. Within Line 2: Select extension in Partition=San Jose Campus (853=Cisco)

    f. Within Call Waiting: select the **Off** option

    g. Within second line: select **Calling Search Space**

    h. Within Forward Busy: input extension in Calling Search Space second line

    i. Within Forward No Answer: input extension in Calling Search Space second line

2 On the admin phone, make the following changes:

   a. Select Line 2: input extension in Partition=San Jose Campus (853=Cisco San Jose Campus)

   b. Select Call Waiting: **Off**

   c. Within second line: select **Calling Search Space**

   d. Within Forward Busy: input extension in Calling Search Space second line

   e. Within Forward No Answer: input extension in Calling Search Space second line

Standard Boss/Admin in Two Locations (Four Phones Total)

Repeat standard boss/admin steps for two new phones.

Known Boss/Admin Feature Limitations

The following are a few admin feature differentiators within the boss/admin configuration. As new versions of CallManager are released, so are new phone features and enhancements. Check with your Cisco engineering team for a list of standard phone features. In the meantime, communicate the differences in features to the end users:

- The Message Waiting Indicator does not display on the boss' phone; instead, you have to look for the Envelope symbol on the display beside the Boss extension to determine whether the boss has a voice mail waiting.

- To check voice mail on the admin phone, select the admin line first; then press the **Messages** button. Depending on the line you are using, just pressing Messages might take the admin to the boss's or user's voice mail box.

- If the boss is using his first line, it is not displayed as in-use on the admin phone. If the boss is using his second line, it *is* displayed as in-use on the admin phone.

Voice-Mail Only Configurations

Use the following procedures to set up users with voice mail only and no desk phone:

1 Search for 0000000 in the appropriate phone cluster.

2 Assign the MAC address of the phone to the next available sequential number.

3 You can then reassign the phone to another user or return the phone to inventory.

Troubleshooting Cisco IP Phones

Use the following tips to troubleshoot Cisco IP Phones.

Problem	Resolution
Rogue phones (extension 4xxxx) on the cutsheet	1. Verify that the MAC address of the phone is configured correctly within the cutsheet and that you've selected the correct CallManager cluster. 2. Disconnect the phone from the network. 3. Delete the phone from the CallManager cluster. 4. Attach the phone to the network, and test.
Rogue phones not on the cutsheet	1. Check whether the MAC address of the phone is configured for a location in any of the other CallManager clusters. 2. If the MAC is configured in a cluster, correct the phone as per rogue phones. 3. If the phone is not configured anywhere, identify the phone location, and include in report.
Duplicate user error when loading BAT	Go to the user's cube to see whether an IP Phone already exists. If so, do not install a new phone and delete the new phone out of CallManager. If a PBX phone exists, go to the user directory and associate the UserID with the new phone.
Mispulled PACBell line in the BDF	Contact team lead with jack information.
Phone does not boot	Is the phone stuck on the opening or recycling screen? 1. Ping the IP address of the phone and disconnect it from the network to ensure that it is getting an IP address. 2. If the phone does not get an IP, and DHCP is disabled on the phone, do **# at the phone to unlock the configuration so that you can enable DHCP.
Analog ports do not work	1. Verify the wiring. 2. Problems can occur if extensions on ports are changed on an FXS card where a reset from the CallManager does not work. Contact the team lead to get the FXS card resets.

War Room FAQ

Use this list to ensure a consistent message to users when they have questions concerning operational policies.

Problem	Resolution
I moved buildings, and my phone does not work.	The move team Telecom help desk supports this. Call xxxxx Option #3.
Will phones work with Oryx?	Oryx is not supported at this time. Future enhancements to Cisco IP Phones will provide all the features of Oryx.
The time is off on the phones.	This is a problem that IT engineering is working on.

Retrofit Project FAQ

Problem	Resolution
My old PBX phone does not work.	After a building is fully retrofitted and the PBX EPN is disconnected, your old PBX phones will not work in the building.
When is my building scheduled for retrofit?	The Retrofit Project will eventually convert all phones on the San Jose campus. You can find the deployment schedule on the AVVID Retrofit project website.
Will my fax machine work after the retrofit?	All faxes and Polycoms will function as usual with no disruption in service.
My boss and I share a phone line. Will this still work?	The same prefix is required for shared lines. (That is, both the boss and admin need to have the same prefix.)
I need to change my phone number.	If an admin wants to change his phone number to support a manager, 48–72 hours are required to request the new phone number to support this configuration.
Who will make sure my shared line with my manager still works?	Boss/admin shared line configurations are not automatic; you must request them in advance.
Can I keep my modem line?	Unapproved modem lines will be terminated.
What do I do with my extra PBX phone?	If you have an extra PBX phone, contact the operations center (555-1212) for pickup.
Will my headset work on the new IP Phone?	Most headsets work on the IP Phone. If not, you must place a new order through the vendor.

continues

Problem	Resolution
How do I set up speed dial?	Your IP Phone will be able to use speed dial after it is retrofitted. The password will be xxxx, yyyy, or cis-coxxx.
Can I use the call forward feature?	The call forward feature can forward to internal and external numbers using the Cisco IP Phone. However, it is not recommended for admin call coverage configuration.
Will Oryx still work?	Oryx is not a supported feature on the IP Phone. In a future IP Phone release, a comparable IP Phone solution (Personal Assistant) for single number reach will be available.
How many lines do I get for a shared line appearance configuration?	Admin configurations for shared line appearances can use up to two lines.
Because I am an admin, do I get a special phone?	The same model of IP Phone will be deployed to all users.
Will my voice mail still work on the new phone?	All voice mail functionality and passwords will remain unchanged.
I want to learn more about the IP Phone.	If you want to use the IP Phone online tutorial, go to http://ipsupport.com.
Where do I call if I have more questions?	You can contact the Retrofit Ops Center team at 555-1212. Help desk cases are not opened during the first 48 hours after a building has been retrofitted. You can send all user questions and concerns to retrofit-case@cisco.com.

Sample Retrofit Issues Log Report

Create an issues log report to capture all outstanding issues and to ensure accurate and timely resolution of all problems. After the operations center is closed, send the issues log to the help desk so that the issues and resolution techniques can be added to their troubleshooting procedures script.

Caller Name	Employee Telephone	Floor/Cube	Problem	Resolution
User A	x-xxxx	2-J6-7	Phone installed in wrong cube	Moved phone to correct cube
User B	x-xxxx	4-G5-7	Cable too short/Headset not working	Replaced cable; reinstalled headset
User C	x-xxxx	2-C7-6	Cable too short	Replaced cable

Appendix 4-G: Cisco IP Phone Test Procedure

Each phone installer uses the Cisco IP Phone test procedure template as a guide on how to manually test each phone to ensure that it meets the operational standards set by the project manager, design engineering, and the customer. This appendix is also available at http://www.ciscopress.com/1587200880.

Floor:_____ Cubicle ID:_____ Phone #:_____ Installer:_____

Step	Procedure
1.	Plug the Ethernet cable into the yellow jack marked 10/100SW on the back of the IP Phone.
2.	Plug the long side of the handset cord into the jack on the bottom-left side of the phone with the handset picture. Plug the other end into the handset.
3.	Plug the other end of the Ethernet cable into the yellow or green jack on the wall or floor.
4.	Verify that the phone is receiving power by observing the front of the IP phone. If the phone is not receiving power, check the connections on the Ethernet cable, and then call for help from a team leader or contact the operations center.
5.	After approximately 2 minutes, the phone should display a number. Does this number match your list and the old phone it is replacing? If not, call for help from a team leader or contact the operations center.
6.	Test the phone by dialing the following numbers and verifying that you can hear using the handset and the speaker. Dial the number listed that matches the first number of the phone you are testing.
7.	Test the phone dial-out capability to verify that you can hear a 1000 Hz tone.
8.	Test the phone by dialing another IP phone and verifying that you can talk to and hear the other person by using the speaker and handset.
9.	Test call the new phone from another phone to ensure that steering is correct.
10.	Using the same person you called in step 8, have that person call your number (do not answer!) to verify that the phone rolls to voice mail after several rings. If the call does not go to voice mail, ask a team leader for help, or contact the operations center.
11.	Call the person's number to repeat the process for his phone. Does the phone roll to voice mail? If it does not, call for help from a team leader or contact the operations center. Notice the ring volume for the phone being tested, and ensure that it is at a moderate level. Then adjust and save the new settings.

continues

Step	Procedure
12.	Place the Getting Started manual, Quick Reference Guide, and Operations Contact Center sheets under the phone.
13.	Place all packing material you removed from the box when unpacking the new phone back into the box, and place it into the trash can in the cube or office.
14.	Unplug the old phone, wrap the cord around it, and take it to the designated drop-off.
15.	Sign this sheet and place it in the designated drop-off location at the operations center.

Appendix 4-H: IP Telephony Retrofit Efficiency Report

The project manager uses the IP Telephony Retrofit Efficiency Report sample to track the progress and pace of the phone installation team. Creation of a metric assists the project manager in determining whether the installation process is becoming more efficient and helps to maintain a consistent momentum during the installation process.

This appendix is also available at http://www.ciscopress.com/1587200880.

Building	Total CallManager Devices Installed	Total Hours Worked	Total Time per Phone	Total Partner Billable	Devices per Billable Hour	IP Phone Installer Hours	IP Phones Installed	IP Phones Installed per Temp Hour
A	133	314.5	2.3647	191.5	0.6945	29.5	107	3.6271
B	433	393.5	0.9088	285	1.5193	89.5	399	4.4581
C	279	345.75	1.2392	281.75	0.9902	86	238	2.7674
D	465	383	0.8237	325.5	1.4286	136.5	404	2.9597
E	359	264	0.7354	256	1.4023	80	294	3.675
F	383	323	1.1857	323	1.1857	82	339	4.134
G	285	238	0.835	238	1.0877	70	262	3.7914
H	278	260	1.0692	260	1.0692	90	262	2.9111
I	417	267	1.5617	267	1.5617	75	382	5.0933

Appendix 4-I: IP Telephony Retrofit Project Gantt Chart

The IP Telephony Retrofit Project Gantt Chart sample is used as a weekly outline of tasks, timelines, roles, and responsibilities for the various activities that must be completed and tracked during the implementation phase. The project manager must ensure 100 percent completion of each task to maintain momentum and efficiency.

This appendix is also available at http://www.ciscopress.com/1587200880.

NOTE	Completion of an AVVID infrastructure readiness audit is a prerequisite for this project.

Day	Time	Task	Assigned To
	3 weeks before	Reserve operations center and staging areas.	Project manager
		Schedule wall phone jack brackets and wiring.	Project manager
	2 weeks before	Send out building notification to users.	Project manager
		Request security escort for access to locked room on Saturday.	Project manager
		Identify escalation contact.	Project manager
	2 weeks before, prior to 3 p.m. Monday's Go/ No Go meeting	Walk buildings, floors, and staging area and verify the following: • All FXS cards are installed in the BDF. • Cabling is in place from the FXS cards to the punchdown block. • Wall cabling is installed. • Ethernet switches are installed in the lab. • Analog cards are ready. • IP phones are available. • The building is ready (from walkthrough). • Work areas are reserved. • Security issues are identified.	Retrofit team

continues

Day	Time	Task	Assigned To
	1 week before, at 3 p.m. Monday meeting	Send out notification to users.	Project manager
		Weekly retrofit meeting. Check off the items in the rows that follow:	WorkPlace Resources
		WorkPlace Resources wiring and wall bracket are ready.	LAN engineer
		The LAN is ready.	Telecom engineer
		Analog cards are ready.	Project manager
		IP Phones are available.	Cisco IP Telephony partner team
		The building is ready (from a walkthrough).	Project manager
		Work areas are reserved.	Project manager
		Security issues are identified.	Project manager
		LAN support is secured.	Project manager
		Locks are installed in operations/ staging room.	Project manager
		Cisco IT staff are on call.	Project manager
		Carts are secured for phone movement.	Cisco IP Telephony partner
		The required cross-connect wire is secured.	Cisco IP Telephony partner
Monday	8 a.m.	Cisco IT starts walkthrough to produce cutsheets.	Project manager
		Verify that operations center is reserved.	Retrofit team
Tuesday	8 a.m. to 5 p.m.	Continue cutsheet production.	Retrofit team
		Move patch cables/punchdown jumpers into IDFs as required.	Project manager
	12 a.m.	Determine the number and type of existing phones.	Project manager

Day	Time	Task	Assigned To
	By 5 p.m.	IP phones brought to secure staging area.	Project manager
		Cutsheet delivered from telecom to Cisco partner.	Telecom operations
	All day	Make available multiple-length LAN patch cables in BDFs as required.	LAN engineer
	By end of day	Clean up and sort cutsheet by type and cluster.	Retrofit team
		Verify that analog cards are programmed correctly.	Retrofit team
		Determine the number of phones required and provide that information to the inventory manager.	Retrofit team
		Distribute copies of the cutsheet to the project manager and others on a need-to-know basis.	Retrofit team
		Order three e-containers per floor.	Project manager
Wednesday	8 a.m. to 12 p.m.	Scan MAC address into batch.	Cisco IP Telephony partner
	12:00 a.m.	Create phone placement spreadsheet.	Cisco IP Telephony partner
		Print floor maps.	Cisco IP Telephony partner
	5 p.m.	Schedule phone pickup for delivery to staging area.	Project manager
Thursday	8 a.m. to 12 p.m.	Scan MAC address into batch input.	Retrofit team
	8 a.m. to 5 p.m.	Verify analog device cutsheet.	Retrofit team
		Convert IP Phone cutsheet to batch input.	Cisco IP Telephony partner
	9 a.m.	Set up operations center.	Cisco IP Telephony partner

continues

Day	Time	Task	Assigned To
		Activate three LAN ports in operations center.	LAN engineer
	2 p.m.	Final building review: • Review special admin configurations. • Verify WorkPlace Resources status (wire and wall mount). • Verify wiring room and staging room. • Final review of cutsheet (adds and changes). • Determine whether additional admin meeting is required. • Final retrofit reminder.	Project team

	By 5 p.m.	Materials preparation:
		• Sort and print cutsheets for IP phone placement.
		• Print floor maps.
		• Print PBX collection documents.
		• Instruct users on how to report problems.
		• Update war room announcement and make copies.
		• Place sign on operations center door.
		• Place three signs on e-container:
		  – "Do not remove"
		  – Equipment count sheets
		  – "Deliver to…"
			Retrofit team

	Start at 5 p.m.	Analog cut starts, one floor at a time: • Perform data entry to CallManager. • Redirect extensions to CallManager. • Cross-connect devices.	Retrofit team
		Perform IP wall phone cross-connects.	Retrofit team
	By end of day	Inform lab owners of switch installation.	LAN team
	8 p.m.	Verify e-container's availability. Notify Cisco partner if missing.	Project manager
Friday	9 a.m.	Move IP phones to each floor (elevator vestibule).	Cisco IP Telephony partner

Day	Time	Task	Assigned To
	5 p.m.	Deliver trouble reporting communique to the Cisco partner.	Cisco IP Telephony partner
		Identify test phones and analog devices.	Cisco IP Telephony partner
		Key analog input.	Cisco IP Telephony partner
		Start cross-connecting analog devices to CallManager port in BDF—at least one per exchange.	Cisco IP Telephony partner
	5 p.m. to 12 p.m.	Cisco IT staff on call.	Project manager
	Start at 5 p.m.	Complete preparation of batch data and run batch programs.	Retrofit team
		Resolve user ID conflicts from BAT run.	Retrofit team
		Restrict dialing of lobby and common area phones and lobby phone access to the directory.	Retrofit team
		Complete analog devices cut from Thursday.	Retrofit team
		Redirect extension to CallManager.	Retrofit team
		Install IP wall phones.	Retrofit team
	6 p.m.	Verify batch run.	Cisco partner
	Start at 8 p.m.	Spot check IP Phone and analog devices, one phone per cluster.	Retrofit team
	End of day	Verify DHCP scope for building.	Retrofit team
Saturday	Beginning of day	Review miscellaneous installation notes with temporary worker.	Temporary leads
	All day	Set all IP Phones[1]: • Place user guide and user trouble reporting instructions with each phone. • Test each phone. (See Test Phone Procedures.)	Retrofit team

continues

Day	Time	Task	Assigned To
		Test phone and technical leads, correcting problems as they are found.	Retrofit team
		Disconnect the PBX phone[2]. Place the PBX phone in the provided box located in the elevator vestibule. Record the number of phones placed in the box.	Retrofit team
		Test the lobby phone and common area dialing restrictions.	Retrofit team
		Cross-connect analog devices to the CallManager port in the BDF.	Cisco IP Telephony partner
		Test each fax, Polycom, and 2500.	Cisco IP Telephony partner
	By end of day	Clean up the building on all floors: • Collect all loose phones and send them to the operations center. • Close any secured doors. • Identify duplicate IP phones. • Identify missed PBX phones. • Secure phones that are not installed.	Retrofit team
	Last thing on Saturday	E-page the Cisco project manager with a status message. If there are any problems, send an e-mail with supporting detail.	Retrofit team
Sunday	All day	Correct problems that were reported on Saturday.	Cisco IP Telephony partner
		E-page the Cisco project manager with a status message.	Cisco IP Telephony partner
Monday	7:30 a.m. to 5 p.m.	Receive trouble calls and resolve problems[3].	Retrofit team
	8 a.m.	Send out speed dialing announcement to building users.	Project IP Telephony manager
	3 p.m. meeting	Attend the meeting directly or by conference call. Discuss both lessons learned and the issues log.	Entire project team

Day	Time	Task	Assigned To
	By end of day	Move staging room stuff to the operations center and clean up.	Retrofit team
Tuesday	7:30 a.m. to 5 p.m.	Receive trouble calls and resolve problems[3].	Retrofit team
	5 p.m.	Provide updated IP phone count, PBX phone count, and total hours worked.	Retrofit team
		Send an e-mail to avvid-docs@cisco.com including the following information: • Retrofit activity report • Retrofit Lessons Learned.doc • IP Phones 12-5.xls • Analog 12-5.xls Forward building cutsheets to the CallManager database administrator.	Project manager
	12 a.m.	Forward lobby IP phone port addresses to the LAN group, requesting them to be restricted.	Retrofit team
	By end of day	Schedule pickup of PBX phone boxes.	Project manager
		Send the operations center location to the move team, WorkPlace Resources, and security.	Project manager
		Move the operations center equipment to a new location.	Retrofit team
		Confirm the removal of operations center locks. Close the operations center and enable voice mail to answer user calls until it reopens, which is scheduled for Thursday.	Cisco partner
	12 a.m.	Distribute reports.	Project manager
2 weeks after wiring room close		Conduct a final PBX dump to ensure that all users are off the PBX.	Project manager
		Remove cross-connects.	Retrofit team

1 IP Phone packing material to be placed in work area trash

2 PBX telephones to be placed in provided containers

3 IT technical staff on call to support problem resolution

Appendix 4-J: Sample Project Plan

Appendix 4-J is available at http://www.ciscopress.com/1587200880.

Appendix 4-K: Sample Project Schedule

Creating a project schedule means identifying the various tasks and timelines to create each phase of the project lifecycle. Use this template as a baseline for creating your own schedule, and be sure to alter the task requirements to meet your specific planning, design, implementation, and operational needs.

You can also find this appendix at http://www.ciscopress.com/1587200880.

Task Number	Task Name	Duration	Start	Finish	Predecessor	Resource Names
1	Project duration (Use this to scale the Cisco project manager time)	91 days	1/3/2000 8:00	5/8/2000 17:00		
2	Initiation phase	20 days	1/3/2000 8:00	1/28/2000 17:00		
3	Appropriate training	2.5 days	1/3/2000 8:00	1/5/2000 12:00		PC1, PE1,PE2, PC2
4	Equipment order	1 day	1/3/2000 8:00	1/3/2000 17:00		SE1, CUST1
5	Equipment shipped	20 days	1/3/2000 8:00	1/28/2000 17:00		
6	Customer requirements document (CRD)	2 days	1/3/2000 8:00	1/4/2000 17:00		SE1
7	Internal / External kickoff	2 days	1/5/2000 8:00	1/6/2000 17:00	6	SE1, CUST1, PC1, PE1
8	Initiation document	1 day	1/7/2000 8:00	1/7/2000 17:00	7	

Task Number	Task Name	Duration	Start	Finish	Predecessor	Resource Names
10	Design workshop	2 days	1/11/2000 8:00	1/12/2000 17:00	9	SE1, PC1
11	Review project timeline against current understanding of scope	1 day	1/13/2000 8:00	1/13/2000 17:00	10	PC1, PE1
12	Detailed design	35 days	1/14/2000 8:00	3/2/2000 17:00		
13	Design assurance (PC team support)	35 days	1/14/2000 8:00	3/2/2000 17:00	11	PC team
14	Lab work on design	10 days	1/14/2000 8:00	1/27/2000 17:00	11	PC1
15	Detailed design draft 1	10 days	1/28/2000 8:00	2/10/2000 17:00	14	PC1
16	Network management system (NMS) detailed design	5 days	2/11/2000 8:00	2/17/2000 17:00	15	PC2
17	Detail design documented and signoff	10 days	2/18/2000 8:00	3/2/2000 17:00	16	PC1
18	Test and acceptance plan	49 days	1/3/2000 8:00	3/9/2000 17:00		
19	Draft network ready for use (NRFU) created	10 days	2/11/2000 8:00	2/24/2000 17:00	15	PE1
20	NMS plan	5 days	2/18/2000 8:00	2/24/2000 17:00	16	PC2
21	Final NRFU created and signed off	10 days	2/25/2000 8:00	3/9/2000 17:00	20	PE1
22	Network implementation plan template created	5 days	1/3/2000 8:00	1/7/2000 17:00		PE1

continues

Task Number	Task Name	Duration	Start	Finish	Predecessor	Resource Names
24	Network staging plan (NSP) creation	5 days	2/11/2000 8:00	2/17/2000 17:00	15	PE1
25	Configuration creation	5 days	3/3/2000 8:00	3/9/2000 17:00	17	PE1, PC1
26	Equipment delivery	0 days	1/28/2000 17:00	1/28/2000 17:00	5	
27	Rack and equipment build	5 days	1/31/2000 8:00	2/4/2000 17:00	26	PE2, PE1
28	NMS build and configuration	5 days	2/25/2000 8:00	3/2/2000 17:00	20	PC2
29	Software, firmware, and configuration load	5 days	3/10/2000 8:00	3/16/2000 17:00	25, 27	PE2, PE1
30	NMS testing	5 days	3/17/2000 8:00	3/23/2000 17:00	29, 28	PC2
31	System and connectivity testing (central office equipment [COE] %)	5 days	3/17/2000 8:00	3/23/2000 17:00	21, 29	PE1, PE2, PC1 [50%]
32	Site surveys×N (number of sites)	8 days	2/11/2000 8:00	2/22/2000 17:00		
33	Site requirements specification (SRS) created	2 days	2/11/2000 8:00	2/14/2000 17:00	15	PE1
34	Survey executed reports issued×N	1 day	2/15/2000 8:00	2/15/2000 17:00	33	PE1
35	Remedial work carried out×N	5 days	2/16/2000 8:00	2/22/2000 17:00	34	CUST1

Task Number	Task Name	Duration	Start	Finish	Predecessor	Resource Names
37	Shipping to site	3.5 days	3/24/2000 8:00	3/29/2000 12:00	31	
38	Network implementation plan (NIP) modified for installation	3.5 days	3/24/2000 8:00	3/29/2000 12:00	31	PE2, PE1
39	Equipment delivered	0 days	1/28/2000 17:00	1/28/2000 17:00	5	
40	Physical installation	3.5 days	2/23/2000 8:00	2/28/2000 12:00	35, 39	PE2, PE1
41	NMS commission	3.5 days	3/29/2000 13:00	4/3/2000 17:00	38, 35	PC2
42	Site commission	3.5 days	2/28/2000 13:00	3/2/2000 17:00	40	PE2, PE1
43	Site test	3.5 days	4/19/2000 8:00	4/24/2000 12:00	59, 42	PE2
44	Installation [Without staging] [Delete one]	64 days	1/28/2000 17:00	4/27/2000 17:00		
45	Configuration creation	7 days	3/3/2000 8:00	3/13/2000 17:00	17	PE1, PC1
46	NIP created for installation	7 days	3/14/2000 8:00	3/22/2000 17:00	15, 45	PE2, PE1
47	Equipment delivered	0 days	1/28/2000 17:00	1/28/2000 17:00	5	
48	Install into racks	7 days	2/23/2000 8:00	3/2/2000 17:00	47, 35	PE2, PE1
49	Software, firmware, and configuration load	7 days	3/23/2000 8:00	3/31/2000 17:00	48, 46	PE2, PE1
50	NMS build and configure	7 days	3/23/2000 8:00	3/31/2000 17:00	20, 46	PC2
51	NMS testing	7 days	4/3/2000 8:00	4/11/2000 17:00	50, 49	PC2

continues

Task Number	Task Name	Duration	Start	Finish	Predecessor	Resource Names
52	System and connectivity testing	7 days	4/19/2000 8:00	4/27/2000 17:00	21, 59	PE1, PE2
53	Acceptance testing	5 days	4/28/2000 8:00	5/4/2000 17:00		
54	NRFU testing	5 days	4/28/2000 8:00	5/4/2000 17:00	52, 43, 41	PE1
55	Acceptance achieved	0 days	5/4/2000 17:00	5/4/2000 17:00	54	PE1
56	Migration [Delete this line if not required]	28 days	3/10/2000 8:00	4/18/2000 17:00		
57	Migration workshop	5 days	3/10/2000 8:00	3/16/2000 17:00	21	PC1
58	Migration plan	5 days	3/17/2000 8:00	3/23/2000 17:00	57	PE1
59	Physical and configuration migration	5 days	4/12/2000 8:00	4/18/2000 17:00	42, 58, 49, 51, 41	PE1, PE2
60	Project closure	2 days	5/5/2000 8:00	5/8/2000 17:00		
61	TAC transition document created	1 day	5/5/2000 8:00	5/5/2000 17:00	55, 59	PE1
62	Lessons learned meeting and report	1 day	5/8/2000 8:00	5/8/2000 17:00	61	PE1
63	Project close	0 days	5/8/2000 17:00	5/8/2000 17:00	62	

Appendix 4-L: Project Risk Assessment Table

The Project Risk Assessment Table is a tool that the project manager uses to determine rules of engagement for the various possible risk triggers. The project team identified a list of possible risk factors and preventive actions during the installation phase. The project manager then determined Go/No Go decisions. Identifying these potential problems early helps to maintain momentum and efficiency.

This appendix is also available at http://www.ciscopress.com/1587200880.

Problem	Preventive Action	Contingency Action	Trigger	Owner
Analog cards are not installed or programmed.	Monitor the installation schedule and inspect the site.	Postpone the analog device retrofit.	(Go/No Go) = No	Cisco IT
IP phones are not available.	Monitor stock and order early.	Continue with analog upgrade.	(Go/No Go) = No	Cisco IT
Power line cards are not available.	Monitor the installation schedule and site inspection.	Install with 110 power supplies.	(Go/No Go) = No	Cisco IT
The LAN infrastructure fails.	Monitor the capacity.	Back out of building retrofit.	Technical issues relating to the LAN arise during the installation.	Cisco IT
The CallManager loads related failures.	Monitor NT.	Back out of the building retrofit.	Technical issues that are related to the LAN arise during installation.	Cisco IT
The batch configuration program fails.	Test.	Call off that week's retrofit.	Friday night's processing fails.	Cisco project manager
There are Cisco partner resource issues.	Meet with your partner early and often. Have a trial run before the first weekend cut.	Postpone the first building retrofit.	The trial run is unsuccessful.	Cisco project manager

continues

Problem	Preventive Action	Contingency Action	Trigger	Owner
Multiple resources are managing the project.	Define responsibilities, deliverables, and customer expectations.	Implement conflict management techniques.	Your partner and customer personnel are unclear of the go-to resource for issue resolution.	Cisco project manager
Your partner lacks resources with a required skill set to successfully install the system.	Meet with customer solutions delivery manager to determine the skill set of your partner. Meet with your partner to define responsibilities.	Implement customer resources to assist in troubleshooting problems.	Technical issues arise during deployment that prevent a successful install.	Cisco project manager

DAY 2 HANDOFF AND SUPPORT

Without a comprehensive, well thought-out support plan, the celebration of a successful implementation will be short lived. Chapter 5 discusses the elements of the Cisco IP Telephony support plan from staffing and training to network management and monitoring tools to troubleshooting and support processes.

Prior to convergence, voice networks, data networks, and servers were managed independently, and administrators could differentiate voice and data service issues fairly easily. Separate groups, each operating in a unique style, typically managed operational processes without a great deal of interaction and often had their own independent support plans with their own goals or service requirements to meet existing needs.

With a converged voice and data network, organizations now need to rethink that support policy. The IP Telephony solution requires groups or individuals that have historically not interacted with one another to work more closely together. New support processes that meet specific IP Telephony requirements to improve availability for voice traffic might be needed. Also, if they are not already in place, new roles and responsibilities to ensure support at each level for all areas of the solution might be required.

To address this highly critical topic, I have turned this chapter of the book over to Cisco Architecture for Voice, Video and Integrated Data (AVVID) Manager for IT Infrastructure, Mike Telang. Mike will discuss how he and his team planned and implemented a support plan that made the Day 2 handoff smooth and virtually seamless for the organization.

In Mike's Own Words...

To fully understand what you need to develop a comprehensive, highly effective support plan, you must stay focused on the primary goal of support, which is to have all issues resolved quickly and effectively. To do that, you need to put the right mix of people in place at the right time to fix the entire spectrum of issues that arise in a converged network environment. If you do not do this with a great deal of thought and preparation, you might end up with highly paid design engineers responding to low-level issues that can be best addressed by Call Center staff.

To streamline this process, we have created a three-tiered internal structure that attempts to resolve problems based on the type of issues that arise matched to the skill set required to resolve them and escalates based on the severity and complexity of the issue.

The three critical components that are required to enable efficient operation and support of the new voice and data converged network are the support team, the support processes, and the support tools. All three components are interactive elements that must blend and coexist to provide effective and responsive support to the new world of Voice over IP (VoIP).

The Support Team

The key to a successful handoff from the implementation stage is a support model that is simple and scalable, along with a support team that has been involved since the beginning of the initiative. Earlier in this book, Stephanie Carhee discussed the importance of developing a Tiger Team with representation from all phases of the initiative that would remain involved throughout the duration. This continuity ensured that when it was time for the handoff from the implementation team to the operations/support team, all individuals would be fully versed on the components of the newly converged infrastructure, especially the CallManager functionality, any issues that arose during the deployment, the upgrade schedule, and the impact on support processes and staff.

The Cisco support team is composed of three levels of increasing responsibility, expertise, training, and capability.

Tier 1

Supported by the Cisco Client Services organization, Tier 1 is the customer-facing arm of the support team. Tier 1 consists of the help desk that takes the initial user call for assistance, opens a support ticket, and routes the call to one of the appropriate Global Technical Response Center (GTRC) technicians who is on call at that time. GTRC performs first-line testing and can normally solve about 40 percent of incoming calls without escalation. Tier 1 support typically is outsourced to a Cisco long-time partner. For Cisco, it is a more cost effective and more efficient use of resources to outsource this type of skill set.

The four Cisco GTRC help desks are located strategically across the globe and follow one standardized operating model to provide real time, "follow-the-sun" user support worldwide. After Cisco deployed IP Telephony throughout the San Jose campus, the GTRC acted as the organization's point guard to answer questions, respond to requests for help, and become the centralized point of contact for user support.

"Although our support processes didn't change, the first thing we did to prepare for IPT [IP Telephony] support was to reorganize ourselves and streamline the support process," says Tracey Mercer, San Jose Corporate GTRC Manager. "We did this by consolidating the Voice Services help desk into the GTRC so that users didn't have to call Voice Services for telephony assistance and then the GTRC for desktop or network assistance."

Integrating IP Telephony into its support processes barely caused a ripple at the GTRC, which typically learns new technology by integrating it first into its own team. "We learn by doing," Mercer says. "We were some of the first pilot users of the new technology, so we had actually used the phones before they were rolled out to the rest of the organization." GTRC also had representatives on the core Tiger Team and worked closely with the team to identify issues, recommend training, and report back to the GTRC as the initiative progressed.

"The Tiger Team came into our staff meetings and gave us regular updates on the deployment," Mercer says. "They showed us the topology, infrastructure, discussed the global deployment, and then when it was time to begin the conversion, they gave our Call Center agents personalized, one-on-one, desk-side training." FAQs, escalation contacts, best practices, and other documentation were developed to help the team further prepare for the Day 2 handoff.

Although the processes, tools, and staff were ready for the conversion to the new technology, change is always a challenge because best practices are still being developed and bugs worked out. "In the initial implementation, the voice quality wasn't yet up to par—but that's the whole point of being the Cisco first and best customer, and we are always willing to take that on," Mercer says. Call Center agents kept both their old PBX and the new IP phones on their desks initially, and as the technology matured, they continued to give feedback, helped build the documentation, and gained the necessary history and experience with it.

"At the end of the day, support is still all about trending the problem, finding ways to resolve as much of the call as possible, and then building escalation contacts," Mercer comments. "And although troubleshooting IP Telephony is different because you're troubleshooting for a desktop problem, the support process and case flow is the same."

Although the GTRC does a terrific job in first-time call resolution in an environment such as ours, the bar is always being raised. Knowledge Management can get you only so far in "first-call" resolution; eventually, you have to face the decision of when to provide CallManager access to Tier 1 so that they can immediately resolve issues, such as password resets. Often, providing access is a trust issue, where the team responsible for uptime needs to be comfortable that the individuals being provided access will neither intentionally nor accidentally stray into areas of the application that might cause a major outage or set the stage for one.

Our choices in providing access to CallManagers include the following options:

A. Complete and unrestricted access

B. Multi Level Access (MLA) and Data Connection Directory (DCD)

C. Integrating MLA with Active Directory

We chose Option A because the GTRC did an outstanding job putting together a business case that clearly defined the value-add both in first-call resolution and in client satisfaction. The GTRC also shared our concerns about the consequences of making unauthorized changes in CallManager and stressed the importance of this to their employees. We needed to resolve this hurdle before we could truly leverage cross-functional teamwork.

Tier 2

Although GTRC can typically resolve the majority of service calls, for those cases in which it is unable to reach a solution for the user or customer, the problem is escalated to our outsourced Tier 2 team. Tier 2 consists of multiple skill sets ranging from the "feet on the field" to dispatchers and includes responsibilities such as moves, adds, and changes trouble ticket resolution and closeout.

Tier 2 is staffed 24 hours per day with rotating personnel. The Tier 2 contact is paged via the on-call duty pager regarding high-priority IP Telephony trouble tickets or issues that Tier 1 cannot resolve. During slack time, the Tier 2 team reviews the IP Telephony queue for lower-priority problems and backfills the Tier 1 team whenever possible and practical. If the Tier 2 support team cannot resolve an issue, it escalates the issue to Tier 3 for consultation on the problem. However, Tier 2 maintains responsibility for the ticket until the case is closed.

Tier 3

The highest level of escalation within IT begins and ends with the Tier 3 team. Tier 3 often leverages the knowledge and expertise of the Cisco IT AVVID design engineers and members of the organization's business units, who were involved in the original design and adaptation of the technology and its applications.

Determining the composition of the Tier 3 team is an issue with which many organizations struggle. The most critical question is whether this group should be composed of data and networking individuals, the original voice team, or a combination of both. After the implementation was complete, we chose to go with a hybrid team, composed of members of both the voice and networking teams.

This is never an easy merger, and it was not an easy one for us, either. Traditionally, LAN and voice teams are separate entities and have not been trained to do each other's jobs. As part of the decision to merge these teams, each member of the team had to be cross-trained on both LAN and voice. This merging of teams and skill sets streamlined the organization and made it much easier to support the new converged network.

One of the most important lessons learned from this experience was not to assume that the learning curve would be steeper for the voice team than it would be for the data team. In retrospect, the inclusion of key fundamental telephony classes would have been extremely helpful to the data folks.

Today when I talk to networking professionals who have made the transition to a converged network, inevitably they tell me that they underestimated the complexity of voice. Make no mistake on what the voice members can bring to the table. Understanding your dial plan, voice routing, and contact center applications (which in some cases are outsourced in the TDM world) is a critical skill set for your success.

You might also hear how the networking team will never understand the complexity, but that again is simply untrue. Given time and dedication, each of these professionals can make a successful crossover. Today we have networking individuals who excel in the new world of IP Telephony.

When IP Telephony issues need to be escalated to Tier 3, Tier 2 maintains ownership of the existing trouble ticket. To ensure consistency and follow-through, however, a separate ticket is opened in TAC's ticketing system. If no solution is available for the problem, Tier

2 support works with TAC to ensure that the problem is listed as a bug report in the Cisco Corporate Defect Tracking System (CDTS) and escalated within the business unit's development engineering team.

Although the three levels of support enable Cisco IP Telephony users to resolve even difficult-to-diagnose issues, users only have to make one phone call to get the ball rolling. (Refer to Table 5-1, "Tiered Support," for additional details on the three levels of Cisco support.)

Support Manager

To ensure that the support program effectively managed network needs and met the Cisco current and future business goals, a Service and Support Manager (SSM) was appointed. To ensure that the support program effectively managed network needs and met the current and future business goals of Cisco, a Service and Support Manager (SSM) was appointed.

SSMs ensure that Cisco Systems provides comprehensive, effective and, as required, customized support services to key strategic accounts. SSMs are placed on select accounts to improve customer satisfaction by facilitating post-sales support and by leveraging resources to increase product, technology, and services absorption into the customer's network.

The SSM serves as a dedicated focal point not only for internal users of Cisco, but also for major strategic Enterprise accounts of Cisco. Following are the SSM's responsibilities:

- Be the customer focal point for support issues.

- Develop a comprehensive "high-touch" support model.

- Ensure successful delivery of all support and services.

- Drive support improvements at Cisco.

- Build relationships and function as a bridge to other business units.

- Ensure customer success.

The SSM function is a critical element in the ability of Cisco to support its users. It acts as an integral member of the team and is an internal and external customer advocate.

Training

The Tiger Team met early and often with representatives from the Cisco support team to ensure that as each building's retrofit was completed, the support team was familiar with the application and could take on the support. Working together, the teams identified the current issues as well as users' needs and challenges, defined what constituted a problem area, and developed a problem statement to match solutions and alternatives to known issues. The teams recommended additional tools, training, and resources, and developed user and support FAQs during the pilot phase to assist in the support development process.

The support team was engaged in all the IP Telephony pilot programs so that it could become familiar with the new technology. The most effective way to increase speed to learning was to give each person an IP phone and let him use it so that he could see it from the users' perspective.

Certification

The benefits of certification include validation of talents that are well versed on Cisco solutions for service providers. In addition, certification helps to identify technology leaders within your organization and demonstrates employee expertise to employers, clients, and end users.

Figure 5-1 illustrates the various levels of certification for support teams responsible for maintaining and supporting AVVID technologies.

Figure 5-1 *Cisco Certification Levels*

The certification levels focus on Cisco technologies and solutions, such as cable, Internet solutions, security, and Systems Network Architecture (SNA)/IP. The following list describes the various certification levels:

- **Cisco Certified Network Associate (CCNA)**—This is an associate-level certification in networking foundations.

- **Cisco Certified Network Professional (CCNP)**—This is a professional-level certification in networking foundations.

- **Cisco Certified Internetwork Expert (CCIE)**—This expert-level certification leads to the highest level of achievement for network professionals.

- **Cisco IP Telephony Design Specialist**—The Cisco IP Telephony Support, Design, and Operations Specialist-focused certifications validate proficiency in designing, installing, and supporting a multiservice network solution.

- **Cisco IP Telephony Express Specialist**—The Cisco IP Telephony Express Specialist certification validates proficiency in installing and supporting a multiservice network solution, with an emphasis on IP Telephony fundamentals and CallManager Express.

- **Cisco IP Telephony Operations Specialist**—The Cisco IP Telephony Support, Design, and Operations Specialist-focused certifications validate proficiency in designing, installing, and supporting a multiservice network solution.

- **Cisco IP Telephony Support Specialist**—The Cisco IP Telephony Support, Design, and Operations Specialist-focused certifications validate proficiency in designing, installing, and supporting a multiservice network solution.

- **Cisco Certified Internetworking Voice Expert**—Certification in the voice track indicates expert-level knowledge in the configuration and maintenance of VoIP networks in the enterprise.

As with all emerging technologies, certification requirements do change. To obtain an updated listing of the suggested certification requirements, review the Cisco certification process at http://www.cisco.com/warp/public/10/wwtraining/.

AVVID Boot Camp

Cisco network deployment boot camps and workshops alleviate the complexity of learning how to deploy and implement a solution for emerging technologies. Using the most up-to-date integration and deployment practices for the technology solution, Cisco networking experts conduct these courses. Attendees will be able to successfully design, implement, operate, and handle the integration aspects of a particular solution and will also receive mentoring and guidance on using the Cisco deployment Best Practices. The boot camps focus on mentoring a student to deploy and operate a complex network solution by providing intensive hands-on lab sessions that include various tasks such as network connectivity from a known network design, configuration of devices, and troubleshooting.

You can find information on the Cisco AVVID boot camp at http://www.cisco.com/en/US/learning/le31/le29/learning_recommended_training0900aecd800d8552.html.

Documentation

The Day 2 handoff from the implementation team to the support team is critical, and all documentation, potential issues, and other relevant information must be provided to the support team ahead of time. "At the time of the handoff, our team gave the operations and support team our cutsheet, which was a spreadsheet listing all of the lines we had cut over," says Chad Ormondroyd, IT implementation team lead. "We also gave them a list of the lines that were not cut over so they could be returned to the pool of extensions assigned for future use."

You can find the following Cisco IP phone FAQ documentation at http://www.cisco.com/univercd/cc/td/doc/product/voice/c_ipphon/english/index.htm:

- Cisco IP Phone 7902G

- Cisco IP Phone 7905

- Cisco IP Phone 7905G

- Cisco IP Phone 7910G and 7910G + SW

- Cisco IP Phone 7912G

- Cisco IP Phone 7914 Expansion Module

- Cisco Wireless IP Phone 7920

- Cisco IP Phone Conference Station 7935

- Cisco IP Phone 7960G and 7940G Series

- Cisco IP Phone 7970

- Cisco IP Manager Assistant

- Cisco CallManager Extended Services

- Cisco IP SoftPhone

- Cisco Conference Connection

- Cisco IP Conference Station 7936

Best Practices: The Support Team

- Ensure operations and support team involvement early and consistently throughout the planning and implementation process.

- Supplement existing staff with external experts where appropriate.

- Ensure that training is provided to meet the needs of each technical level.

- Certifications are an important element of managing and supporting emerging technology. Encourage members of your support team to seek the required level of certification to manage their jobs more effectively.

- Assign ownership and develop standardization of hand-over process and documentation between implementation and operations/support.

The Support Process

A big mistake often made during the implementation of new technology is the temptation to completely reinvent the support model with each new application. Although the IP Telephony support model created the necessity for multiple groups to work closely together to help resolve user issues, it still took advantage of much of the Cisco existing support processes. The newly converged support model was then streamlined so that it could continue to support whatever new future application was deployed throughout the organization.

The tiered support model already in use at Cisco was modified to include expertise in the new technology. The tiered model was cost effective and enabled the resolution of easy-to-solve or repetitive issues, such as phone resets and user access passwords, to be handled by Tier 1. Tier 2 tackled the more complex problems such as software issues, LAN support, and data problems. Tier 3 required the involvement of those individuals who were responsible for the design and engineering of the technology solutions.

Tiered Support

The Cisco tiered support model was designed to give direction and service-level requirements for all IP Telephony-related support issues. The model in Table 5-1 explains the various tiers, the teams responsible, and the targeted time for resolution.

Table 5-1   *Tiered Support*

Support Tier	Responsibility	Goal
Tier 1 help desk/GTRC	Full-time help desk support Answer support calls, place trouble tickets, work on problem up to 15 minutes Document ticket and escalate to Tier 2 support	Resolve 40% of incoming calls
Tier 2 transport team	Queue monitoring, network management station monitoring Place trouble tickets for software problems Provide implementation support Take calls from Tier 1, vendor, and Tier 3 escalation Retain ownership of call until resolved	Maintain ownership of escalated issues until resolution
Tier 3 Technical Assistance Center/ business unit/ design and engineering	Provide immediate support to Tier 2 for all priority 1 issues Agree to help with all problems unresolved by Tier 2 within the service level agreement (SLA) resolution period	No direct problem ownership

With input from design/engineering and the business unit, the support team then designated a severity code (priority level) for each type of issue and directed the request for help accordingly, as shown in Table 5-2. Severity codes define response times and escalation paths.

Table 5-2   *Response Times*

Severity	Definition	Action	Response	Resolution or Workaround
1	25% or more of phones down or functionality severely degraded	Immediate escalation to Tier 2.	Tier 2 5 minutes	4 hours
2	15% or more of phones down or functionality somewhat degraded	Immediate escalation to Tier 2.	Tier 2 1 hour	8 hours
3	Single phone outage or service affecting problem	Tier 1 tries to resolve. If unable within 15 minutes, escalate to Tier 2.	Tier 2 1 hour	1 business day
4	New hire request for installation	Tier 1 responds and resolves.	2 hours	2 business days
5	Request for phone upgrade or new feature	Tier 1 responds and resolves.	24 hours	5 business days

Best Practices: The Support Process

- Develop a support model that best utilizes existing resources and supplements existing staff with external experts when appropriate.

- A tiered support model will most effectively match severity levels with the appropriate technical response staff.

- Ensure a system of checks and balances within the network to increase and sustain network architecture.

- Develop Priority 1 and 2 weekly reports and review them with the implementation and support teams. Reports should include issues, action, and status.

- Capture and summarize lessons learned from trouble tickets and problem cases so that you can provide the information to the implementation and support teams.

- Plan quarterly case summary meetings to discuss the number of cases, number and type of Return Material Authorizations (RMAs), failure analysis information, and other priorities to enable continuous improvement and network optimization.

The Support Tools

Managing and monitoring the new network creates an environment that catches many potential problems and helps to escalate the resolution process before the problems become visible to users. With the right support tools, the network can maintain the highest level of reliability and stability, providing increased performance and availability.

Network Management

Five functional areas of the network are managed to ensure the highest level of availability:

- **Fault management**—Fault management detects hardware or software problems on network elements in the infrastructure that can lead to disruption or degradation of network services. A properly configured network element is capable of forwarding system messages and notifications to a management system, which can then take the appropriate action to minimize the impact on network availability based on the severity of faults reported. Fault management must be implemented properly to ensure the effectiveness of fault detection and the timely resolution of network-related issues.

- **Configuration management**—Configuration management manages configuration files, software, addresses, and detailed inventory information of network elements. An up-to-date configuration management system can significantly reduce the amount of time spent troubleshooting network activities. Complete and detailed inventory information also provides tremendous value in the planning and budget allocation stages of a network rollout.

- **Accounting management**—With increasing user and application traffic in the network, Cisco tracks the use of its network resources on the CallManager. A thorough understanding of traffic profiles allows network planners to prioritize and allocate sufficient bandwidth for different applications. Critical and delay-sensitive applications should receive a higher priority than regular user traffic to satisfy their time and bandwidth requirements. Accounting data collected from network elements typically ranges from simple to detailed records on traffic statistics. This data can be used for planning, or as an input to the billing system for enterprises that need to implement chargeback to internal and external entities.

- **Performance management**—Performance management measures the performance levels of different components of an IT infrastructure. Satisfactory performance levels depend on network, system, and application components of the overall infrastructure. Measuring the performance of different components is crucial and can be accomplished by first defining specific metrics and then collecting them on a regular basis. The collected performance data can be measured against performance objectives or a service level agreement (SLA) established within the organization. Historical performance data also serves as a baseline of normal operating characteristics and utilization of network elements and end systems. Performance data gathered on an ongoing basis provides network engineering with the ability to effectively plan for growth in the infrastructure.

- **Security management**—Security management involves the various aspects of controlling access to resources in the infrastructure. Security measures ensure that only authorized users have access to network platforms, systems, and sensitive business information. The Cisco security policy requires that the Terminal Access Controller

Access Control System (TACACS) handle the network devices. "TACACS provides a way to validate every user on an individual basis before [he] can gain access to the router or communication server," said Shawn Armstrong, IT engineer. "TACACS is used by Cisco to allow finer control over who can access the router in non-privileged and privileged mode. Windows 2000 and CallManager Administration are managed with approved NT accounts and domain memberships."

CallManager monitoring and reporting is an important function to the support process. Figure 5-2 illustrates the various reports, logs, and thresholds that Cisco uses to manage and monitor the network.

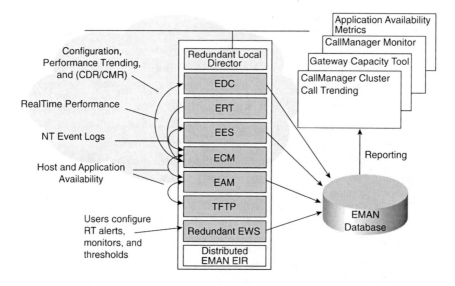

Figure 5-2 *CallManager Monitoring and Reporting*

Clarify Reporting

Cisco uses a service/contact management system that enables multiple, global support organizations to track, manage, and report on customer service and support issues. The issues are tracked by client/contact problem submissions and support requests that are received into GTRC's help desk via the phone, web, and chat sessions used in the early stages of the Cisco IT strategy. However, the solution did not scale and had reached a point where it could not be upgraded for global collaboration, reporting, and integration with

Cisco technology, such as Enterprise Management (EMAN) (an internally developed management system), IP Contact Center (IPCC), and other applications.

To address scalability, a cross-functional team consisting of GTRC, voice services, data center operations, and others researched an IT service/contact management solution. Following a four-month test and trial of several top contenders, the team found a solution to replace the case reporting solution.

The solution rated high among contenders in out-of-the-box usability, integration capability, return on investment (ROI), vendor reputation, track record, and product line. The results generated a smoother case flow, automation of several labor-intensive activities, a web interface that takes the place of a local installation, better tools for root cause analysis, and a more flexible and robust reporting structure.

The decision to integrate this solution will allow IT to streamline business processes, integrate Cisco technologies, fully capture and report on service levels, leverage industry best practices, and prepare us to develop the tools necessary to evolve our service organization to new heights.

The implementation will be one of the first programs to utilize the Internal Contact Center (ICCIT) business model, which is focused on the ability to track and resolve issues, reduce time to resolution of problems, improve productivity, and reduce the cost of support.

CallManager Monitoring/EMAN

Many organizations develop their own monitoring tools that meet unique business needs for availability and quality. The Cisco IT team developed the EMAN tool to further ensure that the new converged network met the Cisco exacting standards. EMAN monitors the CallManager and other related IP Telephony equipment for availability and alarms, collecting historical data for proactive problem identification, trending, capacity planning, and statistical analysis.

EMAN collects availability statistics from both the Cisco CallManager and from any IP-addressable adjunct equipment, including the TFTP server, the Dynamic Host Configuration Protocol (DHCP) server, and the Digital and Analog gateway devices. However, EMAN does more than just monitor the IP Telephony infrastructure. The call detail record (CDR) provides information on who is calling whom (produced by the

CallManager and then reported by the EMAN tool), from what extension the call is being made, whether the call went through, and what the voice quality of the call was.

This essential transition—from measuring time-division multiplexing (TDM) to measuring IP Telephony availability—is an important distinction and provides a true comparison to determine if the device is online, with the sole purpose of measuring host or device availability, similar to the way it is done in a PBX.

A core team lead by Marc Holloman, Cisco IT manager for IP Telephony in the Americas, addressed this issue of measuring availability, as shown in Figure 5-3.

 Refer to Appendix 5-A, "Voice Quality & Availability." Measuring voice quality is a critical component for supporting your converged voice network. The "Voice Quality" document created by Cisco Network Engineers Bill Hennenlotter, Kevin O'Healy, and David Neusdter attempts to offer some guidance and references for industry standards, new methods of consideration, leading causes of poor voice quality, and implementation guidelines.

This appendix is available at http://www.ciscopress.com/1587200880.

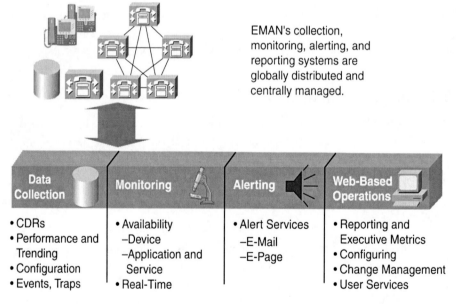

Figure 5-3   *Enterprise Management/AVVID Operations*

Monitoring Tools

With the emergence of new technologies comes the need for additional tools. Cisco developed a network monitoring tool, called EMAN, to manage data collection, monitoring, alerts, and web-based operations. Similar monitoring tools are available to Cisco customers and partners.

Microsoft Performance Monitor

Performance Monitor, a Windows 2000 application, displays the activities and status of the Cisco CallManager system and reports both general and specific information in real time. "It takes certain values on the server, such as the CallManager heartbeat, system uptime, the number of phones and gateways, memory and processor load on the machine, etc.," says Anthony Garcia, Cisco IT AVVID engineer. "It also monitors the number of calls in progress and the number of calls currently passing through a specific gateway. We want to make sure that if there's any problem with the IP phone service, we know about it as soon as the first user is affected."

Performance Monitor collects and displays system and device statistics for any Cisco CallManager installation. You can set up monitoring within a short amount of time without significant load on the server. After adding the Cisco CallManager parameters, the support team defined the terms under which Cisco CallManager displays statistics and alerts administrators. Performance Monitor shows both general and Cisco CallManager-specific status information in real time.

Microsoft Event Viewer

Microsoft Event Viewer, a Windows NT Server application, displays system, security, and application events (including Cisco CallManager) for the Windows NT Server. "Most of the time, we use that tool after the fact to see what the root cause of the problem was," Garcia says. "When there's a problem, it is listed in the Event Viewer. For example, if you tried to log into our server and you didn't have authorization, it would give you three tries and then kick you out. I could look in Event Viewer to see what happened in the last hour, and it would show me that your username tried to log in unsuccessfully three times."

CallManager

CallManager traces are local log files. You can use the IP address, TCP handle, device name, or time stamp when reviewing the CallManager trace to monitor the occurrence or the disposition of a request. "Within the CallManager is a database that stores traces of everything that happens in the system," Garcia says. "Whenever there is a problem, we look through these traces that include CCM traces, SDL traces, CTI traces, etc."

Sniffer Trace

Sniffer is a software application that monitors IP traffic on a network and provides information—such as quantity and type of network traffic—in the form of a trace. Sniffer traces also can help identify high levels of broadcast traffic that could result in voice audio problems or dropped calls. "For example, say we're having problems with our circuit number one," says Dennis Silva, voice services senior network design engineer. "We'll get a Sniffer on it and see what's happening and do some test calls over it. It analyzes at the packet level, and we get the results immediately."

Troubleshooting

The Cisco manual "Operating the IP Telephony Network" addresses some common problem categories that might occur with Cisco CallManager and related devices. Each problem category suggests troubleshooting tools that you can use to help isolate and troubleshoot problems. Although Table 5-3 is not an exhaustive list, it does present some of the more common problem categories.

Table 5-3   *Troubleshooting Problems and Symptoms Case*

Problem Category	Description
Voice quality	Lost or distorted audio during phone calls.
Phone resets	Phones power cycle or reset due to one of the following: • TCP failure connecting to Cisco CallManager, or • Failure to receive an acknowledgement to the phone's KeepAlive messages.
Dropped calls	Occur when a call is terminated prematurely.
Cisco CallManager feature issues	Caused by configuration errors or a lack of resources. These issues might include Conference Bridge or Media Termination Point.

Table 5-3   *Troubleshooting Problems and Symptoms Case (Continued)*

Problem Category	Description
Slow server response	Mismatched duplex, screen savers (that consume all of the CPU when active), and third-party software.
Reorder tone through gateways	Occurs when users try to make a restricted call, when users call a number that Gateways have blocked, or when users call a number that is out of service. This problem also occurs if the PSTN has an equipment or service problem.
Gatekeeper registration problems	Sometimes occurs when IP connectivity is lost within the network.

When the GTRC encounters a problem that it cannot resolve using the troubleshooting tools and utilities, it calls the Tier 2 transport team for assistance. The GTRC then provides CallManager administration details, in addition to any diagnostic information that it was able to gather, and we take it from there.

Power Backup

Power backup provides UPS power and is typically either installed to support IP Telephony devices or has already been installed to support critical network devices and servers located in data centers. All CAT 6Ks and CallManager servers that support IP Telephony at Cisco are on UPS power located in the data centers. However, smaller devices, such as the 3524-PWR switches, are generally located in secondary wiring closets (SDFs) and are not on UPS power. "A minimum of two hours of UPS battery backup is supplied to support the phones in a power outage," says Al Valcour, construction planning project manager. "The CallManager servers are located in the data centers and have both UPS and generator backup, while the 6509 switches require 2500 watt power supplies to provide power for the phones."

Managing risk includes identifying all of the critical network components that will be affected during a power failure, including power requirements and availability requirements. The power matrix in Table 5-4 gives a summary of how Cisco managed its power requirements and standards.

Table 5-4   Power Matrix

	Reliable Networks	**High-Availability Networks**	**Non-Stop Networks**
IP phones	Inline power with surge protection and eight-hour UPS battery backup recommended	Inline power with surge protection and eight-hour UPS battery backup recommended	Inline power with surge protection and eight-hour UPS battery backup recommended
CallManager and Gateways Data center internetworking infrastructure	30-minute UPS battery backup recommended Equipment BTU determination and environmental provisioning process recommended Power provisioning process recommended	One-hour UPS battery backup recommended Equipment BTU determination and environmental provisioning process recommended Power provisioning process recommended UPS Simple Network Management Protocol (SNMP) management process required	Eight-hour UPS battery and generator backup recommended for CallManager servers and Gateways Four-hour UPS battery and generator backup recommended for data center and internetworking infrastructure Equipment BTU determination and environmental provisioning process required Power provisioning required UPS SNMP management process required

Serviceability—Five 9s

Availability and performance goals and standards set the service expectations for the Cisco support team and help to define service and support requirements for the IP Telephony network. We included performance factors such as delay, jitter, maximum throughput, and bandwidth commitments. Availability for a converged network includes IP Telephony and gateway availability, in addition to overall network availability.

Cisco developed performance goals based on IP Telephony or VoIP requirements and created availability goals based on business requirements, keeping in mind relevant technical constraints and cost. The following areas determine the potential availability of the IP Telephony solution:

- Hardware path mean time between failure (MTBF) and mean time to repair (MTTR)

- Software reliability

- Power/environment availability, including disaster preparedness

- Carrier or link availability

- Network design, including redundancy and convergence capabilities

- User error or process considerations, including the time it takes to isolate and resolve technical problems

After we defined the service areas and service parameters, we built a matrix of service standards. We also defined areas we thought could be confusing. For example, round-trip maximum response time will be very different for a ping from what users might experience on a voice call. Availability was based on expected availability defined by investigating each of the previous areas and the expected support capabilities.

To ensure that availability agreements were in place to reflect the new network for Cisco, availability standards had to be created for the support teams. The metrics in Table 5-5 share the standards and response times that Cisco targeted for its data-only network.

Table 5-5 *Availability Target for Data-Only Network*

Network Area	Availability Target	Measurement Method	Average Network Response Time Target	Maximum Response Time Accepted	Maximum Jitter Accepted
LAN	99.99%	Ping monitoring	Less than 50 ms (round trip ping)	250 ms	20 ms
WAN	99.9%	Ping monitoring	Less than 100 ms (round trip ping)	250 ms	20 ms

Similar to the availability requirements for the data-only network, a standard needed to be targeted for the voice and data converged network. The standards were similar to the data-only network, but the WAN requirements were slightly yet distinctively different, as Table 5-6 indicates.

Table 5-6 *Availability Target for Voice and Data-Converged Network*

Network Area	Availability Target	Measurement Method	Average Network Response Time Target	Maximum Response Time Accepted	Maximum Jitter Accepted
LAN	99.99%	Ping monitoring	Less than 50 ms (round trip ping)	250 ms	20 ms
WAN	99.99%	Ping monitoring	Less than 100 ms (round trip ping)	250 ms	20 ms

Note: Ping does not always accurately measure the response time for round trip ping or voice traffic due to quality of service (QoS) configurations for round trip ping and ping process priority for many platforms. Instead, round trip ping traffic performance is measured with the Cisco Internet Performance Monitor (IPM), which is bundled with CiscoWorks2000.

Device File Backups and Recovery

The potential always exists for device file corruption or loss due to hardware problems. We prepared for this by developing a defined process for backing up network devices and CallManager systems. Most network devices, including IOS gateways and MGCP gateway devices, support TFTP for configuration file backups. DT-24 gateways keep their configuration on the CallManager, so if a new one is required, a new MAC address is configured on the CallManager. The CallManager system might require a system software load, as well as a set of configuration files for recovery; therefore, these should be on hand in case of a needed recovery. You can perform CallManager backups using a supported tape drive backup or network backup to another system.

Part of the Cisco support policy includes defining when backups should occur, who can perform the backup, where the backup tape or directory can be found, and who is responsible for recovery. Table 5-7 shows the Cisco file backup and recovery plan.

Table 5-7 *Cisco File Backup and Recovery Plan*

Device	Backup Method	Backup Responsibility	Backup Period	Recovery Responsibility
CallManager	Network-CallManager utility to backup server XX	Tier 2 NT operations (no remote CallManagers backed up)	Full backup daily at 6:00 a.m.	Tier 2 NT operations
Cisco IOS gateway	Network TFTP	Data network Tier 2 operations	After configuration changes	Tier 2 data network operations
IP phone	None—information stored on CallManager	N/A	N/A	N/A
DT-24 gateway	None—information stored on CallManager	N/A	N/A	N/A
Other network devices	Network TFTP	Data network Tier 2 operations	After configuration changes	Tier 2 data network operations

Because the CallManager is a Windows 2000 server, the Cisco server administration group was assigned the responsibility for managing CallManager configuration and change. This included the following:

- Track, manage, and archive all CallManager change control logs.

- Maintain CallManager configuration consistency.

- Maintain CallManager software consistency, including versions and patches. (Note: Although the operations and NT team were a converged team, an NT expert was responsible for managing and supporting the operating systems.)

- Back up schedule.

- Back up recovery procedure.

Support Frequently Asked Questions

It always helps to have a list of FAQs available for your end users that will answer their most common questions. This strategy also reduces the number of "nuisance" calls that would otherwise dilute the resources of your first-level support team. Cisco put the following list of questions together for its end users and made them available online on the project website:

- Where can I purchase an IP phone?

- How can I get an IP phone expansion module?

- How do I request an analog line?

- Where can I get a headset for my IP phone?

- Why can't I receive calls from external callers?

- Why can't I make calls to a specific area code?

- Why am I unable to transfer/hold/conference multiple calls?

- Why are phone calls going into my voice mail when I am on the phone?

- Why doesn't my phone show up under the drop-down menu at the URL for speed dial?

- Why isn't my caller ID working?

- How many people can be conferenced on a call using my IP phone?

- How do I disable a conference call on an IP phone?

- What can I do about the static/distortion/popping noises on the phone line?

- How can I get the guest phone in the cube to display correctly?

- How can I get a new person starting in my department a phone and voice mail?

- How do I request support for Cisco IP SoftPhone?

Resources

Appendix 5-A, "Voice Quality & Availability": http://www.ciscopress.com/1587200880

Appendix 5-B, "Cisco CallManager 3.2 Software Upgrade Checklist": http://www.ciscopress.com/1587200880

Cisco Certification Process: http://www.cisco.com/warp/public/10/wwtraining/

Cisco IP Phone FAQ documentation: http://www.cisco.com/univercd/cc/td/doc/product/voice/c_ipphon/english/index.htm

Change Management White Paper: http://www.cisco.com/warp/public/126/chmgmt.shtml

Summary

A carefully thought-out support plan will keep the new IP Telephony network running smoothly and resolve any problems quickly. The Cisco support model includes a combination of tiered technical expertise and response processes, network monitoring, network backup and recovery, and an effective change management model. A support plan should consider the following components:

- **The support team**—Early engagement of the operations and support team ensures familiarity with the new technology and converged network as well as issues and special configurations. Three tiers of response should be staffed with increasing expertise and ability to solve routine to complex problems.

- **The support process**—Whenever possible, the support model that was already in existence served as the Cisco baseline for IP Telephony support. The Cisco model included tiered support, escalating priority designations, and associated response times. The network management model covered fault, configuration, accounting, performance, and security.

- **The support tools**—EMAN monitors CallManager and other IP Telephony equipment for availability and alarms, collecting historical data for problem identification, trending, capacity planning, and statistical analysis. Determine service thresholds and use an automatic paging system for all alerts. Other monitoring tools include Performance Monitor, Event Viewer, CallManager Trace, and Sniffer Trace.

- **Power backup**— All CAT 6Ks and CallManager servers that support IP Telephony at Cisco are on UPS power. However, smaller devices, such as the 3524-PWR switches, are generally located in secondary wiring closets (SDFs) and are not on UPS power.

- **Serviceability**—Availability goals are based on business requirements. Cisco CallManager availability standards are currently set for 99.99 percent LAN and 99.9 percent WAN based on MTBF, MTTR, software, power/environment, carrier/link availability, redundancy, and fault isolation.

- **Backup support and recovery**—Most IP Telephony network devices, including IOS gateway and MGCP gateway devices, support TFTP for configuration file backups.

Chapter 6, "Final Piece of the Conversion," covers the retrofit cleanup, PBX lease returns, software upgrades, disaster recovery, and network planning for the future.

Appendix 5-B: Cisco CallManager 3.2 Software Upgrade Checklist

The following is a sample of a software upgrade checklist created by Anthony Garcia, AVVID network design engineer. Columns A–H represent the servers being upgraded. Place a check in boxes A–H to indicate that the task has been completed for each server.

A	B	C	D	E	F	G	H	Task Number	Upgrade Task
								Pre-Upgrade Tasks	
								1	Put new device loads in TFTP path.
								2	Configure Data Connection Directory (DCD) on subscribers and TFTP.
								3	Disable Trend Micro Service. (Stop and then disable.)
								4	Dump CDRs. This process can take a long time.

									5	Reduce msdb/dbo.sys replication alerts.
									6	Run Backup and verify completion.
									7	Turn off PerfMon alerts.
									8	Get current gateway, phone counters, and TFTP file count.
									9	Clean up disk space. Trace files, c:\templ, perf logs, empty Trash, and copy upgrade files to servers.
									10	Upgrade Routing Information Base (RIB) configuration. Done at console and via web browser.
									11	Reboot process guidelines.
									12	Fix RIB configuration. Done at console via web browser.
									13	Create PC BIOS, RAID Firmware CD #2.
									14	Perform OS update (win-S-Upgrade.2000-1-3.exe).
									15	Stop CallManager.
									16	Apply Microsoft SQL Service Pack 3.
									17	Run QCHAIN.
									18	Create RIB driver for W2K.
									19	Set win32time on each server. Run this command: **net time/ setsntp:ntp02**.
									20	Perform disk swap routine.

continues

									Upgrade Tasks	
									21	Log on as Administrator.
									22	Upgrade Publisher, and reboot at end.
									23	Verify database tables and stored procedures.
									24	Upgrade TFTP.
									25	Change CMTFTP login name in Services.
									26	Reboot TFTP.
									27	Verify TFTP file generation and verify that CMTFTP login name is correct.
									28	Disable Rogue via web browser.
									29	Upgrade Primaries. Do *not* reboot. Stagger every 5 minutes.
									30	Simultaneously reboot Primaries and…
									31	Simultaneously stop CallManager service on backups.
									32	Verify CallManager Heartbeat, tables, and stored procedures DB totals on Primaries.
									33	Upgrade Backups, reboot, and end.
									34	Verify CallManager Heartbeat, tables, and stored procedures DB totals on Backups.

Post-Upgrade Tasks										
									35	Change SQLSvc and Administrator passwords.
									36	Verify CallManager Heartbeat, tables, and…
									37	Edit voice mail message waiting indicator (MWI) configuration.
									38	Perform full cluster reboot (Pub, TFTP, Primaries, and then Backup).
									39	Verify auditing.
									40	Disable Telnet service.
									41	Remove Software Message Transfer Parts (MTPs), Conf Bridges, and MOH that were built with Hawkbill.
									42	Enable Rogue via web browser.
									43	Enable Trend Micro Service.
									44	Reset IIS Security.
									45	Check IP Services (on phone, services button).
									46	Reset Gateways, Digital PBX Adapter (DPA) Voice Mail Gateways, and VG200s.
									47	Test calls.
									48	Test voice mail.
									49	Test PA (if installed).
									50	Verify and enable PerfMon alerts.
									51	Verify that *cisco_main\domain admins* is in the local administrators group.
									52	Verify DCD search and update functionality.

continues

FINAL PIECE OF THE CONVERSION

You have almost arrived. You can see your destination, and it is a fully converged voice and data network with all users migrated to IP Telephony. However, you still need to address a few more things before you can start celebrating. This chapter discusses how Cisco manages changes to the network, implements software upgrades, and takes steps to ensure continuous and uninterrupted service on the new network. This chapter also discusses PBX disconnects and returns, disposal of Cisco-owned equipment, the final cleanup effort, new technologies, how IT is preparing the network for future applications, and how the Cisco portfolio of services and support helped to fill in the gap.

Certificate

Congratulations to the San Jose IP Telephony Retrofit Project Team for Above and Beyond Customer Service

The San Jose retrofit project team has just completed the largest deployment of LAN infrastructure and IP Telephony in industry history. At a Herculean pace of one building per week, the project team completed the entire upgrade and conversion of the San Jose campus, with its 55 buildings and nearly 20,000 users. As the PBX leases came up for renewal, the team successfully rebuilt the entire desktop LAN infrastructure, retrofitting the San Jose campus in just one year. The financial impact resulted in $2.5 million annual savings in competitor-leased equipment and $425 thousand annual savings in PBX maintenance cost.

The implementation team installed more than 500 CAT6K and CAT3500 switches during the upgrade. The project team counted, packaged, and returned 10,000 PBX legacy phones and physically removed 22 leased PBXs and 2500 ancillary parts and components—all within the lease deadline.

When the exploration of IP Telephony began at Cisco in 1999, IP Telephony technology was still in its infancy. As part of a combined cross-functional project team effort, customer solutions, best practice principles, product workarounds, and system fixes were developed to ensure that an immature product would be a viable solution in a large campus environment. The project team worked closely with the business unit to identify bugs, fixes, and solutions that ultimately resulted in the evolution of today's Cisco IP Telephony solution.

Today, the San Jose retrofit project team has set the standard for a multicluster CallManager implementation and a way to successfully migrate to cutting edge technology. Not only was this team the first to use IP Telephony on such a large scale, but they also did it with minimal customer impact.

Our sincere thanks,
The Cisco Committee for IT Quarterly Award for Excellence
for Above and Beyond Customer Service

Refer to Appendix 5-B, "Cisco CallManager 3.2 Software Upgrade Checklist," which appeared in Chapter 5, "Day 2 Handoff and Support." This is a software upgrade checklist created by Anthony Garcia, Architecture for Voice, Video and Integrated Data (AVVID) network design engineer. Please note that after new software is released, you might need to alter this checklist to reflect the changes.

You can also download this appendix at http://www.ciscopress.com/1587200880.

But We're Not Done Yet

Cisco has come a long way since 1999 when the IP Technology exploration process first began. In addition, those of us on the Tiger Team had come a long way since that first meeting when we met to decide on the goals, processes, and plans that would result in the year-long Cisco migration to a new voice and data converged network. But we were not done yet—there was still work to do.

To complete the conversion, we still needed to conduct a final cleanup of analog and modem lines, package and return the remaining leased PBX equipment, implement new processes that would keep the network clean and stable, and leverage Voice over IP (VoIP) into the organization's disaster recovery plans. Never one to stand still, Cisco was already looking ahead and preparing the new network for future innovations, new technologies, and new applications such as personal assistant, SoftPhone, conference connection, extension mobility, and unified messaging. Although the team had upgraded the LAN and WAN for IP Telephony, installed the IP phones, and put the support plan in place, the initiative would not be complete until the team had taken those final steps.

Change Management

An IT network is a constantly changing landscape with software upgrades, bug fixes, new applications, and other changes continuously being introduced. To keep the network stable in the midst of constant change, we needed to implement a process that would provide a level of control, authorization, accountability, and monitoring of each change request.

A change management process helps to ensure that changes to the network do not have a negative impact. When a change to the network is needed, requestors must follow the Cisco internal change management process to maintain network integrity. The process is controlled and managed by the Cisco network operations center's (NOC) change management committee, which reviews the request, identifies the impact to the network, and determines the fit and timing with other changes and upgrades that are already in the funnel. Cisco identified the process for change management as follows:

1 Change controllers facilitate change management review meetings, receive and review change requests, manage change process improvements, and act as a liaison for user groups.

2 Periodic change review meetings bring together system administrators, application developers, network operations staff, facilities groups, and general users.

3 Change input requirements identify the change owner, business impact, risk level, reason for change, success factors, backout plan, and testing requirements.

4 Change output requirements document updates to Domain Name System (DNS), network map, template, IP addressing, circuit management, and network management.

5 A change approval process verifies validation steps for higher-risk change.

6 Postmortem meetings are held to review unsuccessful changes and to determine the root cause of the change failure.

The flowchart in Figure 6-1 demonstrates the process of change management that Cisco uses, as well as each step along the way from submitting a request to the change management committee to acceptance and implementation of the change.

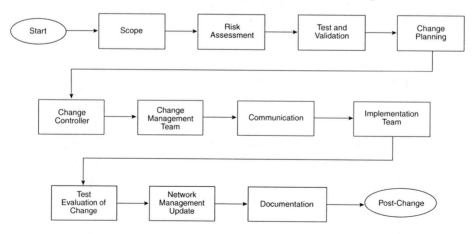

Figure 6-1 *Change Management Process Flowchart*

Change management is the toughest process to maintain when your new network is in place. The reason for that is not because of the routine changes or software upgrades; rather, after you get comfortable, it is quite easy to take for granted the principles that make change management so important. Maintaining a strict yet manageable and scalable process is key to your success. Not only do your methods and procedures require a solid plan of execution, but the standards for which you communicate the plan are also paramount.

In an attempt to provide a deeper understanding of the change management principles, the following provides an overview for change management that promotes high-availability networks. Specifically, the following information provides the critical steps that Cisco uses to create a change management process, a high-level process flow for planned change management, an emergency change process flow, and a general method to evaluate the success of your process.

Critical Steps for Creating a Change Management Process

Change management can be divided into two basic areas: planning for change and managing change. These areas are defined as follows.

Planning for Change

Change planning is a process that identifies the risk level of a change and builds change-planning requirements to ensure that the change is successful. The key steps for change planning include the following:

Step 1 Assign a risk level to all potential changes prior to scheduling the change.

Step 2 Document at least three risk levels with corresponding change planning requirements. Identify risk levels for software and hardware upgrades, topology changes, routing changes, configuration changes, and new deployments. Assign higher risk levels to nonstandard add, move, or change types of activity.

Step 3 The high-risk change process that you document needs to include lab validation, vendor review, peer review, and detailed configuration and design documentation.

Step 4 Create solution templates for deployments that affect multiple sites. Include information about physical layout, logical design, configuration, software versions, acceptable hardware chassis and modules, and deployment guidelines.

Step 5   Document your network standards for configuration, software version, supported hardware, DNS, and supported device naming, design, and services.

Managing Change

Change management is the process that approves and schedules the change to ensure the correct level of notification and minimal user impact. The key steps for change management are as follows:

Step 1   Assign a change controller who can run change management review meetings, receive and review change requests, manage change process improvements, and act as liaison for user groups.

Step 2   Hold periodic change review meetings to be attended by system administration, application development, network operations, facilities groups, and general users.

Step 3   Document change input requirements, including change owner, business impact, risk level, reason for change, success factors, backout plan, and testing requirements.

Step 4   Document change output requirements, including updates to DNS, network map, template, IP addressing, circuit management, and network management.

Step 5   Define a change approval process that verifies validation steps for higher-risk change.

Step 6   Hold postmortem meetings for unsuccessful changes to determine the root cause of change failure.

Step 7   Develop an emergency change management procedure that ensures an optimal solution is maintained or quickly restored. Refer to the following URL for additional information on emergency change management procedures. You can find the "Change Management Best Practices" white paper at http://www.cisco.com/warp/public/126/chmgmt.shtml#3#.

High-Level Process Flow for Planned Change Management

The steps that you must take during a network change are represented in the flowchart previously shown in Figure 6-1. The sections that follow explain each step in detail.

Scope

The scope of a proposed change should include a complete technical definition and the intent or purpose of the change. In addition, the person or department who is requesting the change should include information describing who will be affected, both during the change period and after deployment. This can include business units, user groups, servers, and applications. In general, you can categorize most changes as one of the following:

- Network expansion

- Addition of LAN segments at existing site(s)

- Addition of new sites

- Connection to existing networks

- Connection to the Internet

- Corporate mergers and acquisitions

- Design and feature enhancements

- Software release upgrade

- Host software

- Distributed client software

- Configuration changes

- Support for additional protocol(s)

- Implementation of enhanced features

Risk Assessment

Every network change has an associated risk. The person who requests the change should assess its risk level. Modeling the change in a lab environment or with a network modeling tool can also help assess the risk of a change. We recommend assigning one of the following risk categories to each change request:

- **High-risk**—These network changes have the highest impact on user groups or particular environments, and they might even affect an entire site. Backing out of this type of change is time consuming or difficult. You can research high-risk changes using the tools available on the Cisco Technical Assistance Center (TAC) website (http://www.cisco.com/tac), including the Bug Navigator (http://www.cisco.com/cgi-bin/Support/Bugtool/launch_bugtool.pl) and product release notes. Then you can implement the change in conjunction with Cisco support personnel. Make sure management is aware of the change and its implications, and notify all users. Cisco TAC provides online documents and tools for troubleshooting and resolving technical issues with Cisco products and technologies. You can access the Cisco TAC at http://www.cisco.com/en/US/support/index.html.

TIP	The risk factor of change has multiple dimensions, such as the impact on users and probability of failure. A change could have a high impact if it fails yet have a low probability of failure. Identify the various risk factors and include these considerations in the risk plan.

- **Moderate-risk**—These network changes can critically impact user environments or affect an entire site, but backing out of this type of change is a reasonably attainable scenario. You can research moderate-risk changes using tools such as the Bug Navigator (you must be a Cisco registered user and be logged in to use this tool), and possibly review the change with Cisco support personnel. Cisco recommends notifying all users of a moderate-risk change.

NOTE	Access the Cisco Bug Navigator tool at http://www.cisco.com/cgi-bin/Support/Bugtool/launch_bugtool.pl.
	This tool is available to registered users only. If you need to register, visit the registration site at http://tools.cisco.com/RPF/register/register.do.

- **Low-risk**—These network changes have minor impact on user environments, and backing out of this change is easy. Low-risk changes rarely require more than minimal documentation. User notification is often unnecessary.

You can choose to have additional risk levels to help identify the correct level of testing and validation undertaken prior to a change. Table 6-1 shows five different risk levels that help identify testing and validation requirements.

Table 6-1   *Risk Levels*

Risk Level	Definition
1 Extremely High	High potential impact to numerous users (500+) or business-critical service because of introduction of new product, software, topology, or feature; change involves expected network downtime.
2 High	High potential impact to numerous users (500+) or business-critical service because of a large increase of traffic or users, backbone changes, or routing changes; change might require some network downtime.
3 Moderate	Medium potential impact to fewer users or business service because of a nonstandard change, such as a new product, software, topology, features, or the addition of new users, increased traffic, or nonstandard topology; change might require some network downtime.
4 Minimum	Low potential impact, including adding new standard template network modules (building or server switches, hubs, or routers); bringing up new WAN sites or additional proven access services; and all risk level 3 changes that have been tested in the production environment. Change might require some network downtime.
5 Low	No user or service impact, including adding individual users to the network and standard configuration changes such as password, banner, Simple Network Management Protocol (SNMP), or other standard configuration parameters; network downtime is not expected.

Test and Validation

After you have assessed the risk level of the potential change, you can apply the appropriate amount of testing and validation. Table 6-2 demonstrates how you can apply testing and validation to the five-level risk model.

Table 6-2 *Testing and Validation Recommendations Applied to the Risk Model*

Risk Level	Testing and Validation Recommendations
1	Requires lab validation of new solution, including documented testing, validation, and what-if analysis showing impact to existing infrastructure; completion of an operations support document, backout plan, and implementation plan; and adherence to the change process. Recommend solution pilots and a preliminary design review prior to testing.
2	Requires what-if analysis performed in lab to determine the impact to the existing environment with regard to capacity and performance; test and review of all routing changes; backout plan, implementation plan, and adherence to change process; and design review for major routing changes or backbone changes.
3	Requires engineering analysis of new solution, which might require lab validation; implementation plan; and adherence to change process.
4	Requires implementation plan and adherence to change process.
5	Optional adherence to change process. Note: Optional is only for those changes that do not affect the network. Similarly to major changes and the potential impact, all minor network changes should also adhere to the standard change process.

For changes with risk levels of 1 to 3, two types of lab validation are important: feature and functionality testing, and what-if analysis.

Feature and functionality testing requires that you validate all configurations, modules, and software with lab-generated traffic to ensure that the solution can handle the expected traffic requirements. Create a test plan that validates configuration parameters, software functionality, and hardware performance.

TIP	Be sure to test behavior under real-world conditions, including spanning-tree changes, default gateway changes, routing changes, interface flaps, and link changes. Also validate the security and network management functions of the new solution.

"What-if" analyses seek to understand the affect of the change on the existing environment. For instance, if you add a new feature to a router, the what-if analysis should determine the resource requirements of that feature on the router. This type of testing is normally required when you are adding additional features, users, or services to a network.

Change Planning

Change planning is the process of planning a change, including identifying requirements, ordering the required hardware and software parts, checking power budgets, identifying human resources, creating change documentation, and reviewing technical aspects of the change and change process. You should create change-planning documentation such as maps, detailed implementation procedures, testing procedures, and backout procedures. The level of planning is usually directly proportional to the risk level of the change. A successful project should have the following goals for change planning:

- Ensure that all resources are identified and in place for the change.

- Ensure that a clear goal has been set and met for the change.

- Ensure that the change conforms to all organizational standards for design, configuration, version, naming conventions, and management.

- Create a backout procedure.

- Define escalation paths.

- Define affected users and downtimes for notification purposes.

Change planning includes the generation of a change request, which you should send to the change controller. We recommend including the following information on the change request form:

- Name of person requesting change

- Date submitted

- Target date and time for implementing change (including project start and end time)

- Change control number (supplied by the change controller)

- Help desk tracking number (if applicable)

- Risk level of change

- Description of change

- Target system name and location

- User group contact (if available)

- Lab tested (yes or no)

- Description of how the change was tested

- Test plan

- Backout plan

- If successful, will change migrate to other locations (yes or no)

- Prerequisites of other changes to make this change successful

TIP	Perform high-impact changes after hours, and only implement them within a certain window to ensure that you establish stability after the change. That way, if the change is not going well, the implementation team has a specific amount of time to move forward with the backout plan.

The technical description of the change is an important aspect of the change request. This description might include the following: current topology and configuration, physical rack layouts, hardware and hardware modules, software versions, software configuration, cabling requirements, logical maps with device connectivity or VLAN connectivity, port assignments and addressing, device naming and labeling, DNS update requirements, circuit identifiers and assignments, network management update requirements, out-of-band management requirements, solution security, and change procedures. You should present all this information for both pre- and post-change.

A change request should reference any standards within your organization that apply to the change. This helps to ensure that the change conforms to current architecture or engineering design guidelines or constraints. Standards can include the following: device and interface naming conventions, DNS update requirements, IP addressing requirements, global standard configuration files, labeling conventions, interface description conventions, design guidelines, standard software versions, supported hardware and modules, network management update requirements, out-of-band management requirements, and security requirements.

Change Controller

A key element to the change process is the change controller. This person is usually an individual within your IT organization who acts as a coordinator for all change process details. Normal job functions of the change controller include these:

- Accepting and reviewing all change requests for completeness and accuracy

- Running periodic (weekly or biweekly) change review meetings with change review board personnel

- Presenting complete change requests to the change review board for business impact, priority, and change readiness review

- Preventing potential conflict by maintaining a change schedule or calendar

- Publishing change control meeting notes and helping to communicate changes to appropriate technology and user groups

- Helping to ensure that only authorized changes are implemented, that changes are implementedinanacceptabletimeframeinaccordancewithbusinessrequirements,that changes are successful, and that no new incidents are created as a result of a change

In addition, the change controller should provide metrics for the purpose of improving the change management process. Metrics can cover any of the following:

- Volume of change processed per period, category, and risk level

- Average turnaround time of a change per period, category, and risk level

- Number of relative changes amended or rejected per period and category

- Number of relative change backouts by category

- Number of relative changes that generate new problem incidents

- Number of relative changes that do not produce desired business results

- Number of emergency changes implemented

- Degree of client satisfaction

Change Management Team

Create a change management team that includes representation from networking operations, server operations, application support, and user groups within your organization. The team should review all change requests and approve or deny each request based on completeness, readiness, business impact, business need, and any other conflicts.

First, the team should review each change to ensure that all associated documentation is complete, based on the risk level; then the team can investigate the business impact issues and business requirements. The final step is to schedule the change. After the team has approved a change, it is responsible for communicating the change to all affected parties. In some cases, user training might be needed.

TIP	The change management team does not investigate the technical accuracy of the change; technical experts who better understand the scope and technical details should complete this phase of the change process.

Communication

After the team has approved a change, the next step is to communicate details of the change by setting expectations, aligning support resources, communicating operational requirements, and informing users. The risk level and potential impact to affected groups, as well as scheduled downtime as a result of the change, should dictate the communication requirements.

We recommend creating a matrix to help define who will be affected by a change and what the potential downtime might be for each application, user group, or server. Keep in mind that different groups might require varying levels of detail about the change. For instance, support groups might receive communication with more detailed aspects of the change, new support requirements, and individual contacts, whereas user groups might simply receive a notice of the potential downtime and a short message describing the business benefit.

Implementation Team

Create an implementation team consisting of individuals who have the technical expertise to expedite a change. The implementation team also should be involved in the planning phase to contribute to the development of the project checkpoints, testing, backout criteria, and backout time constraints. This team should guarantee adherence to organizational standards, update DNS and network management tools, and maintain and enhance the toolset used to test and validate the change.

Specifically, the implementation team should fully understand the following testing questions and include them in the change documentation prior to approval by the change control board:

- How thoroughly should we test the change?

- How will we roll out the test?

- How long will testing last, and at what point can we make the decision that the change has been implemented successfully?

The implementation team should be fully aware of all backout criteria, time constraints, and procedures. The team should answer the following questions as part of the change documentation for high-risk change prior to approval by the change control board:

- How will we remove the change?

- At what point will we make the decision to back out the change?

- What information should we gather before backout occurs to determine why the change needed to be backed out or why it affected the network adversely?

During the implementation of any change, it is key to follow the change management team recommendations on how to make the change. If anything is performed on the network that deviates from the recommendations, the implementation team should document and present these steps to the change controller after the change is complete.

Test Evaluation of Change

Testing and verification can be critical to a successful change. Identify testing steps after defined change checkpoints and final change completion. In addition, allocate sufficient time for testing, both during and following the implementation and backout, if necessary. In some cases, you can do testing prior to the change when new service is involved, such as new circuits or links that are not currently in production. The following additional testing and verification procedures might be pertinent to a network change:

- Extended pings for connectivity and performance (might require many to many)

- Traceroutes

- End-user station network and application testing

- File transfers or traffic generation for performance-related changes

- Bit error rate tester (BERT) testing for new circuits

- Interface statistic verification

- Log file verification

- Debug verification

- **show** command verification

- Network management station availability and verification

After you have achieved some level of comfort with the change, evaluate what you have accomplished. Does the change make sense? Did the change address the network problem? What should you do differently the next time a change is warranted?

Network Management Update

Operational readiness requires that you update all network management tools, device configuration, and DNS to reflect the change. In addition, your organization might have tools for fault management, configuration management, availability measurement, inventory management, billing, and security that require updates. The following are some typical network management update requirements following change:

- Router loopback address with DNS primary name following naming standard

- Router interface addresses with DNS primary/interface names following naming standard

- Removal of DNS entries and network management system (NMS) management for devices removed from the network

- Standard SNMP configuration entered on devices, including community string, location, support contact, syslog server, trap server, and SNMP server host

- Trap source, syslog source, and SNMP source configured for loopback0

- Fault management tool update

- Inventory management tool update

- Physical network diagram update

Documentation

Possibly the most important requirement in any network environment is to have current and accurate information about the network available at all times. During the process of changing the network, it is critical that documentation is kept up to date. Network documentation should include the following:

- Detailed physical layer drawing displaying all network devices that have a medium risk (or higher) on the network; this includes rack layouts, cable connections, and devices.

- Detailed network layer drawing of all network devices that have a medium risk (or higher) on the network; this includes addresses, IP subnet, and VLAN information.

- Out-of-band management access maps and documentation.

- Solution templates.

- Detailed IP and Internetwork Packet Exchange (IPX) numbering plans and assignments.

- VLAN numbering plans and assignments.

- Naming standards for all network devices.

- Software code and hardware types currently implemented and supported.

- Protocol filtering criteria and methodologies.

- Routing protocol standards and supported modifications from default settings.

- Global configuration standards.

- Inventory database for all physical connectivity and contact information.

In addition, we recommend that you develop a matrix containing information about user groups, the applications they require, and the servers (addresses and locations) that host these applications. This information is necessary to ensure that users continue to have the level of access and performance they require during and after the change. In addition, previously used test plans assist in simplifying future changes, and they might assist in troubleshooting problems that have occurred because of a change.

High-Level Process Flow for Emergency Change Management

Unfortunately, not all situations that occur in a network environment are conducive to the extensive research and planning described in the previous section. Sometimes you will need to make more immediate changes to restore network connectivity following a network outage.

The procedures you put in place to handle emergency changes should be flexible enough to facilitate rapid resolution of the problem, including documentation of who is authorized to make emergency changes to the network and how to get in touch with these individuals. You should either have a sufficient number of people who can resolve network emergencies, or those people should be easily accessible at all times to prevent a roadblock in the problem resolution process.

You must maintain both communication and the integrity of documentation through an emergency change. This is the time when you need documentation the most, so documenting the steps taken to resolve the problem is of paramount importance.

Finally, when you are considering changes, think not only about whether the change will resolve the existing problem, but also about whether the change will cause other network problems. Figure 6-2 shows a flowchart that documents the steps that are critical for an emergency change process.

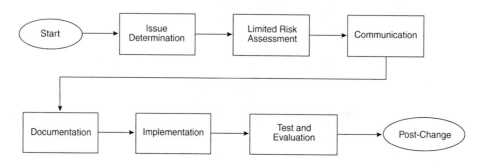

Figure 6-2　*High-Level Process Flow for Emergency Change Management*

Issue Determination

It is usually obvious when an emergency change is required in a network environment. However, exactly what change is required might not be obvious. For Cisco equipment, include the appropriate Cisco support personnel in the troubleshooting process.

For all customers, partners, resellers, and distributors who hold valid Cisco service contracts, Cisco provides around-the-clock, award-winning technical support services, both online and over the phone. You can reach the Cisco worldwide technical contacts at http://www.cisco.com/warp/public/687/Directory/DirTAC.shtml.

When you are taking corrective action, implement only one change at a time. Otherwise, if you resolve the problem by multiple changes, pinpoint which change actually fixed the problem. If other problems are introduced, you cannot determine which change was the cause of the new fault. Each change should go through the full change management process outlined previously before you begin the next change. If a change is shown to have no effect, back out of it before beginning the next change. (The single exception to this is when the initial change is a prerequisite to the next change under consideration.)

Limited Risk Assessment

In most cases, the amount of risk assessment done in an emergency situation is directly proportional to the scope of the change and inversely proportional to the effect of the network outage. For example, the scope of changing a router software release is much greater than that of changing a protocol address. Similarly, the same change would go through increased scrutiny if a single user were unable to access the network rather than if an entire site had lost connectivity.

Ultimately, risk assessment is the responsibility of the network support person who is implementing the change. This person should rely on his own personal experience, as well as that of associated support personnel. You can adapt many of the ideas provided in the section "Change Management: Planned Change Management White Paper" (see the "Change Management" white paper website reference) to the emergency change environment, but on a more limited scale. For instance, you can use the Cisco Bug Navigator tool (as long as you are a logged in, registered user) or even a limited test bed simulation, depending on your situation.

Finally, as part of the limited risk assessment, you should determine which users might be affected by the change.

Communication

Although it is not always possible to notify all users of all changes (especially in emergency situations), the user community will certainly appreciate any warning you can provide. Also communicate the details of any emergency changes with the change controller, allowing that person to maintain metrics on emergency changes and root causes. The information might also affect the scheduling or rollout of future changes.

Documentation

Updating documentation is critical to ensure valid, up-to-date information. During unplanned changes, it is easy to forget to make updates because of the frantic nature of emergencies. However, undocumented change solutions often result in increased downtime if the solution is unsuccessful.

In emergency situations, it helps to document changes from a central location before you make them, perhaps at the change controller level. If a central support organization does not existtodocumentchangesbeforetheyoccur,differentindividualsmightmakechangesatthe same time, not knowing about each other's activities. Following are types of documentation that often require updates during a change: drawings, IP/IPX/VLAN databases, engineering documents, troubleshooting procedures, and server/application/user matrices.

Implementation

If the process of assigning risk and documentation occurs prior to implementation, the actual implementation should be straightforward. Beware of the potential for change coming from multiple support personnel without their knowing about each other's changes. This scenario can lead to increased potential downtime and misinterpretation of the problem.

Test and Evaluation

In this phase, the person who initiated the change is responsible for ensuring that the emergency change had the desired affect, and if not, restarting the emergency change process. Steps to take in the investigation of the change include the following:

Step 1   Observe and document the impact of the change on the problem.

Step 2   Observe and document any foreseen or unforeseen side effects of the change.

Step 3   Determine whether the problem has been resolved, and if so, make sure all necessary documentation and network management updates occur to properly reflect the change.

Step 4   If the change is unsuccessful, back out, and continue the emergency change process until the problem is resolved or a workaround is in place.

After the change has been deemed successful, send all emergency change documentation to the change controller for review and documentation by the change control team. The change controller and change review team should perform a postmortem on the problem to determine potential improvements to prevent future emergency changes of this type. You should also bring the information to engineering or architecture groups for review. Allow them the opportunity to change solution templates, standard software versions, or network designs to better meet the goals or requirements of your organization.

Performance Indicators for Change Management

Performance indicators provide the mechanism for you to measure the success of your change management process. Review these indicators monthly to ensure that change planning and change management are working well.

To access detailed descriptions for each of the following, refer to the "Cisco Change Management Best Practices" white paper at http://www.cisco.com/warp/public/126/image2#image2.

- Change management metrics by functional group

- Targeting change success

- Change history archive

- Change planning archive

- Configuration change audit

- Periodic change management performance meeting

Change Management Metrics by Functional Group

Change management metrics by functional group include the percentage and quantity of change success by functional group and risk level. Identify emergency changes separately in the metrics by functional group, including the success rate for attempted fixes. Functional groups include any IT teams that are making changes, possibly encompassing server administration, network administration, database groups, application teams, and facilities. Risk level is important because higher risk changes generally fail or create incidents. You can define change failure as any change that is backed out or causes a problem incident, resulting in user downtime.

Determining change-related incidents can be difficult. Contact the user who is identified on the change request form following the change to get an understanding of change success. The change controller might also have a help desk database available that includes problems closed because of change-related issues.

Targeting Change Success

To target change success, start with a baseline of change management metrics. The change controller can then identify potential issues and set overall goals. A reasonable overall goal for change success in high-availability networks should be 99 percent across all functional groups. If your organization is experiencing a higher rate of change failure, target it for improvement.

Change History Archive

The change controller is also responsible for archiving the change history. Creating a spreadsheet with functional group success and failure columns and month rows is sufficient for archival. Change history archives can help identify current issues based on past change rates and available resources. The information can also help investigate change rates in general for overall planning purposes.

Change Planning Archive

The change controller should archive change planning documentation, such as network engineering documents, to create a reference of examples for future successful projects. If the change controller notices change problems, he can refer to the change planning document to investigate how well the particular issue was documented before the change. Over time, the change controller might ask to have additional information added to future change planning documents for higher-risk changes to help ensure success.

Configuration Change Audit

Investigate the quantity and risk level of undocumented changes. In networking environments, this requires the implementation of user Terminal Access Controller Access System (TACACS) and network time protocol (NTP), in addition to a configuration file archival process and application. The Cisco Resource Manager Essentials toolbox (found at http://www.cisco.com/warp/public/cc/pd/wr2k/rsmn/index.shtml) has a configuration file utility that can help log configuration file changes. For example, the TACACS can log who accessed a device and whether NTP was used. It also provides an accurate time stamp of what someone accessed. This data might be useful when troubleshooting difficult network cases.

Undocumented change is a common problem in almost all organizations. Continually reiterate the requirement for team members to use the required change control process, even though it adds time and effort.

Periodic Change Management Performance Meeting

Review the metrics you collect monthly, including the following: change quantity and risk level, change failure quantity and post mortems, emergency changes and post mortems, change management goals, and undocumented changes. The functional manager should review the metrics and report to the appropriate teams for improvement.

NOTE	For more information on change management, refer to the "Change Management Best Practices" white paper at http://www.cisco.com/warp/public/126/chmgmt.shtml.

Quarter End Freeze

Change to the network must always be carefully monitored and managed, but system stability is especially critical during a fiscal quarter end close. Because change inherently induces risk, which has the potential to reduce system stability, it is important to put a process in place that minimizes the number of changes being made to the network at that point in time. If you do not carefully plan this, the impact to the network and other systems in preparation for fiscal quarter end processing can cause a devastating slowdown or halt to those critical business activities.

Change is fundamental to staying current and providing the best service to the business. The quarter end freeze policy is designed to allow some leeway for as long as possible prior to the close. However, you never want to allow last-minute changes to the network immediately prior to the freeze start date. At Cisco, changing out phones was considered a low-risk project, but we were sensitive to those buildings that required 100 percent reliability during quarter end freeze, such as those whose users performed financial or accounting activities. Altering the schedule to retrofit only those buildings less affected by the quarter end freeze ensured that the retrofit could continue to move forward while minimizing risk to those business-critical buildings.

The Cisco change management committee considered the impact of all requested changes and identified in advance all affected systems and users who would be impacted. Representation at the change management meeting was mandatory for all change requests submitted, and the policy required that changes affected by the quarter end freeze would *only* be approved as a result of discussion in the change management meeting.

Best Practices: Change Management

- Emergency change requests that involve work to be completed before the next change management meeting require the approval of the requestor's manager and director, the operations duty manager, and the senior director of enterprise operations and hosting.

- Consult with management regarding changes being planned and how the business financial quarter end freeze period might affect those changes.

- If a change is being made to an information system (IS) within the quarter end freeze period, obtain written approval from the IT director or above in advance of the change management meeting.

- The senior director of enterprise operations and hosting, or his designee, will review all change management requests submitted for work during the quarter end freeze.

- Be sensitive to those buildings that incur heavy activity during quarter end freeze, and try not to conduct phone swap out of those buildings during that time.

- Prepare for quarter end freeze (and fiscal end freeze) in the project schedule, and plan the migration schedule around it.

Software Upgrades

To accommodate the massive, enterprise-wide IP Telephony deployment, we used a program created by Cisco called Strategic Program Management (SPM), which became the model for large implementations. Because we faced the challenge of trying to get everything synchronized in terms of all currently active software versions, the program focused on a chain release of software upgrades. SPM provides a process of managing multiple projects across different disciplines and assigns a project manager who is responsible for coordinating all the projects.

According to Doug McQueen, manager of SPM, "Waves of new applications at Cisco are frequent because we're a technology-driven company, and these new technologies often come with frequent change/upgrade cycles. You have to time the various activities so that you can make progress deploying the current upgrade before getting hit with a new release. Ideally, you want to have plenty of time to lab test the upgrades before they enter production."

After conducting a thorough review of the new software load and reviewing the new architectural design, the team reviewed the release notes and selected the smallest CallManager cluster to test in a lab environment. When the new load was stable and viable, the team scheduled the remaining CallManager clusters for upgrade.

Because the technology was new and the deployment schedule was aggressive, the team had to come up with a way to make the process workable and manageable.

Dennis Silva, voice services senior network design engineer, agreed. "Some upgrades can be quite complex," says Silva. "So this is actually the first time we've ever had to put something together that documents each step that needs to be done, in what order it needs to be done, and provides checks and balances along the way." A maintenance upgrade or a maintenance patch is simpler, according to Silva. "Basically, you just click on it and off it goes, but a major upgrade is much more complex."

The voice services design and engineering team created a checklist that provides high-level steps to help ensure that the release process goes smoothly and to prevent or minimize business disruption.

 Refer to Appendix 5-B in Chapter 5. It is a software upgrade checklist created by Anthony Garcia, AVVID network design engineer. Note that after new software is released, you might need to alter this checklist to reflect the changes.

This appendix is also available at http://www.ciscopress.com/1587200880.

Communication is critical in this stage. The implementation team was on the e-mail alias for all change management requests so that they were kept in the loop on all network changes, including new software loads.

Communication between the engineering, change management, and implementation teams ensures a smoother transition during any change. We also kept the change management committee apprised of building conversions by submitting a change management request along with their deployment schedule.

TIP	Work closely with the change management team. You do not want to lose momentum by finding out it is necessary to cancel a scheduled site conversion due to a network freezeout.

NOTE	To track known software bugs and associated release notes, go to http://wwwin-metrics.cisco.com/FAQ.html. (A Cisco.com login is required.)

Best Practices: Software Upgrades

- Make sure the upgrade team represents expertise in both voice and data. The overall value will be a simplified network, and ultimately, a simplified organization.

- Training is essential. Find out where the gaps are, and make sure the team has access to the appropriate training.

- Try to control the number of upgrades occurring at the same time. Testing too many systems at once means that you will lose track of what you are trying to achieve. Also, you might complicate diagnostics if multiple upgrades do not go as planned.

- Do not conduct an exhaustive test of everything. Monitor the upgrade, decide where the time will be spent most wisely, and focus on doing that well.

- Never introduce a new software load on the production network first. Use the lab to conduct a thorough preliminary test.

- Ensure that the implementation team is on the e-mail alias for all change management requests.

- Try to mimic the production environment in the testing lab as close to your budget as possible. If your new network will accommodate 300 phones, test that same number of devices in the lab. Cutting corners now increases the chances of unhappy surprises later.

Disaster Recovery

A disaster recovery plan covers the hardware, software, and processes required to run critical business applications that enable business continuity in the case of a disaster. The IP Telephony application created new implications for disaster recovery because the voice and data networks are converged.

Every organization has different needs and different views for an appropriate disaster recovery plan. For example, finance-based companies are required by law to have a hot standby site, whereas the retail industry is more focused on inventory protection. "Our focus has been to identify IP Telephony-based solutions for several scenarios," says Jayne McKelvie, IT project manager. "Although some of these are still in the pilot stage, we've taken advantage of the IP phones' ability to reconnect and create a virtual office wherever the user happens to be."

If a single key building is unsafe, the Cisco disaster recovery plan moves call center agents to another building on campus. This takes advantage of the flexibility of the CallManager to "plug and play" phones anywhere on the LAN. "In case we can't retrieve the regular phone sets, we have spares available in secure locations" McKelvie adds. If the campus is unsafe but the CallManager is still operational, disaster recovery leverages the IP Telephony telecommuting tools—such as Virtual Private Network (VPN) and SoftPhone—and instructs employees to use their IP phones at home if they can continue working.

For example, during the September 11 crisis in 2001, many employees chose to work at home, using the Cisco VoIP network to conduct business. In addition, Cisco identified those employees who were traveling, determined if any of them were unable to make connections to get home, and then ensured that they had access to IP Telephony tools to keep them in constant communication. In an emergency situation, the ability to communicate is critical, and IP Telephony plays a vital role at Cisco.

If the campus is unsafe and the CallManager is unavailable, those same telecommuting tools can be used but redirected to a different CallManager. "We'll be piloting this variation soon for IT Ops' application and using 800-number rerouting to get calls to the group, wherever they might be located," McKelvie says. "The most important elements addressed for the new disaster recovery [DR] plan were flexibility and maintaining communications within the DR and IT Ops teams during an outage. If they can't talk to each other, we can't react to a disaster."

No matter how many scenarios the disaster recovery team can envision, actual disasters can be a surprise that can encompass anything from virus attacks to natural disasters. However, with the conversion of IP Telephony technology within the San Jose campus, ensuring LAN, WAN, and Internet network security and availability has become extremely important. "The technology and products are still evolving, and we're always on the lookout for new products and new ways to use existing products," McKelvie says.

TIP	Make sure you test your E911 solution often, especially after an upgrade, a move/add/change, or a network change. To make it easier, consider scheduling the test automatically after a change to ensure that it is operational. This basic functionality needs to be online and ready to go if an emergency or disaster hits. For additional information, refer to the Cisco E911 documentation at http://www.cisco.com/en/US/products/sw/voicesw/ps842/products_administration_guide_chapter09186a00800d768a.html.

Resiliency and backup services form a key part of disaster recovery and require diligent reviews to meet the criteria for business continuity. A high-availability design (such as multiple clusters, design resiliency, and so on) is often the foundation for disaster recovery. Key tasks for resiliency planning and backup services include an assessment of the current situation and a review of existing backup support services. Vendor support services, such as specific managed "hot standby sites" or onsite services with rapid response times, can also add a strong value to disaster recovery planning.

Best Practices: Disaster Recovery

The Cisco IP Telephony disaster recovery plan is an evolving process that will continue to develop. The preliminary best practices covered in the section that follows have been identified as critical to its success:

- Identify and make a list of the top ten potential disaster types and the impact on the business. Review the list with senior management, build management awareness, and obtain sign off from management for disaster recovery planning process and funding.

- Establish a disaster recovery planning group to perform risk assessments and audits, establish priorities for network and applications, develop recovery strategies, create up-to-date inventory, document the plan, develop verification criteria and procedures, and prepare an implementation strategy.

- Ensure that members of the IP Telephony team are part of the disaster recovery team, and leverage their expertise and knowledge of the VoIP network.

- Conduct system backups on a daily basis Monday through Saturday. Hold overnight backup tapes onsite, weekly backups offsite for 35 days, and monthly backups for seven years. In a disaster situation, tapes would be used for recovery at an alternate mirror site.

- Look at disaster recovery from the new IP Telephony perspective, and ensure that the disaster recovery elements traditionally found on a data network (such as viruses) are addressed.

- Include IP Telephony's features in disaster recovery plans because they will provide new levels of flexibility and increased uptime.

- Continually identify new potential disaster scenarios and how to address them.

- Ensure that your backup plans allow you to provide two-way backup exchange to the alternate site or systems that offer you backup. Redundancy can be a two-way process.

- During a disaster, your E911 solution will be critical. Test your E911 solution often—especially after a system upgrade or move/add/change—to ensure that it is operational.

NOTE	Consult "Operating the IP Telephony Network" document for more information: http://www.cisco.com/en/US/products/sw/voicesw/ps556/ prod_installation_guide09186a008015a006.html.

PBX Lease Returns

At the time of the implementation, 22 of the 55 Cisco Expansion Port Network (EPN) PBXs were leased, which meant that the IP Telephony implementation schedule was largely dictated by the PBX lease return dates. To keep the massive effort of returning the large quantity of leased equipment organized and on schedule, the team leader who was responsible for the retrofit cleanup effort entered all the Cisco PBX leases onto a spreadsheet and developed a Microsoft project plan to keep the returns on track. The initiative involved returning each leased PBX, along with its ancillary parts, throughout the San Jose campus.

In 2003, the two main leased PBXs were removed and fully disconnected. Chapter 7, "Moving Forward: Continuing to Be Cisco's First and Best Customer," outlines that process in more detail.

"Getting the equipment out of the buildings was the easy part," says Reid Bourdet, SPM IT project manager and team lead who was responsible for returning all the Cisco leased legacy PBX equipment. Like a lot of large enterprises, Cisco had taken each lease agreement and allocated that lease to various buildings. "Because of the sheer size of the deployment, we had to pull all of the equipment back together to rebuild the original lease, ensuring that it was all there, and matched the original equipment list before we returned it," Bourdet recalls.

The other challenge was to ensure that when the PBX deinstallations were conducted, steps were taken to prevent creating alarms from the equipment that remained. Cisco developed a procedure that entailed removing the software, removing all the trunks—the lines coming into the PBX—and then removing the cabinet from the CPU. "You have to tell the CPU that the cabinets are no longer there. If you don't, the CPU is always looking for them and will alarm the system," Bourdet cautions.

Each PBX hardware deinstallation took an average of one working day, whereas the software removal required an additional three to four hours. Staffing involved four technicians who were familiar with the PBX network and knowledgeable on trunking technology. An additional telecom administrator removed the phone sets from the software configuration. "It's really important that the individuals doing the actual deinstalls are qualified and familiar with this type of network," Bourdet said. "We were fortunate enough to have the necessary resources on staff. If we didn't, we would have outsourced that part of the initiative to PBX-certified individuals."

Although the equipment disconnection and retrieval went smoothly for the team, they did experience a problem reconciling their equipment list with the vendor's. "We followed the lessor's instructions to the letter, but we still ended up with disagreements about the quantities of equipment that we returned," Bourdet says. The leasing company did not inventory the equipment when it arrived at the facility, instead turning it over to a secondary market vendor. "The secondary vendor then either miscounted it, or things got lost between here and there, because our records and their records did not match. If I had it to do over, I would have gone an additional step that included a box level inventory of the equipment, rather than a consolidated list," Bourdet adds.

Results of PBX Lease Return Initiative

STATUS:

- 99.9 percent of all leased equipment up for renewal was returned.
- More than U.S. $3.5 million dollars (market value) of equipment was returned, including 22 PBX EPNs and 10,000 phones.
- U.S. $128,888 per month was saved in leased equipment cost.
- All final leftover equipment was inventoried and identified for lab testing use or reselling opportunities.

RESULTS:

- The San Jose campus is completely retrofitted and is now 100 percent IP Telephony-ready.

Best Practices: PBX Lease Returns

- Enter all PBX lease renewal dates and associated equipment onto a spreadsheet for tracking purposes, and build a project plan that schedules the deinstallations and returns.

- Develop a process that prevents alarms when removing cabinets from the PBX.

- Ensure that only PBX-certified technicians are involved in the deinstallation.

- Carefully match the equipment list on the original lease agreement to the inventory being returned, create a box-level inventory list, and get a signed receiving list from the vendor.

Vendor Rules of Engagement

Maintaining a good relationship with the PBX vendor is especially critical at this point of the process. Despite the fact that discontinuing the lease arrangements, returning the equipment, and migrating to new technology is not good news for the vendor, honesty, trust, integrity, and continuing to treat the vendor as a valued member of the team enable the process to go as smoothly as possible.

"We shared our deployment schedule with them and kept them up to date monthly," says Fran McBrearty, IT project manager. "Before the deployment began, we always had weekly project meetings and were working with them on several different projects in terms of growth, management of systems, call center issues, etc. So when we started doing the PBX disconnects, the same process continued."

By the time the retrofit was complete and the team began to disconnect the PBXs, the vendor had already reassigned its resources to other customers. "As the team shrank, we had to learn how to deal with the right people at the right time in order to keep the initiative moving forward," McBrearty says.

We understood that the vendor could not keep its project managers, software engineers, and technicians assigned to us because the level of their business was undergoing substantial reduction. At this point, it was important to understand the contract requirements. We reviewed the original service level agreements we had signed with the vendor, and although we were flexible about allowing the vendor to begin pulling and reallocating resources it had dedicated to Cisco, we leveraged the maintenance contract to obtain the support we needed from those vendor resources that remained.

TIP	Read your current PBX vendor contract and know the terms of the agreement. Pay close attention to the support and data access parameters. Make sure you have access to the data stored in the PBX (such as your configuration files) and that your contract allows you to have unrestricted access to this data. Honesty and clear communication are critical for a successful transition.

"We used the same PBX vendor to do the disconnects," says Reid Bourdet, SPM IT project manager. "But we made sure that we had a mutually agreed-upon scope of work and negotiated the pricing on disconnects for a one-time charge rather than on an as-needed basis. We gave them the schedule, the scope of work, and then negotiated the price."

Due to the massive size of the enterprise-wide initiative, the IP Telephony rollout took place in phases. "Many companies will opt to do the cutovers as a flashcut," McBrearty says. "Basically, the PBX is here on Friday, gone on Monday. That scenario is not going to require the vendor to keep existing resources on staff throughout the implementation." But whether the retrofit is conducted in phases or flashcut in a single event, honesty, integrity, and adherence to the contract help to maintain a good relationship on both sides.

Best Practices: Vendor Rules of Engagement

- When disconnecting the PBXs, discontinuing the lease arrangements, and returning the equipment, continue to treat the vendor with honesty, trust, integrity, and as a valued member and partner of the team.

- Understand the existing service agreement before you begin the migration, and ensure that the resources you need to assist with the migration are consistent with the terms of the agreement.

- If the PBX vendor is contracted to assist with the disconnects, make sure there is a mutually acceptable and agreed-upon scope of work and schedule.

- Negotiate the disconnect price as a one-time charge rather than on an as-needed basis to keep costs down.

Nonleased Equipment Disposal

Not all the equipment that the IP Telephony migration replaced was leased. For the nonleased equipment, Cisco made the decision to sell the equipment, transfer it internally to other locations and engineering labs inside the organization, or discard it and write it off. Following is the procedure used by the Tiger Team's financial representatives to collect, mark, and dispose of the nonleased equipment.

For write-offs (equipment not able to be redeployed or sold):

I. Information that *must* be provided to financial analyst:

    a. Serial number of the asset, asset tracking number, tag number, or department number where original asset was purchased (at least one of these four must be provided)

    b. Current location of the asset (state, city, building)

    c. Brief asset description

II. Provide other information if known:

    a. Approximate cost of asset when purchased originally

    b. Approximate date of original purchase

    c. Department number where original asset was purchased

III. Send asset to the system resource center after it is written off

For sale of asset:

I.   See section I. A, B, C for required information to be sent to financial analyst.

II. Customer should be notified to send the check payment to the following:

Cisco Systems, Inc.

Attn: PBX Equipment Disposal Financial Analyst

Room XXX

170 West Tasman Drive

San Jose, CA 95134-1706

III. Purchaser must write asset number on the check so that fixed asset accounting can apply the proceeds to the original department charged with the depreciation expense. Contact your financial analyst if you do not know the asset number.

For transfer of asset within Cisco: (that is, equipment redeployed to a lab)

I.   See section I. A, B, C for required information to be sent to financial analyst.

II. Provide financial analyst with the department number to which the asset will be transferred and e-mail confirmation from the transferee department accepting the ongoing depreciation charges.

Retrofit Cleanup

When the implementation team began the conversion to IP Telephony, an IP call center solution was not yet in place. The decision was made to remove as many lines off the PBX as possible, conduct a partial retrofit, and convert everyone except for call center agents, their backups, and any business-critical analog lines. The team conducted a final cleanup at the end of the conversion to ensure that it would have ample time to carefully review all analog lines housed in the same buildings as call center agents.

It would have been detrimental to the implementation team if we had accidentally removed a business-critical phone line used by our call center team. Because we were careful in our decision to remove only those lines that were traced and identified, we are proud of the fact that during the course of the year, we did not bring down any call center agents or their designated analog lines during the retrofit.

After the retrofit was over and the dust was settled, the cleanup phase began. "We had to examine each situation separately and make the decision, for example, whether to pull out an analog line or replace it with CallManager," Bourdet says. "If a line was designated 'critical use,' we replaced it with an outside line." Other situations included engineering lab applications with call-in numbers for product demos and high-speed modem lines.

The cleanup ensures that all lines removed and disconnected from the PBX are not business critical and provides ample time to carefully review all the "unidentified" analog lines and trace them in an attempt to find owners. By doing this, the implementation team was able to carefully remove nearly 17,000 ports from the PBX—3000 of which were analog lines. Most enterprise companies like Cisco have thousands of lines that, through the years, have either been forgotten about or are simply unused. By being mindful of this extra step, the Cisco cleanup effort eliminated thousands of unused lines and resulted in annual cost savings of up to U.S. $42,000.

TIP	Keep your original cutsheets so that you have a working list of the various lines that you need to review again during the cleanup phase. Maintaining this log saves you time during the cleanup process.

TIP   Seldom is there the opportunity or time to trace every unverified or questionable line on your network. Use the cleanup phase to ensure that every line going onto your network is viable, and disconnect those lines that are no longer in use. Note all untraced lines on your cutsheets for future reference.

Because of the accelerated pace of the project, a guest phone might be functioning incorrectly, or a legacy phone or missed wall bracket might get lost in the shuffle. The cleanup effort provides an opportunity to walk the floor once more to ensure a clean 100 percent campus conversion.

"One of the things that made it much easier for us was that the implementation team gave us a printout of what was remaining in the PBX," Bourdet says. "We started working with that and then went through a period of discovery with the users to determine the best course of action." Paying close attention to the applications that were left running through the PBX and working with users to determine what their needs were allowed the cleanup team to tailor a solution that fit the needs of the user and of the organization.

Using the same individuals for the cleanup effort as for the PBX lease returns, the team conducted the cleanup building by building, concentrating on Cisco-owned equipment only after the lease return efforts were completed. As of April 2001, San Jose still had more than 22,000 ports remaining on the PBX. One year later, those ports were reduced to less than 2000. Today, both G3R PBXs have been removed, and not a single PBX port remains active. Chapter 7 provides a complete review of the PBX removal process and the final cleanup effort.

Preparing Your Network for the Future

UTOPIA (or "PBX-free in 2003") is the unofficial name of an official Cisco project at Cisco that involves decommissioning all the legacy phone equipment, migrating the entire organization across the globe to IP Telephony, and planning for growth, scalability, and integration of future applications.

"Of course, it's not as simple as that," cautions Paul Molyski, IT LAN project manager. "We have to have the solutions in place, and UTOPIA is our plan for doing that." Figure 6-3 represents the Cisco old-world network applications and the new network that demonstrates the capability of a converged voice and data network with applications either currently in place or those in the implementation plan.

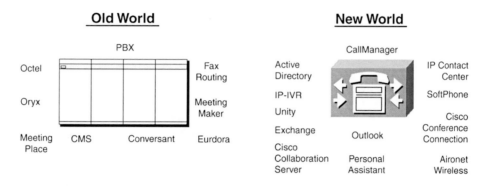

Figure 6-3   *Old World/New World*

As new technology evolves, so should the systems or processes that manage them. As Cisco prepares for the UTOPIA stage, team members are developing a system that will analyze the new IP technology for applicability, test it for feasibility, provide an adoption position, and ensure that all impacted teams are involved and in agreement.

The Cisco business philosophy has always been based on a first-to-market strategy. However, business decisions are driven more by what meets the needs of the organization than by dates or schedules. Certain technologies need to scale to meet our global 40,000+ user community, and because of that, we needed to take our time to make the final IP Telephony conversion right the first time. After the San Jose campus conversion was complete, we identified many components that still hung off the PBX. Therefore, instead of focusing on removing the PBX in 2003, we ensured that every possible solution was in place to lessen the need for it until we were indeed PBX free.

The chart in Figure 6-4 outlines all the cross-functional teams affected by the rollout of new applications and identifies an interception point to which the product development stage will need to evolve before the applications are ready for deployment. New technologies are designed to provide employees with even more flexibility and productivity than ever before. As a result, the chart provides a method of determining at which point each application is ready for deployment, without creating silos and duplication of work between cross-functional teams. The chart demonstrates how applications are integrated and developed into the new IP-enabled network.

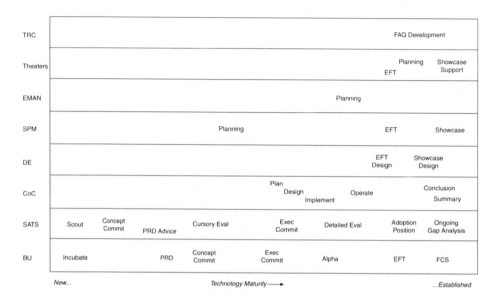

Figure 6-4   *Technology Maturity Swimlanes*

The flexibility of IP Telephony opens the floodgates to many new applications. Looking at how quickly you can integrate these applications yet maintain compatibility between hardware and software versions is the challenge. Cisco technology experts work closely with its business units to determine compatibility and feature requirements. Understanding the needs of the various cross-functional teams will enable the team to continue to identify innovative product development requirements, adoption positions, and timing for implementation. Cisco will always be its first and best customer, and piloting these new applications will be a primary directive.

Operate Phase

The first step after transitioning from the implementation phase is the operate phase. The goals of the operate phase are to ensure that your systems continue to run efficiently and that they remain highly available. The Cisco Steps to Success portal offers the following best practices and steps for managing the operate phase.

TIP	Take advantage of a variety of Cisco services and support programs in the ongoing operations and management of the IP Telephony system. The portfolio of Cisco services is outlined within this chapter.

NOTE	The Steps to Success portal requires a Cisco.com login. You can access it at http://www.cisco.com/go/stepstosuccess.

Step One: System Management

Develop processes to manage the system in ongoing operations mode, including system administration and backup, asset management, and scheduled maintenance.

The tasks required for this step are as follows:

1 **Administer and back up system components**—Develop procedures to back up system components, including servers, operating systems, telephony applications (including dial plans), software, databases, gateways, switches, and routers. Test recovery from backups on a scheduled basis.

2 **Manage the assets**—Establish a database of record to enable quick, restricted access to inventory information for the following:

- Hardware components (models, versions, and capabilities)
- Software components (version and release warranty information, such as dates, entitlements, and processes)
- Service contracts (dates, entitlements, and processes)
- Maintenance information (schedules, actions, and results)

Maintaining good records of system components is vital to an effective network management operation.

3 **Perform routine maintenance**—Advise the customer of the processes associated with scheduled maintenance of systems components and software updates to ensure sound operational practices. Benchmark the scheduled procedures against a log of

actual executed procedures. Verify that the network operations center (NOC) understands which logs to monitor for each interprocess communications (IPC) product and which resources are available to explain recommended actions for items that appear on the logs.

4 **Manage system trouble** — This is another core NOC/customer response center (CRC) responsibility. Guides, tools, training, and experience are required for success. In addition to troubleshooting and resolving problems, NOCs should provide a mechanism for tracking each incident and ensuring a satisfactory resolution. Usually the same tool for tracking moves, adds, and changes is used for tracking issues, and the same tool for cost accounting for moves, adds, and changes is used in this area. A key entitlement of Cisco service and support contracts is access to the Cisco TAC. The Cisco TAC has the skills and capabilities to assist customers and partners in resolving the most complex issues. Determine the priority level of the problem and assess the impact on the customer's network (priority 1, 2, or 3). Follow established escalation procedures for level-3 support from the Cisco TAC. These contracts also provide for the replacement of hardware. The following contract options are available for the delivery of replacement parts:

Next business day

Within 4 hours during an 8–5 business day

Within 4 hours around the clock (24×7)

Within 2 hours around the clock (24×7)

Cisco SMARTnet Onsite also provides a certified technician to install the replacement part. Every hardware component should have a Cisco SMARTnet contract, and every software product should have software application support.

NOTE   For a complete list of the Cisco and partner IP Telephony services and support programs that have been described, visit http://www.cisco.com/en/US/products/svcs/ps2961/ps2664/serv_group_home.html.

5 **Maintain system security** — Confirm that all security policies have been implemented according to the requirements, and set up ongoing monitoring processes to identify new security issues. Emphasize to the customer that sufficient security of networks, servers, software, and data is essential and is an ongoing process. Note: Cisco Security Agent provides threat protection for server and desktop computing systems, also known as endpoints. It identifies and prevents malicious behavior, thereby eliminating

known and unknown ("Day Zero") security risks and helping to reduce operational costs. The Cisco Security Agent aggregates and extends multiple endpoint security functions by providing host intrusion prevention, distributed firewall capabilities, malicious mobile code protection, operating system integrity assurance, and audit log consolidation, all within a single product. Because Cisco Security Agent analyzes behavior rather than relying on signature matching, it provides robust protection with reduced operational costs. You can find additional Cisco Security Agent information at http://www.cisco.com/en/US/products/sw/secursw/ps5057/index.html.

NOTE   For more detailed information about providing security to the network, visit the Steps to Success for Cisco Network Security and VPN Solutions at http://www.cisco.com/partner/WWChannels/technologies/Security/index.html. (A Cisco.com login is required.)

Step Two: Change Management

Determine how to manage and perform system changes, and integrate them into the operational environment.

Recognize that system changes can be challenging for a customer's operations, and offer to assist the customer in planning for future upgrades and defining the overall change management process.

The tasks required for this step are as follows:

1 **Plan and perform product upgrades**—Upgrade products for the customer, or work with him to make sure that he has sufficient skills to upgrade a product himself. Monitor announcements of upgrades and new releases, and discuss with the customer whether to apply them and what the costs would be. Emphasize the importance of version release control, especially if the customer has multiple sites or servers. If possible, plan to perform upgrades based on scheduled maintenance windows. Be sure to follow backup, rollback, and recovery strategy.

2 **Develop processes for moves, adds, and changes**—Cisco IP telephony products greatly change the moves, adds, and changes process compared to the legacy model. If set up properly, the labor and administration that are associated with legacy moves, adds, and changes for desktop phones are all but eliminated in areas where Ethernet service is already in place. Processes and work functions are still required when moves,

adds, and changes are performed for servers, switches, Gateways, and other components. Ensure that there is a process for accepting and processing orders for moves, adds, and changes. Give consideration to the tool(s) used by the customer's help desk or NOC to accept, assign, dispatch, and track functions that are associated with moves, adds, and changes. Ensure that there is an agreed-upon process for change control. For example, if it is necessary to bring down a primary call processing system for memory or software upgrades, you must have a process for scheduling the change so that it does not disrupt work functions and agreed-upon service-level agreements. (See the "Change Management" section earlier in this chapter for additional details on managing change.)

3 **Perform moves, adds, and changes**—This process involves many of the same processes as with installation. Use the installation URLs for the components involved in the move, add, or change. Size and complexity dictate the need for a project manager and project plan.

4 **Perform post-move, add, and change help desk/NOC functions**—To complete this task, ensure successful completion of moves, adds, and changes in the production environment; help the customer cost account/bill for moves, adds, and changes; and update records/databases impacted by the move, add, or change procedure.

5 **Conduct move, add, or change knowledge transfer**—Assist the customer in socializing change within the user community and implementing any training redesign caused by the move, add, or change. Assess training impacts from both an end-user and system administrator perspective.

Step Three: Performance Management

Assist the customer in identifying best practices to monitor system performance and respond to trouble reports. While you are assisting the customer with performance management, watch for opportunities to assist in addressing network optimization needs as well.

The tasks required for this step are as follows:

1 **Monitor the health and performance of the system**—Examine the customer's network performance-monitoring process and identify opportunities for improvement. Consider the customer's existing processes, tools, and staff for monitoring warnings and errors, performance trends, and incidences of exceeding threshold performance targets.

2 **Produce network availability reports**—Assist the customer's system administrator in defining and automating a process for scheduling network outages and reports and making the reports available online for system users.

3 **Monitor service level agreements (SLAs)**—Assist the customer in monitoring the SLAs established with vendors and users of the systems. Ensure that Cisco SMARTnet and Software Application Support (SAS) agreements are in place.

4 **Conduct customer satisfaction surveys**—The system owner surveys users in the customer's organization to ensure that system performance and functionality meet business needs. Use the survey results as a basis for refining the performance management process and as input for optimization planning. Use baselining to manage performance goals pre- and post-installation so that you can measure good and bad performance.

NOTE	You can find templates and resources that support the operate phase at http://www.cisco.com/partner/WWChannels/technologies/IPT/operate.html. (A Cisco.com login is required.)

Optimize Phase

After the IP Telephony solution is up and running, you need to keep it functioning as efficiently as possible and with high availability, while resolving problems quickly as they arise. Evaluate the customer's network design to determine if opportunities for optimization exist. Review the output to assess whether the solution maximizes the desired business results. When you have identified significant deviations, offer optimization recommendations for the current solution, to minimize or eliminate impacts and to maximize business results delivery. The following steps outline the key components for executing the optimize phase.

Step One: Optimization Planning

After the customer stabilizes the operational solution, work with him to identify and prioritize system improvements. Optimization can generally be defined as post-installation services that are not under a remote or onsite maintenance contract, including but not limited to performance audits, major software/hardware upgrades, and applications development. The main goal is to assess new business functionality gaps between solution functionality and apparent business gaps.

The tasks required for this step are as follows:

1 **Establish an optimization process**—Help the customer establish an optimization process for identifying areas for improvement under the optimization guidelines. If these guidelines are not defined clearly, determine what optimization means to the organization and what its goals are. Guidelines should include best practices around the backup, rollback, and recovery strategies; software and hardware upgrades; and system maintenance improvements.

2 **Evaluate optimization needs**—Help the customer manage the findings that emerge from the optimization process. Process output might be in the form of an issue log. Evaluate the impact of the issues that are relative to the customer's goals.

3 **Identify opportunities for optimization**—Help the customer assess the effort and benefits related to specific optimization opportunities. Determine the business value of optimizing the existing system. Provide value by working with the customer to build the financial justification for optimization, and propose the plan for execution.

Step Two: Optimization Execution

As optimization opportunities emerge during the system operations, you can assist the customer in planning and implementing enhancements, which take the solution to the next level.

The tasks required for this step are as follows:

1 **Devise optimization solutions**—After the customer decides to pursue optimization opportunities, present the solution alternatives to meet the optimization goals. These alternatives can be rooted in technology or process improvements to meet the operational and business objectives. Include the high-level implementation plan for the viable solution approaches.

2 **Test the optimization solution**—After the customer makes the final decision for the optimization approach, build and test the solution in a test environment that models the production environment. The customer can then conduct user testing to validate the design and his expectations of the optimization implementation.

3 **Perform optimization**—Upon confirming a successful test of the optimization approach, move forward with implementing the solution in the production environment. This task essentially mirrors, on a smaller scale, the deployment plan of the implement phase, including site preparation, staging/installation of any new equipment, configuration, integration, and acceptance testing of the solution.

4 Conduct optimization knowledge transfer—Hand off the optimization implementation to the system administrator given a successful implementation. Based on the scope of the improvement, there might be opportunities to assist with a retraining effort and documenting lessons learned for future initiatives. This completes the final customer acceptance of the optimization.

NOTE   You can find templates and resources that support the optimize phase at http://www.cisco.com/partner/WWChannels/technologies/IPT/ optimize.html. (A Cisco.com login is required.)

Cisco IP Communications Services and Support Programs

"We can now troubleshoot 99.9 percent of our locations remotely."

The importance of developing a comprehensive business plan for service and support is critical to leveraging the successful implementation of your new converged voice and data network. Through these services, your organization benefits from the experience gained by Cisco and its partners in deploying some of the world's largest and most complex IP Telephony systems. Taking advantage of this valuable experience, organizations can create and maintain a resilient converged network that will meet your business needs today—and in the future.

IP communications covers Cisco IP Telephony, contact center, and unified messaging. The Cisco IP communications service and support solutions are designed for one purpose—to ensure your success by delivering a suite of proactive services. Cisco and its partners provide strategic and consultative support that maps to each stage of the solution life cycle: planning, design, implementation, operations, and optimization (PDIOO). The award-winning Cisco service program enables the alignment of a converged IP communications network infrastructure with customers' unique business strategies and goals, utilizing Cisco expertise, experience, processes, tools, and resources to reduce time, cost, and complexity of implementing an IP Telephony solution. Advanced services and technical support services covering the entire network life cycle might be delivered directly by Cisco, or via its ecosystem of best-in-class partners.

InfoTech developed a recent white paper called "The New Converged Applications Support Model," which you can find at http://www.nwfusion.com/whitepapers/cisco/CiscoSept2003.pdf. The authors point out that many companies do not have the resources required to adequately plan, design, implement, and manage a converged communications environment. They suggest that when making the investment in an IP-based network, organizations need to look closely at the vendor's ability to provide post-installation service and support.

According to InfoTech, implementing and optimizing IP-based communications consists of the following best practices:

- **End-to-end PDIOO capability**—This capability covers the full range of lifecycle needs. These needs include a network and telecom traffic analysis, technology evaluation and migration, network application performance and optimization, remote deployment support, ongoing software release assessments, network troubleshooting, and security management.

- **Expert support partners**—Carefully chosen partners must be able to offer a wide-ranging set of expert choices in application expertise, vertical specialization, geographic coverage, and tools that encompass testing and analysis.

- **Cutting-edge management tools**—Tools that enable remote monitoring and management of the network, combined with trouble resolution services, provide a proactive approach to expert network support.

- **Knowledge management and transfer**—Communication is vital to any partner relationship, and equally so in this situation as you work in tandem with your partner.

- **Global coverage**—Ensure scalability by enabling the expansion of business on both global and virtual levels through consistent, transparent global service capabilities.

Cisco Systems has created the Cisco IP communications services blueprint (see Figure 6-5) to provide partners and customers with a comprehensive guide that outlines the standard services that should be offered as part of a Cisco IP communications solution.

A comprehensive service and support plan optimizes IP communication deployments and was an integral part of our own Cisco IP Telephony implementation.

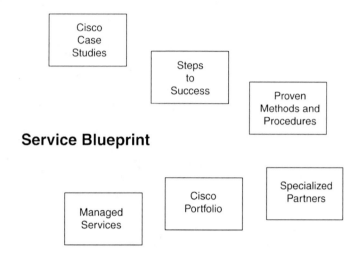

Figure 6-5   *Cisco Blueprint for Success*

The blueprints provide the service descriptions and deliverables associated with the PDIOO phases. The complexity level of the solution ultimately drives the PDIOO service deliverables required for the engagement. Therefore, Cisco has provided the standard PDIOO service descriptions and deliverables associated with low- and medium- to high-complexity Cisco IP communications solutions.

NOTE	You can access the Cisco blueprints at http://www.cisco.com/partner/ WWChannels/technologies/IPT/resources/doc/IPC_Services_Blueprint.doc. (A Cisco.com login is required.)

Table 6-3 is an example of some of the deliverables associated with an IP Telephony engagement and for which services can be provided.

Table 6-3 *Cisco IP Telephony Services Blueprint—Service Requirements for Success*

Service Requirements	Service Benefits
Planning	
IP Telephony network infrastructure readiness assessment	Identifies explicit infrastructure and application requirements and assesses readiness for IP Telephony applications Avoids additional planning cycles by identifying gaps and risks in the earliest phase of the planning process
IP Telephony solution planning	Ensures success of the solution
Design	
IP Telephony detailed design review	Thoroughly plans for the successful introduction of new technology or new services into your network through a comprehensive network design process that meets your technical and business requirements Lets you take advantage of leading practices and expertise
IP Telephony proof-of-concept support	Provides you with an IP Telephony expert who is familiar with the planning and design of your IP Telephony solution to help ensure that the pilot process verifies that the design can be implemented in the production environment
IP Telephony detailed design development	Translates requirements into details necessary to engineer the network
Implementation	
Installation: • Project management coordination • Site survey(s) system configuration • Onsite staging installation plan • Installation • Implementation testing • Administrator of knowledge transfer • End-user training • Cutover and post cutover support	Streamlines communication by providing a single point of contact Ensures an efficient process and a successful installation Mitigates risks associated with the site that might delay installation and postpone the introduction of services Supplements customer networking staff, enabling the optimization of internal resources Ensures functionality and meets customer requirements and expectations Reduces onsite installation time Accelerates knowledge transfer and reduces risk

Table 6-3 *Cisco IP Telephony Services Blueprint—Service Requirements for Success (Continued)*

Service Requirements	Service Benefits
Implementation plan review	Ensures that the implementation plan is complete and contains critical elements that are required for a scalable and predictable deployment that meets your expectations Minimizes migration issues, deployment time, and service disruptions
Ongoing remote deployment support	Streamlines deployment processes so that unnecessary bottlenecks are eliminated, improving productivity and speed to migration Minimizes risk during critical phases of the IP Telephony deployment
Acceptance of test plan review	Offers assurance that no critical parts are missing in the plan regarding IP Telephony, additional features, and other applications Provides targets to perform the acceptance testing thoroughly and efficiently, leading to proper test coverage to avoid future issues and delays
IP Telephony implementation engineering	Assists with the collection of deliverables and activities for planning and execution of the IP Telephony implementation
IP Telephony deployment project management	Provides experienced network project management assistance during the planning, design, and implementation of a major IP Telephony deployment project
Operational	
Technical support services: Maintenance, bug fixes, and software updates or upgrades	Maximizes and protects your technology investment Reduces the cost of ownership by taking advantage of Cisco expertise and knowledge Ensures that your network benefits from the latest functionality, security, performance, and more Provides timely problem resolution 24×7 through access to Cisco technical expertise

continues

Table 6-3 *Cisco IP Telephony Services Blueprint—Service Requirements for Success (Continued)*

Service Requirements	Service Benefits
Remote network operations: • Monitor of systems 24×7 • Proactive maintenance • Fault notification, isolation, and resolution • Logical moves, adds, and changes • Configuration management • Performance management	Offers lower total cost of ownership versus PBX Offers proactive notification, decreasing time to resolution and increasing network uptime Takes advantage of years of in-depth VoIP and network expertise Offers coordination and execution of soft moves, adds, or changes Offers online access to availability and service-level reports
Physical moves, adds, and changes	Supplements customer networking staff, enabling the optimization of internal resources
Optimization	
Ongoing network application performance and optimization	Helps you lower the total cost of ownership by preventing solution-level issues through proactive support focused on keeping applications running at optimal capacity Simplifies network expansion and optimization by providing ongoing network configuration updates and recommendations, as well as proactive design consulting and application technology expertise Lowers operational costs and provides for less business interruption by helping you identify how to respond to performance-degrading events and resolve issues faster
Ongoing design support	Keeps the network design up to date with the needed changes, avoiding obsolescence Provides leading practices when making changes, avoiding potential outages Results in a robust network application with satisfied and productive users
Knowledge transfer	Improves the IP Telephony knowledge base and troubleshooting techniques of your staff Improves the ability to solve small problems proactively before they become major issues, saving operating expenses in the long term

Table 6-3 *Cisco IP Telephony Services Blueprint—Service Requirements*
for Success (Continued)

Service Requirements	Service Benefits
Ongoing software release assessment	Provides optimal feature set to maintain a robust network and meet your requirements at the same time Helps you achieve gains in productivity by operating a seamless network
IP Telephony onsite support	Helps you realize the full benefit of proactive, consultative support

For a complete list of the Cisco and partner IP Telephony services and support programs that map to the service requirements described in this table, visit http://www.cisco.com/en/US/products/svcs/ps2961/ps2664/serv_group_home.html.

In addition to the IPC blueprint, high-level and detailed requirements are assured via presales readiness assessments based on partner and Cisco tools and methodologies. Technology application support (TAS) and partner consultative support (PCS) services have also been designed to supplement and complement partner and in-house IT staff services with a set of system engineering and consultative support components.

Cisco IP telephony service and support solutions are designed to ensure customer success by delivering a suite of proactive services. Rapid deployment, core, and advanced service and support covering the entire network lifecycle can be delivered directly by Cisco Systems, or through its ecosystem of best-in-class partners working closely with your internal resources.

This comprehensive portfolio of services is available directly from Cisco or through Cisco IP Telephony specialized partners who are trained and qualified in Cisco IP Telephony. Cisco IP Telephony specialized partners have the expertise to deliver planning, design, and implementation services for the most basic and complex network environments. These partners have demonstrated skills in project management, ensuring consistent delivery of services on demanding projects and strong customer satisfaction records.

NOTE   For a list of qualified technology specialized partners, visit the Partner Locator tool at http://tools.cisco.com/WWChannels/LOCATR/jsp/partner_locator.jsp. (A Cisco.com login is required.)

To learn more about the Cisco Services and Support portfolio, contact your local Cisco account manager or log onto http://www.cisco.com/en/US/products/svcs/ps2961/ps2664/serv_group_home.html.

Lessons Learned

A long-term, complex deployment of emerging technology that involves multiple groups and a tightly controlled schedule is a learning experience where bumps, bruises, and mistakes are turned into lessons learned and documented to enable others to benefit from the experience. The IP Telephony implementation initiative was no exception. Following is a consolidation of the lessons we learned throughout each stage of the initiative, contributed by members of the IP Telephony Tiger Team, who were front and center from beginning to end.

Communication

- Without senior management support and sponsorship, the integration and acceptance of new-world technology will be harder to reach and might inhibit an earlier user adoption curve.

- Decisions made in a vacuum will not be integrated easily. Maintain consistent communication among design, implementation, and support.

- Communication is fundamental to enabling the rapid introduction of new technologies. Use the web to communicate with users and team members and to manage all processes and procedures so that you can maintain the project pace and schedule.

- Change is always difficult. Users will be less likely to commit to the project if they do not know who, what, when, and why. Set clear expectations within the user community to ensure a smoother migration.

- Beware of terminology differences. Overlapping terms and acronyms from different technology tracks have different meanings. Develop a glossary of terms and consistently check for understanding.

- Incorporate the business value behind the migration in your communication plan so that users know how the new technology will improve the company's bottom line.

Team/Relationships

- Those involved in the original design and engineering of the new solution know the technology intimately. Involve the engineering team when making strategic implementation decisions to leverage their expertise for unique configurations and workarounds.

- The Cisco LAN was upgraded in preparation for the new converged voice and data network. Save time and maintain project momentum by working closely with the LAN infrastructure team to ensure that the infrastructure you require is in place before the implementation team is ready to begin the retrofit.

- The implementation team was made up of Cisco partners who managed the company's old-world telephony network. Having core members of the implementation team who best know the existing network makes the process more efficient and helps to maintain the pace and schedule of the project.

- Depreciation variables, lack of monitored budget control, and the potential for over-ordering equipment are sure ways to invite out-of-control costs. Assign a financial analyst to monitor the entire project and work with you to keep the financial aspect on track.

- Cross-functional training between the transport and voice teams is essential to ensure effective troubleshooting and reduce adverse changes made in the network.

- Understand the value that each cross-functional team brings to the initiative. Involve voice services to help integrate customer requirements into the design and functionality; the LAN team to help monitor the sensitivity of voice traffic and provide a stable network infrastructure; and the Windows team to provide guidance in management of application resources.

Planning/Strategy

- Starting the implementation before you know the "must-have" features and configurations identified and ready can cause an immediate slowdown while fixes are developed and put into place. Do your homework and learn who your users are to identify the product/design features that are "must have" versus "nice to have" before you begin.

- Administrative assistants use their phones differently from most users. Understand their special needs and the boss/admin relationship, and work with them to ensure that their IP Telephony setup accommodates those needs.

- Because senior management and their admin support team are heavy phone users and often hold highly visible or customer-critical positions, they might require a different procedure or support plan than that used for the rest of the organization.

- To make the process more efficient and manageable, define your migration strategy (that is, by organization, by user, by building, by technology, and so on) and incorporate the new technology three ways: new hires, moves/changes, and by building.

- Determine which elements will drive the project pace (PBX leases, new building openings), and design the schedule to accommodate those variables.

- Know your business-critical phone users and their "critical lines" within your network so that the implementation team is prepared to take special care not to disrupt their business operations. This includes call centers, modem lines, 1-MB lines, analog lines, and so on.

- Software upgrades are a fact of life and, in Cisco's case, were sometimes deployed at the same time as the IP Telephony retrofit. Ensure that the project schedule allows time for routine software upgrades. Select areas with less than critical applications to retrofit while the upgrade is underway.

- Introducing new software releases on the production network before testing the software in a lab environment can have a negative impact on the network.

- Because the IP phones use a new pair of wires on the CAT3 cable, have wiring experts on call to correct the cabling in case you run into wall phone wiring/jack problems. Have someone from the LAN team onsite for the lab cabling.

- Ensure that security access to locked offices is authorized before the implementation team arrives to begin the retrofit to prevent avoidable delays.

Strategic Placement of Equipment

- Place servers in diverse data centers on campus, equally balancing the load and failover redundancy. Ensure adequate UPS and generator backup.

- Place Gateways on NOCs for diverse routing from the local and long-distance providers. Ensure UPS and generator backup.

- Each part of the IP phone has been designed to work optimally when it is set up correctly. The phone cord will curl and knot if it is installed incorrectly or backward. Pay close attention even to the small details.

Understand Current Environment

- Each department and group uses its phone system differently. Study customer usage or patterns and business requirements.

- Understand voice mail requirements to identify which options are required, which are obsolete, and which are best suited in a different platform.

- Understand the grade of service that is being provided. Engineer a solution to aggregate traffic and trunking together to take advantage of more efficient and cost-effective solutions.

- Study dial plans to fully understand existing requirements.

- Understand the network infrastructure to ensure that it is ready to deploy voice.

- Standardize across CallManagers. In a multicluster environment, standardization between systems helps in administration, troubleshooting, and problem resolution.

Technology

- The Cisco standard for desktop Ethernet service provides two 10/100 live jacks at each CAT5 wall plate. The IP phone, with the desktop PC connecting to the phone, uses one.

- Do not underestimate the convenience of not having to use an external power adapter. The use of inline power for the IP Phones is highly recommended.

- Beware of PC/workstation interruptions when those devices are plugged into the phone. Create a standardized process for the implementation team to ensure that this is done properly (that is, standardize which jacks are used).

- Cutsheets should include jack numbers, be scanned for duplicate phone numbers, and be sorted so that offices and cubes are grouped together for greater efficiency.

- If voice mail problems persist during an upgrade, try a server system reboot after the upgrade to remedy the problem.

- Contact the lab administrators ahead of time to verify jack numbers for the lab phones. Provide lab administrators with the new jack numbers and phone numbers after the conversion. Provide the lab team with documentation for how new LAN switches are connected and cabled.

Operations

- Use the "clean network" philosophy when defining your implementation guidelines. The retrofit is a perfect opportunity to start out with a clean network. Operational policies will accommodate the new voice and data converged network and keep it clean and stable.

- Create configuration and speed dial backups for key administrative personnel in case someone's phone is accidentally deleted and needs to be re-created.

- The benefits of IP Telephony allow you to conduct most of the key function of the operate phase remotely. Use the various Cisco services and support programs to take advantage of this new option.

- E911 is an often-neglected solution. Use the operate phase as an opportunity to validate and test the system often, especially after performing routine moves, adds, and changes.

- Optimize after the IP Telephony solution is up and running. It is important to keep it functioning as efficiently as possible and with high availability, while resolving problems quickly as they arise.

- When you identify significant deviations, seek optimization recommendations for the current solution to minimize or eliminate impact and to maximize business results delivery.

Resources

"Change Management Best Practices" white paper: http://www.cisco.com/warp/public/126/chmgmt.shtml#3#

Cisco Bug Navigator tool: http://www.cisco.com/cgi-bin/Support/Bugtool/launch_bugtool.pl

Cisco Security Agent: http://www.cisco.com/en/US/products/sw/secursw/ps5057/index.html

Cisco Resource Manager Essentials toolbox: http://www.cisco.com/warp/public/cc/pd/wr2k/rsmn/index.shtml

Cisco Technical Assistance Center for Support: http://www.cisco.com/en/US/support/index.html

Cisco Technical Assistance Center website: http://www.cisco.com/tac

Cisco's Worldwide Technical Contacts: http://www.cisco.com/warp/public/687/Directory/DirTAC.shtml

"Operating the IP Telephony Network" document: http://www.cisco.com/en/US/products/sw/voicesw/ps556/prod_installation_guide09186a008015a006.html

QDDTs FAQ (Software release notes): http://wwwin-metrics.cisco.com/FAQ.html

NOTE	Accessing all the tools on the Cisco TAC website requires a Cisco.com user ID and password. Obtain a user ID and password with your valid Cisco service contract at http://tools.cisco.com/RPF/register/register.do.

Summary

- **Change management**—To maintain the integrity of the network, requestors follow the Cisco internal change management process whenever a change to the network is required. Change requests are reviewed for impact to the network, fit, timing, and upgrades that are already in the funnel.

- **Software upgrades**—Cisco created a CallManager software upgrade checklist focused on managing a chain release of software upgrades to keep upgrades synchronized with all the versions that were currently active.

- **Disaster recovery**—A disaster recovery plan covers the hardware and software required to run business-critical applications. The IP Telephony application created new and positive implications for disaster recovery, providing a level of flexibility that was not readily available within the legacy systems.

- **PBX lease returns**—The PBX lease return dates largely dictated the IP Telephony implementation schedule. The initiative involved removing 55 EPN PBXs, each containing different cabinets throughout the San Jose campus. A comprehensive inventory and detailed tracking log of all equipment are key to the return process.

- **Vendor rules of engagement**—Discontinuing the lease arrangements, returning the equipment, and migrating to new technology change the relationship with the PBX vendor. Know what your contract states from a support and data access perspective before the migration. Honesty, trust, integrity, and continuing to treat the vendor as a partner and valued member of the team enable the process to go more smoothly.

- **Nonleased equipment disposal**—For the nonleased (Cisco-owned) equipment, the decision was made to sell the equipment, transfer it internally to other locations and use it inside the organization, or discard it and write it off.

- **Retrofit cleanup**—After the retrofit was over, the cleanup phase began, and decisions were made whether to disconnect the remaining analog lines or steer them onto the CallManager. Migrate what you use, not what you have, so that you keep the network clean.

- **Preparing your network for the future**—Preparing for the future means that as new IP Telephony applications become available, a system must be in place to analyze the technology for applicability, test it for feasibility, provide an adoption position, and ensure that all teams are involved and in agreement.

- **Operate phase**—The goals of the operate phase are to ensure that your systems continue to run efficiently and remain highly available. Cisco offers tools that allow you to conduct most of this process remotely.

- **Optimize phase**—Review the output from your network to assess whether the solution maximizes the desired business results. When you identify significant deviations, seek optimization recommendations for the current solution to minimize or eliminate impact and to maximize business results delivery.

- **Cisco services and support**—The Cisco IP communications services blueprint is a comprehensive guide that outlines the standard services that should be part of an IP Telephony solution. This service and support plan optimizes IP communication deployments and was an integral part of our own Cisco IP Telephony implementation. The blueprints provide the service descriptions and deliverables associated with the PDIOO phases.

- **Lessons learned**—Planning and scheduling are critical to the success of any large initiative, but trial and error are part of implementing any new technology. The team learned and documented lessons learned throughout the entire implementation for use in future deployments.

MOVING FORWARD: CONTINUING TO BE CISCO'S FIRST AND BEST CUSTOMER

It has been nearly two years since Cisco successfully retrofitted its San Jose campus to IP Telephony. Today, 2004, our San Jose campus continues to be the largest IP Telephony site in the world. Also, although we have more than 23,000 IP Phones (54,000 worldwide) and 500 CAT 6K and CAT 3500 switches, the journey certainly does not stop there. Throughout this book, you have read an expression that explains why Cisco migrated to IP Telephony called "being our first and best customer." This is not just a motto within Cisco but a commitment that keeps Cisco moving forward. This chapter outlines the additional technologies that Cisco has rolled out as a result of its initial IP Telephony migration and the benefits of a converged, IP-enabled network. In addition, I have summarized the key questionnaire I used to get the team thinking.

Looking Back and Moving Forward

The late 1990s were booming years for Cisco, as they were for many in the high-tech industry. By 2000, we were growing at an amazing pace—purchasing new buildings, relocating to larger office buildings, hiring new employees, and acquiring new businesses. It was an exciting time, and we were in an environment of constant change. To keep pace with that change and to showcase our new technology, Cisco began looking for ways to increase the organization's flexibility and agility, and that is how we embarked on the journey toward an enterprise-wide IP Telephony migration.

As we started the migration and moved into 2001, however, times had changed. The economy had begun to soften, high-tech was the first to feel it, and the terrorist attacks on September 11 had dramatically changed the political and economic environment. As with all industries, the tech industry started a surge of layoffs, belt tightening, and changing strategies. Suddenly, our focus expanded to include cost reduction, office space consolidations, increased operational efficiency, and ways to do more with less. However, although the focus expanded, the solution did not change. Rather than charging off to find another way to accomplish those additional goals, we realized that IP Telephony would achieve them all.

Today, when we look back on the past two years, we can say without hesitation that IP Telephony was a supremely successful initiative that has reaped benefits beyond what we had even hoped. At the Burton Group EMEA conference in October 2003, Cisco IT Director Vladeta Marjaonovic presented the real business benefits that Cisco has realized through our migration to IP Telephony and a converged network.

"Today, IP Telephony is an integral part of our converged network, delivering better quality and service to our employees, driving higher productivity, and reducing costs to the business," Marjaonovic says. "We have achieved cost reduction by converging to a single network, reducing cabling costs and management overhead, and nearly eliminating the cost associated with adds, moves, and changes."

Marjaonovic went on to describe how IP Telephony not only achieved the original goals that senior executives established, but the technology enabled unexpected benefits as well.

"We discovered some surprises after deploying IP Telephony throughout Cisco," Marjaonovic says. "Not only did it save money, especially in new offices, but it made a big difference in supporting employee mobility. It enabled our employees to take advantage of new mobility functionality that included using their Cisco IP Phones to relocate themselves to any available workspace, or wherever they could turn on their laptops. This mobility, coupled with some new phone functionality and web-based application services, has improved employee productivity."

Mobility has been a significant driver, not only in increasing operational efficiency, but also in employee motivation. Cisco employees often work from multiple locations in and around the San Jose campus. IP Telephony enables employees to establish a virtual office no matter where they are—even if they are working from home. Employees can receive calls as if they were sitting at their designated office space and be equally productive and accessible from alternate locations.

Since completing the project, we have installed more than 54,000 IP phones worldwide. Our robust, scalable, converged network delivers better quality and service to our employees and enables us to reach higher productivity levels and lower operational costs. Following are specific annualized benefits that Cisco has realized in the past two years:

- U.S. $500 million in increased productivity and employee mobility

- U.S. $1.45 million in reduced call costs resulting from unified messaging, outbound call management, audio conferencing, and extension portability

- U.S. $1.6 million in real estate space management and workspace efficiencies

- U.S. $630 thousand cost reduction in support, administration, Media Access Controls (MACs), cabling, and maintenance

Other benefits, such as cultural enhancement, are real but difficult to place a dollar figure on and include employee retention, geographic flexibility, competitive positioning, faster application deployment, and voice business continuity.

I would like to update you on each piece of the migration, what the team has done since completing the initiative in 2002, and where Cisco is going from here.

PBX Removal Complete

In 2002, the Cisco San Jose campus disconnected its last non-IP–enabled PBX. At the time of the implementation, 22 out of 55 of the Cisco Expansion Port Network (EPN) PBXs were leased, which meant that the IP Telephony implementation schedule was largely dictated by the PBX lease return dates. To keep the massive effort of returning the numerous leased equipment organized and on schedule, the team leader responsible for the retrofit cleanup effort entered all of the Cisco PBX leases onto a spreadsheet and developed a project plan to keep the returns on track. The initiative involved returning each leased PBX, along with its ancillary parts, throughout the San Jose campus.

Although the entire campus was routing calls on the new CallManagers, the two main PBXs remained connected because several critical applications depended on the main PBX, preventing Cisco from disconnecting them. A separate project team was assembled to manage the final PBX removal after the migration was complete. In 2002, the two Cisco-owned main PBXs were removed and fully disconnected. John Chambers, president and CEO of Cisco and the project sponsor for the IP Telephony migration, attended a celebration at which the last switch was disconnected, thus decommissioning the PBX (see Figure 7-1).

In addition to managing the return of all leased equipment, the team had to remove all ancillary solutions and systems that were tied to the PBX. The project was titled UTOPIA, which spelled out Unity, Telephony, & Other Powerful IP Applications. The overall objective of Project UTOPIA was to completely disconnect the PBX and Octel voice mail solutions. The final phase of Project UTOPIA will be to replace the Octel voice mail solution with Cisco Unity, scheduled for completion in late 2004.

Figure 7-1   *John Chambers Congratulates the Team on the Removal of the Final PBX on the San Jose Campus*

Left to right, kneeling: Joe Pontes, Sergio Quezada. Standing from left to right: Adam Downing, Fran McBrearty, Bob Bernal, John Chambers, Dennis Silva, Stephanie Carhee, Marisa Chancellor, Doug McQueen, (Bill Lowers in photo), Bernie Caro, Mike Telang, and Reid Bourdet.

The PBX disconnect was a bit more complicated than we expected. Our research identified some critical applications that hung off the PBX that required decommissioning, rerouting, or identifying a new solution before we could disconnect the PBX. A year of activities included complete removal of all call center applications, such as automatic call distributor (ACD) functionality, digital and analog circuit decommissioning, fax server migration, PBX trunking rerouting, a revised security solution, and some TI lines.

NOTE   You can find Cisco resources for managing a PBX migration on the Cisco Steps to Success website at http://www.Cisco.com/go/stepstosuccess. (A Cisco.com login is required.)

TIP   Select the PBX disconnect project lead by his experience with the current PBX vendor. Having a project lead who has the knowledge of how the PBX functions saves you time and prevents you from making critical and costly mistakes.

TIP   Run a PBX dump report that reveals all the solutions and applications that run off of it. Create a project plan for each application or solution to ensure a smooth and easy migration. Removing some of the applications will take time; therefore, run your PBX dump report early, be patient, and schedule the disconnect only after you have identified a solution.

TIP   The PBX disconnect project dependencies were vast, and in some cases complicated. Run a PBX report that identifies all the variables hanging off of it.

The Cisco PBX decommission team (Project UTOPIA) created a project plan to address all the dependencies so that the disconnect would become a smooth non-event, as shown in Figure 7-2.

What's Next for Cisco

Project UTOPIA offered Cisco the flexibility to utilize a more cost-efficient option for running all its voice systems on a new fully converged IP-enabled network. Quantifiable benefits and improvements have resulted in cost savings and support improvements. As Cisco pushed ahead, the plan to run all voice applications on Voice over IP (VoIP) started with the migration of its contact center solution.

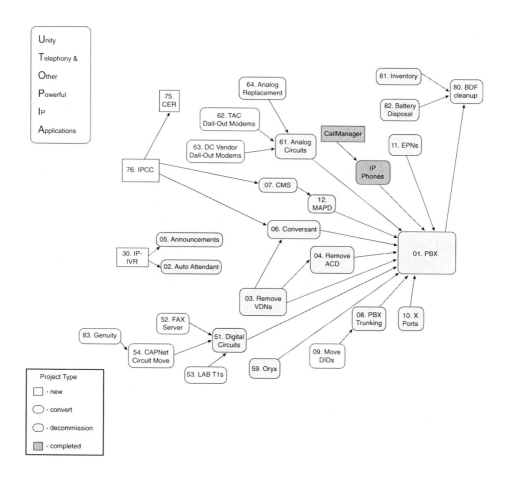

Figure 7-2   *PBX Disconnect Project Dependencies*

Figures 7-3 and 7-4 provide a comparison of the San Jose campus before and after the migration.

The old campus topology illustrates the San Jose campus just before the final PBX was decommissioned. At this point, although the PBX was still in place, all voice traffic was running (except for a 5300 WAN router) on the Cisco CallManager. The new campus diagram illustrates the final stage and how the Cisco San Jose campus looked after the PBX was completely removed and 100 percent of the campus was running voice traffic on the Cisco CallManager.

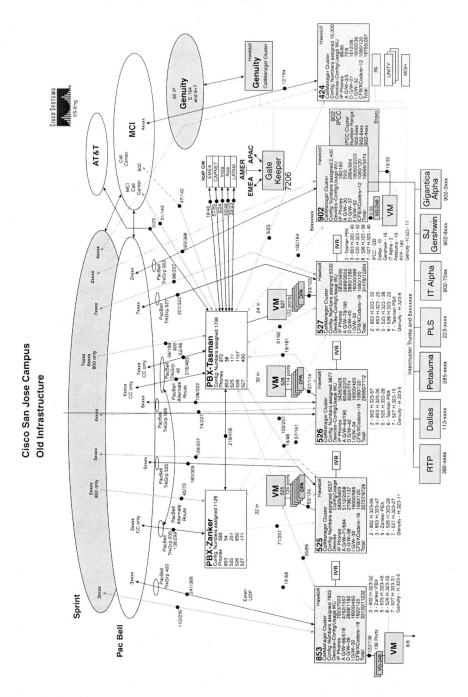

Figure 7-3 *Old Campus Topology*

Thanks to Bill Lowers for this topology diagram.

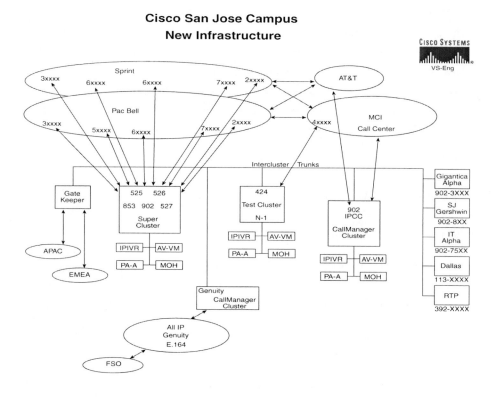

Figure 7-4   *New Campus Topology*

Thanks to Bill Lowers for this topology diagram.

Cisco IP Contact Center Migration

Cisco has long been recognized as the leader in Internet networking. As such, it knows firsthand the importance of leveraging a VoIP network to improve all aspects of its business—from delivering "best-in-class" customer service, support, and sales to assisting employees with internal help desk, travel scheduling, and benefit-related inquiries. As the "face" of Cisco to its internal and external customers and partners, Cisco contact centers rely on leading-edge technology to resolve customer issues quickly and thoroughly. A worldwide organization, Cisco has more than 35 internal and outsourced locations handling customer support and service functions. More than 600 customer service agents working in Cisco contact centers handle more than 100,000 calls per week as well as a multitude of e-mails and web requests.

How We Started

The success of the Cisco Technical Assistance Center (TAC) deployment of advanced customer contact software and the deep conviction that Cisco had in the benefits of an IP infrastructure caused Doug Allred, senior vice president of customer advocacy, to issue a challenge to Cisco global contact centers. The challenge was to follow the Cisco TAC lead and dramatically improve the ways in which customers are serviced across all Cisco contact centers worldwide—but take it one step further and deploy it all on IP.

This mandate resulted in the creation of a cross-functional team to ensure clear communication and synergy among the more than 35 contact centers (see Figure 7-5). Key team leads included LaVeta Gibbs, director of the technical support group, and Cindy Mike, global program manager for the Cisco IP Contact Center (IPCC) Enterprise Edition and Cisco IPCC Express Edition deployment.

Although the migration was targeted for a fast track, the process and structure for managing the migration was well thought-out and concise. The project team used the following methods to complete the migration:

- Utilize core team experience.

- Identify and create standards.

- Uncover support concerns.

- Ensure two-way client feedback.

- Communicate constantly.

- Utilize Cisco employee communication (CEC) web announcements.

- Conduct weekly program meetings and team meetings.

- Create e-mail alias—IPCC program (status updates, planning), IPCC steering committee, IPCC support, IPCC applications, IPCC hardware, IPCC clients, and IPCC outsourcer.

- Create a project web page with team contact information, support resources (including escalation path), administrative tools, project schedule, contact center client information, on-call help, training links, project documents (including sharepoint location), and so on.

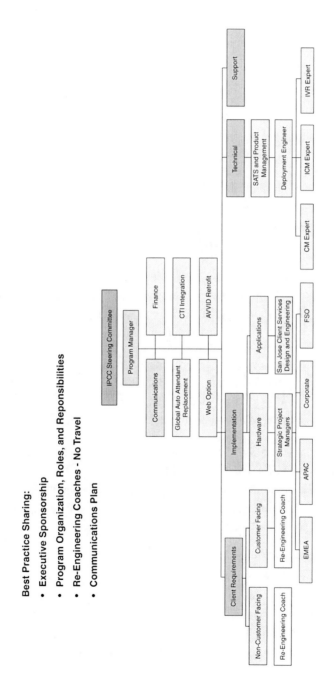

Best Practice Sharing:

- **Executive Sponsorship**
- **Program Organization, Roles, and Reponsibilities**
- **Re-Engineering Coaches - No Travel**
- **Communications Plan**

Figure 7-5   *IPCC Migration Program Structure*

"The exciting part of moving toward a pure IPCC environment is that it changes how we interact with customers. When we combine the web, data, and voice as a way to interact with our customers, the voice part becomes complementary—not the main event," says LaVeta Gibbs.

The Cisco IPCC achieved the next step in improving customer service and provided a comprehensive customer interaction network. Our goal was to migrate all of our front line contact centers to a cross-functional, virtual organization that could showcase Cisco products, best practices, and the power of the Internet.

In 1999, as a result of numerous acquisitions, our call center environment consisted of many small, independent call centers that were "stovepiped" due to inconsistent tools and service levels and no standard naming conventions or standard skills. The front line contact centers had 26 unique group names, 42 unique department codes, 23 unique vendors, 22 Cisco sites, 1000 employees, and 539 different dial-in numbers.

In addition, the contact centers worked from different platforms, and we had no reporting visibility into those who were outsourced. It was clear that we needed to integrate the entire operation and establish standardization, operational efficiency, and a clear reporting mechanism that would improve service to our customers.

Our Intelligent Call Management (ICM) project launch began in October 1999 and included time-division multiplexing (TDM) PBX-based call centers in 10 locations with TDM-based reporting. It gave us 100 percent call throughput with a fully redundant infrastructure, provided flexibility, and reduced transport and support costs.

However, that was only the first step. Going one step further, we have now integrated our IPCC that wraps around our newly installed Cisco Call Manager technology, utilizes automatic call distribution and standardized call routing rules, and queues calls through our Cisco IP interactive voice response (IVR). Reporting is performed in the Cisco Webview reporting package, and the call control is managed by the Cisco agent desktop rather than the phone.

This solution enables us not only to showcase Cisco products, but also to provide feedback to the business units to enable immediate and continuous improvement. We have completely removed competitor technology and have not only reduced our transport and support costs even further, but laid the foundation for changing the way we interact with customers. Our new customer contact solution offers a more streamlined and efficient system. We can route calls more easily to the right skilled agent and decrease caller on-hold time by seamlessly routing callers to the right solution based on their answer selection.

Site Deployment Design

Figure 7-6 illustrates how the production CallManager integrated with the new customer contact center solution.

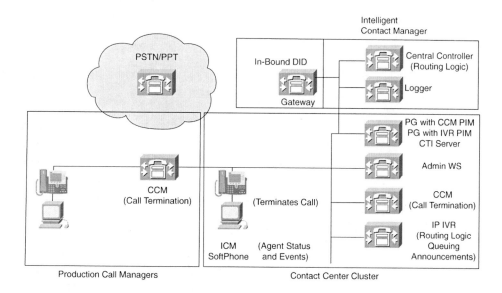

Figure 7-6 *Site Deployment Design*

An example of a Cisco contact center relying on Cisco IPCC Enterprise is the Global Call Center (GCC), a worldwide organization composed of multiple teams, each with a distinct functionality. These teams include the customer response center (CRC), which provides customer support through basic level technical assistance; service relations, which manages customer entitlement to Cisco support; GCC escalations, which resolves issues escalated by the CRC; and acquisitions and special handling (ASH), which provides customized support for the Cisco service provider and other customers. Contact centers are maintained in Research Triangle Park, North Carolina; San Jose, California; Sydney, Australia; Brussels, Belgium; Salt Lake City, Utah; Jacksonville, Florida; and Milton-Keynes, United Kingdom, supporting more than 50 countries, 82 toll-free and in-country numbers, and more than 80,000 calls per month. More than ten large contact centers in the Americas, Asia Pacific, Europe, and the Middle East were included in the migration to an IP infrastructure, with Cisco IPCC Enterprise serving as the backbone. Another 13 sites were migrated to Cisco IPCC Express.

Cisco IPCC Express provided the necessary capabilities to bring online all the smaller Cisco contact centers, including some TACs and GCCs in Latin America, Asia-Pacific, and Europe; and some internal Cisco help desk operations, including stock administration, Cisco capital leasing, investor relations, and corporate travel. The Cisco IPCC Express solution provides these organizations with simplified call routing options, easy scripting and administration, agent flexibility, as well as detailed reporting for small teams. Figure 7-7 shows the resulting Worldwide Contact Center.

Implementation Approach

Following the best practices we learned during the IP Telephony implementation, we once again developed a team based on executive sponsorship, a Tiger Team deployment strategy, and a well-formed communication plan. The entire initiative, deployed across all theaters, involved no travel.

Twelve agents were deployed in the first two months with our new 902 exchange. (We created a separate cluster for our San Jose contact center agents so that we could better manage them.) The deployment integrated 12 groups of agents, seven server CallManager clusters, four IP interactive voice responses (IPIVRs), 6 Peripheral Gateways (PGs), ICM SoftPhone and Webview software, and Cluster Management Suite software (CMS). In the first two months, more than 2700 calls per month were taken.

The implementation approach as shown in Figure 7-8 followed a phased approach and allowed us to strengthen our migration strategy after each increasingly critical phase was completed.

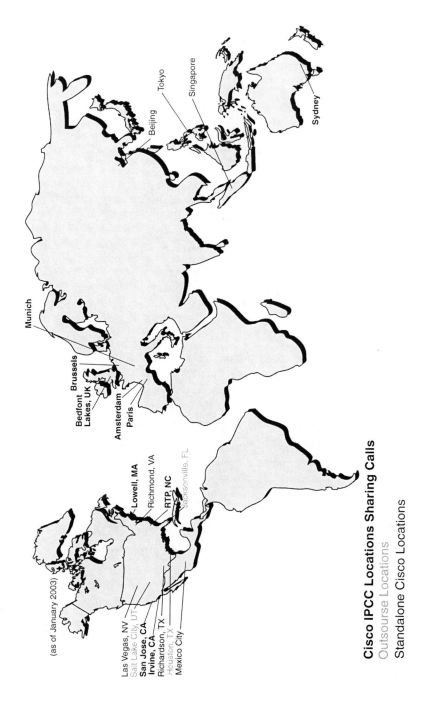

Figure 7-7 *Worldwide Contact Center*

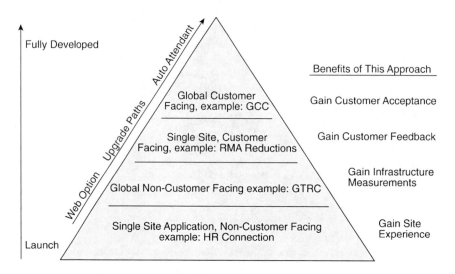

Figure 7-8 *Application Implementation Approach*

TIP   Create an agent survey to measure the success of the migration. Use this data to adjust your strategy and to fix mistakes in your implementation approach.

The contact center migration included project challenges, unique design solutions, and specific measurable results, all attributing to a successful contact center migration. The following sections detail a few of the variables that the team identified and resolved during the migration.

Challenges

The list that follows documents some of the challenges identified during the contact center migration:

- Technical

    - Maintaining consistency globally

    - Client use of features—that is, line appearance

    - Standardization

- Support

    - Overlay understanding of the call process

    - Repeat training, draining resources

    - Upgrade process moving forward

    - Global education and planning

Design Solutions

The list that follows documents some of the unique design solutions deployed during the contact center migration:

- Telephone system is Cisco CallManager (IP PBX).

- Automatic call distributor (ACD) is software in the Cisco Intelligent Call Management (ICM).

- Call routing rules are in ICM.

- Queuing of calls is in the Cisco IPIVR.

- Reporting is in the Cisco Webview reporting package.

- Call control is handled by the Cisco agent desktop, not the phone.

Results

The goals and benefits of this initiative were clear:

- Provide a worldwide test platform for Cisco IPCC Enterprise and Cisco IPCC Express technology for further testing and improvement.

- Implement the contact center solutions on time and on budget.

- Remove all TDM equipment at all Cisco contact centers.

- Drive outsourced call centers into Cisco IPCC solutions and integrate their IP environments into the Cisco enterprise IPCC platform.

- Increase feature functionality—including the ability to have supervisor functions at the desktop; the ability to have multichannel agents handling voice, e-mail, and web interactions; and the ability to close a contact center from a desktop in case of an emergency.

- Reduce support requirements.

- Reduce transport costs.

Cisco has seen its customer satisfaction levels increase substantially since installing Cisco IPCC Enterprise in its contact center environment. Cisco IPCC Enterprise replaced Lucent/Avaya ACDs at more than ten Cisco contact center sites.

"This has been an incredible effort," says Gibbs. "The project has been a real Cisco-wide endeavor encompassing resources from throughout Cisco: the business units, TAC, AVVID design/engineering and voice services, as well as all the individual contact center managers—internal, external, and outsourced. Everyone has truly worked together in the spirit of meeting this challenge!"

"We wanted to become free of traditional PBX hardware and remove contact center dependencies in Cisco's effort to be a complete IP voice and data network company," says Cisco Global Program Manager Cindy Mike. "We're now well on our way to achieving that goal. The project also enabled us to truly understand our global contact center landscape and have significant insight and 'best practices' to share with our customers."

Benefits

Following are some benefits from the Cisco IP customer contact implementation:

- Increased customer satisfaction scores

- One seamless experience regardless of access point

- Reduced call duration

- Increased usage of the web for reporting problems

- Decreased call volume by nearly 50 percent

- Improved holistic approach to customer entry

- Reduced transfers, not bounced around the company

- Increased first contact resolutions

- Capture of the customer experience

- Critical mass coverage 24×7

- Segmentation opportunity

- Smoother consolidation opportunities and success

- One point for vendor negotiations

- One point for third-party product selections

- Easy, successful optimization

- Position to grow front line skills

- Better negotiation opportunities

- Quality feedback, content, and design

- Capture of sales opportunities

- Shared use of LANs and WANs for voice, messaging, and data; economies of scale

- Public switched telephone network (PSTN) toll bypass via VoIP networking

- Centralization of communication servers and administration in a distributed enterprise

- XML application deployment to phones—that is, alerts, front end to internal help desks

- Consistent reporting and training of agents and supervisors

- Showcase of Cisco contact center products

"We also created a new Internet best practice with this project," says Mike. "The entire deployment was managed using the web as a project platform. Software was posted for the contact centers to download, avoiding the need for travel; status reports and directives were shared on the web; training, support resources, implementation details, and client information were all available to all team members via the Internet. It was truly a 'virtual' project—and that contributed greatly to our ability to meet the aggressive deadlines that were set."

"Phase one is just the foundation," says Doug Allred. "Only after we have the foundation in place can we begin to dream and change the way we interact with our customers."

NOTE   You can find more information about the Cisco IPCC migration at the following sites:

- http://www.cisco.com/en/US/products/sw/custcosw/ps1844/ products_case_study09186a00801534e2.shtml

- http://www.cisco.com/warp/public/cc/pd/cucxsw/prodlit/glob_sc.pdf

You can find Cisco best practices for an IPCC migration at http:// www.cisco.com/partner/WWChannels/technologies/IPCC/index.html. (A Cisco.com login is required.)

Cisco Wireless LAN Migration

Wireless LAN technology offers a path toward "anywhere, anytime" network connectivity, increases employee flexibility and mobility, offers increased productivity, and ensures greater workplace utility. In October 2001, we began to deploy the Cisco Aironet wireless LAN solution within the organization throughout 300 sites in more than 100 countries around the world.

Our challenge was in designing a truly global, scalable, and secure wireless end-to-end solution that would seamlessly integrate into our existing network infrastructure. We had to address issues such as integration into our existing enterprise management framework, global authentication, authorization, and accounting (AAA) architecture, and a common "user experience" regardless of geographical location. With the phased migration from NT to Active Directory running concurrently to our planned deployment schedule, active cross-functional teamwork between the entire IT organization and the Tiger Team was essential.

We had to address security issues that were inherent in deploying a wireless solution while keeping usability and operation seamless. Emphasizing one at the expense of the other would result in either an unusable but extremely secure wireless LAN, or a "wide open" but insecure wireless network. Careful reconciliation of these two considerations was essential.

A global and increasingly mobile workforce meant that architectural, procedural, and user standards were critical. User experience should be the same from San Jose to Sydney, and from London to Tokyo.

Finally, because wireless LANs are an emerging technology, it was critical that Cisco develop a solution and best practices that enterprise customers could leverage so that they, too, could achieve the significant productivity benefits that wireless LANs offer.

An architectural team was created to define business and user requirements, global architectural standards, support plans, and an ongoing management framework.

Pilot Testing

In early 2001, pilot testing resulted in the development of significant security enhancements to the Cisco Aironet product suite. These security enhancements, based on a Cisco developed Extensible Authentication Protocol (EAP) mechanism and known as EAP-Cisco Wireless (or LEAP), addressed known weaknesses in 802.11 security and immediately put Cisco Aironet at the forefront of wireless LAN technologies and the global WLAN marketplace.

At an early stage, the team decided that the wireless LAN in Cisco should be considered a productivity tool and mobility enabler. Therefore, ease of use and a common and pleasant user experience were essential. The Cisco worldwide wireless network would be architected along global scalable standards, effectively providing a single global wireless network.

Upon agreement of core business goals and design considerations, the architectural team went on to define a specific global architecture. The architectural team agreed that the theatre teams would have freedom to make local deployment decisions as long as they followed the minimum global standards. In this manner, Cisco ensured that our worldwide wireless LAN maintained a common global architecture, while providing for country- and theatre-specific considerations (such as aesthetic mounting of the access points).

Architectural Standards

The global architectural standards focused on security, network integration, naming standards, AAA, and physical installation considerations. The most important of these were as follows:

- Access Point 350 (AP)

- 802.11b standard (2.4 GHz offering 11 Mbps)

- Use of EAP-Cisco Wireless (aka LEAP) for security

- Separate VLAN for wireless network

- 25:1 user to AP ratio

- Global naming standards

- Integration into the Cisco EMAN system

- Use of Cisco Access Control Server (ACS) for AAA

A global deployment team was organized along theatre lines. Each theatre had a local project manager who was responsible for managing his regional deployment, implementing global design standards, and reporting to the global program manager. The global team met on a weekly basis to review architectural developments and to ensure global compliance with agreed standards and architecture.

Deployment began in early 2002. Trusted vendors and partners were engaged on a theatre-by-theatre basis for cabling and physical AP installation, while an experienced Cisco staff resource controlled and managed network integration and configuration. In this manner, the team achieved a rapid deployment pace. By August 2002, the global program team had completed more than 300 Cisco sites in more than 100 countries. A handful of additional sites have come on line since that time, mainly due to regulatory delays during the initial deployment (such as Cisco sites in India).

Results

The Cisco wireless LAN is now a fully deployed end-to-end solution in widespread use around the globe that includes the following:

- 3000+ Access Points

- 300+ sites

- 100+ countries

- 32,500+ clients and rising

- 802.11b wireless LAN standard (2.4 GHz, 11 Mbps)

- 13 ACS hubs for a globally distributed AAA architecture

In total, the team installed more than 3000 Access Point 350s within approximately eight months. Each AP was configured in line with global standards and differs only in the local ACS server to which it passes client authentication requests. In all, 13 ACS "hubs" are located in strategic places around the globe. This distributed architecture has resulted in reduced login times and offers the added benefit of a fully redundant AAA infrastructure.

Entitlement is all-inclusive and, as such, every Cisco employee receives a wireless NIC or wireless-enabled laptop. At present, Cisco has more than 32,500 wireless users, and this number is rising. Cisco now has the largest single enterprise deployment of a global wireless network.

At this stage, the wireless LAN is considered a secondary network; that is, it is not meant to replace or supercede our wired infrastructure. By its very nature, a wireless network based on unlicensed spectrum is subject to unforeseen service impacts. Mission-critical applications and services should still rely on our wired network. As architected, the Cisco Aironet WLAN is not ideally suited, for example, for video on demand, large-scale multicast services, latency-sensitive applications, and so on. However, it has been extremely successful in addressing its core business drivers: productivity enhancement and user mobility.

EMAN, the Cisco Enterprise Management framework, manages and maintains the wireless network. It provides configuration management, automated firmware updates, host monitoring, and other services. EMAN continually scans the network for rogue APs, which are a recurring threat for all wireless LANs and one of the challenges we had to address during deployment. Rogue APs are now uncommon, due to ubiquitous WLAN coverage, and are mitigated upon detection.

Next Steps

The future for the Cisco global wireless network is bright. Cisco IT shall continue to develop the solution, and we expect 2004 to bring several evolutionary developments, including the following:

- Provision of integrated guest WLAN hotspots by using Aironet's wireless VLAN functionality

- Introduction of wireless telephony using the latest Cisco wireless AVVID handset—the 7920

- Enhanced security, based on the upcoming 802.11i standard (which includes Advanced Encryption Standard, or AES, for U.S. Federal Information Processing Standards compliance)

- Wireless quality of service (QoS) (through 802.11e standards)

- Introduction of "higher speed" wireless radios—802.11a and 802.11g (both offering up to 54 Mbps bandwidth)

- The San Jose Mobile-Wireless Extended Remote Access (ERA) project to try and evaluate the viability and usefulness of a mobile data service for San Jose, the U.S., and Canada-based employees

The Cisco vision for a global wireless network aims to deliver a service-rich environment of persistent voice, video, and data applications and content to users of any device, via any access in any location. This vision enables high productivity and segmented services by maximizing the presence and leverage of Cisco technology in terminal devices, remote access networks (RANs), physical aggregation, service elements, network cores, and management.

NOTE   You can find Cisco best practices for deploying a Cisco wireless solution at http://www.cisco.com/partner/WWChannels/technologies/Wireless/index.html. (A Cisco.com login is required.)

Adoption has been more widespread and much more popular than anticipated. Although a "priority level 4 (P4) service (explained in more detail in Chapter 5, "Day 2 Handoff and Support"), day-to-day usage is significant and continues to rise. Users appreciate being untethered from their desks. User mobility and productivity have improved significantly. Based on an independent National Opinion Poll (NOP) world study, and given a reported average salary of U.S. $64,000, our findings indicate that the annual productivity improvement per user is worth, on average, U.S $7000. For the average large corporate organization, this productivity improvement is worth as much as U.S. $6.3 million per year.

Furthermore, by providing ubiquitous coverage, Cisco IT has successfully reduced the number of rogue APs. With universal access, users no longer need to set up their own noncompliant access points. Additionally, our global WLAN solution has provided "walk-in, online" access in any Cisco office across the globe, as well as network connectivity to areas that have traditionally been unwired or had limited network access. These include meeting rooms, executive briefing center areas, cafeterias, and reception areas. Even network communication rooms benefit from WLAN access because support staff is free to roam data centers without being limited by having to physically connect their laptops to—and possibly impact—production network switches.

Figure 7-9 depicts the Cisco mobility vision.

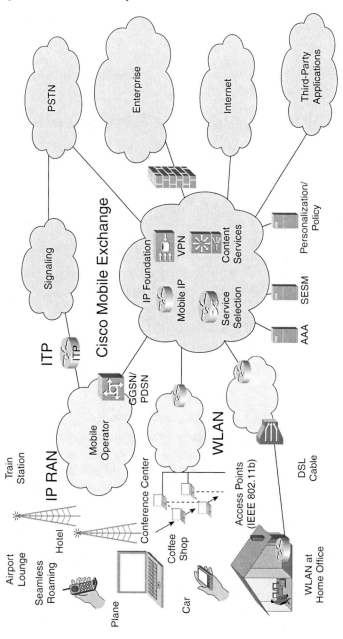

Figure 7-9   *The Cisco Mobility Vision*

Overall, the global deployment of wireless LANs within Cisco has been a complete success. By carefully defining our business goals, agreeing on a scalable global architecture and support framework, and continuing to add value and evolve the network, Cisco has shown and reaped the significant benefits that wireless technology brings to the enterprise.

Maintaining Five-9s on the New Network

A smooth migration and a new network are tremendous accomplishments. However, if a network is unreliable, unstable, and unavailable, all the positive effects and goals set for organizational improvements will never be realized. For an update on how Cisco maintained its new network, I have turned this section over to Darrell Root, Cisco network engineer. Darrell will tell you how his team has been able to extract almost unheard of availability from the new LAN. In Darrell's own words...

July 1, 2003 marked the first day that the network devices in the San Jose CallManager LAN cluster had been up for a full year with 100.000 percent availability. That's right—not 99.999 percent availability, but 100.000 percent availability. In addition, the LAN networks in the data centers in San Jose 12 and San Jose D have been up for a full year with 99.999 percent availability. That means that they have had unscheduled outages totaling less than 5.3 minutes for the entire year.

How did the Cisco IT network operations San Jose team do it? The success required good design, a solid change management process, reliable tools, effective processes, and the discipline to apply these processes consistently and continually.

The Cisco IT LAN in San Jose is enormous, spanning more than 55 buildings and supporting 18,000 people. Maintaining this complex LAN is the responsibility of the Cisco IT LAN San Jose team. From July 2002 through June 2003, this team achieved a significant and enviable accomplishment: 99.995 percent availability across the entire San Jose LAN. The IT LAN San Jose team achieved 99.998 percent availability in data centers during the same time period. That is less than 11 minutes of downtime for the entire year.

Because the network is a critical enabler of employee productivity, Cisco must achieve at least four 9s to function efficiently. But five 9s is the availability that businesses aspire to reach. This is another example of Cisco leadership, demonstrating new levels of IT excellence in the networking industry.

Achieving high availability is a result of optimizing people, processes, and technology. Cisco IT has achieved high availability by using a combination of these factors. As a result, business efforts around increasing productivity can continue uninterrupted by network outages and downtime. This is quite an achievement, considering all the Cisco leading-edge technologies we deploy and showcase on our global production network. For example, traditional telecommunication demands five-9s availability due to its business-critical nature. With the advent of IP Telephony, high availability is paramount to sustaining business operations. Now Cisco can show its converged network approaches the reliability of a telecommunications network, which will spur faster adoption of IP Telephony in the marketplace.

Spanning 55 buildings throughout San Jose and serving desktops, data centers, laboratories, and manufacturing, the Cisco IT LAN San Jose network consists of 900 switches, 200 routers, 250 console servers, 800 Cisco Aironet access points, and an assortment of content-switching devices inside the Cisco firewall.

Despite its size and complexity, the San Jose network approached 99.999 percent availability in 2002. During the second calendar quarter of 2003, in areas where a 100 percent uninterruptible power supply (UPS) and generators reinforce the network, Cisco IT LAN San Jose achieved 99.99853 percent availability.

If you would like to know more about how we accomplished this availability, you can read about it in my recently published white paper, "How Cisco IT-LAN-SJ Achieved High Availability." You can download the full 39-page PDF version of the white paper from http://www.cisco.com/en/US/tech/tk869/tk769/tech_white_papers_list.html. Note: Cisco practices are specific to the Cisco environment; their use elsewhere does not ensure that the same results will be obtained in a different environment.

Cisco Unity Voice Mail Migration

Program Unity, a joint initiative between the IT organization and the voice technology group, will begin implementing Cisco Unity voice messaging across Cisco in February 2004. The first phase of the global deployment will include the campuses at Sydney, Amsterdam, London, Research Triangle Park (RTP), and San Jose, as well as some sites to be serviced from their data centers. As project sponsors of the Cisco Unity migration, Lance Perry, Cisco vice president of IT, and Don Proctor, Cisco vice president of voice technology group, anticipate that more than 75 percent of the Cisco user population will be migrated to Unity voice messaging by the end of the first phase.

Cisco Unity voice messaging will offer advanced networked voice messaging functionality, including the ability to send and receive voice messages from a web browser. Integration between the phone and PC interfaces will provide users with greater flexibility to manage their voice messages.

The Cisco Unity program will be the largest global deployment of Unity to date, replacing 160 Avaya Octel systems with 45 Cisco Unity voice messaging systems, eliminating more than U.S. $7 million paid annually to a Cisco competitor. With Unity voice messaging, Cisco users will have the same set of conversation features across all theatres, simplifying the current environment, which consists of two different Avaya Octel systems.

This is a voice messaging-only solution. Although Cisco Unity as a product is scaleable to support unified messaging (UM) through integration with Microsoft Exchange and Lotus Notes, a corporate-wide UM solution will not be implemented in Cisco in fiscal year 2004. Meanwhile, we continue to demonstrate the use of UM at showcase sites in San Jose, the Americas, and EMEA.

Global Implementation Strategy

The Cisco Unity voice mail deployment is a phased approach for which every user throughout Cisco will be affected. The following highlights the global implementation strategy used in the deployment.

Global Implementation—Phase 1

1 Build out core infrastructure—alternate mark inversion (AMI), APAC, EMEA, San Jose

2 Migrate clients at small AMI site—Grand Rapids, Michigan (17 clients)

3 Migrate clients at small APAC site—8 sites in Australia and New Zealand (approximately 200 clients)

4 Migrate clients at medium AMI site—Atlanta, Georgia (250 clients)

5 Migrate clients at a campus—Sydney, Australia (approximately 900 clients)

6 Migrate clients at RTP and San Jose on the same weekend (approximately 20,000 clients)

7 Migrate clients at London, England and Amsterdam, The Netherlands campuses (approximately 8000 clients)

Global Implementation—Phase 2

1 Build remaining infrastructure — AMI, APAC, EMEA

2 Migrate remaining clients — AMI, APAC, EMEA

Cisco Unity Architecture Summary

- Consolidate from 160 current Octel systems to 45 centralized Cisco Unity voice mail systems.

- Cut the largest populated sites (75 percent of users, high volume network traffic) first.

- Cut remaining sites (25 percent of users, low volume network traffic) as feasible. These sites will leverage a combination of Octel and Cisco Unity Bridge technology during "hybrid" state.

- Utilize separate Active Directory Forest and Exchange infrastructure to speed up the deployment process.

TIP	The key to ensuring that you have the most optimal voice mail design is to pay close attention to the power phone user and not the typical phone user. For those who rarely use e-mail but are constantly on the phone, voice messaging is their primary method of communication, and their usage should help dictate the user feature requirements.

This major global deployment of Cisco Unity voice messaging represents a further return on investment (ROI) from our acquisition of Active Voice. We are pleased to be able to offer the benefits of yet another leading Cisco technology to our Cisco users.

NOTE	You can find Cisco best practices for deploying a Cisco Unity solution at http://www.cisco.com/partner/WWChannels/technologies/Unity/index.html. (A Cisco.com account is required.)

Cisco Unity Architecture (Pre/Post)

As Cisco prepares for the Cisco Unity deployment, the project team will have to convert more than 160 voice mail solutions located around the world, as illustrated in Figure 7-10.

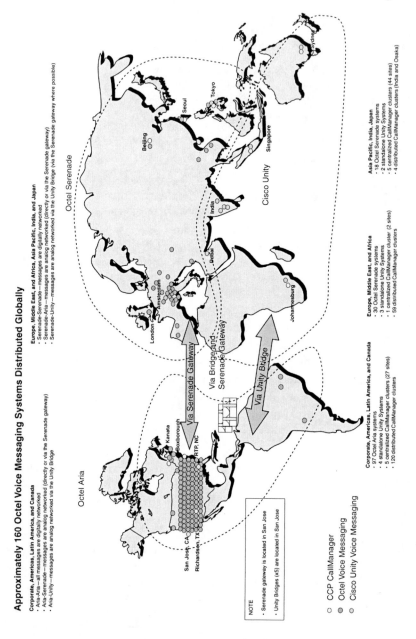

Figure 7-10   *Cisco Voice Messaging Environment During Migration*

(338)

When the Cisco Unity deployment is complete, 45 Cisco Unity voice messaging systems will be distributed globally, as illustrated in Figure 7-11.

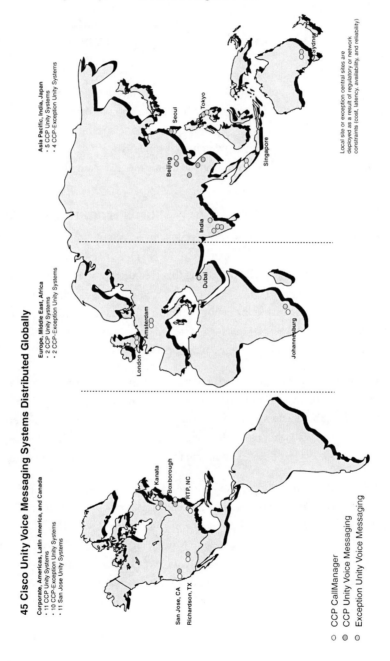

Figure 7-11 *Cisco Voice Messaging Environment After Unity Deployment*

(339)

Conclusion

We have come a long way since 2000. Just three years ago, the Cisco telephony system was based on an all-PBX infrastructure. Today, we have deployed more than 54,500 IP phones and 234 IP CallManagers worldwide. In San Jose alone, 23,700 IP phones operate in a single cluster, with availability of 99.999 percent.

Pushing forward continues to keep Cisco IT busy. The deployment of a centralized call processing model, preparation for video, and implementation of the wave of existing and future XML applications are projects that peak on the Cisco horizon. However, pushing the envelope and finding more ways to be even more productive, efficient, and mobile is part of Cisco culture and will always be our organization's biggest strength.

What It Has Meant to Me... A Few Words from the Author

It has been almost two years since Cisco completed the retrofit of our San Jose campus, and I never get tired of telling the story of how we did it. I still remember the day my manager informed me that I would be project managing this Herculean endeavor. I recall my concerns and questioning of whether I was experienced enough, whether I would be able to lead the team, and whether I knew enough about IP Telephony to lead the charge. Of course, the answer to all these questions was yes. I just needed to remember all the lessons I had learned from my 10 years of managing projects.

It all comes down to this. Plan the plan. Build a strong team around you. Communicate the vision. Identify the risk. Develop and maintain key relationships. Do not try to do too much. Build confidence within the teams. Do not be afraid to ask stupid questions. Keep copious notes. Keep the obstacles clear so that the team can do what it was assigned to do. Always remember that this project is not just about the technology; it is about the people.

This project really tested my abilities and allowed me to prove to myself that if I could do this, I could do anything. I cannot tell you how many times I needed to call in a favor, calm down an anxious end user, or ask the team to keep going when it wanted to slow down. My focus was clear, and my mission was eminent: Migrate the campus, and do it right the first time. Of course, we made some mistakes along the way, but we captured many best practices and lessons learned. I am so proud that we were not only the first to use IP Telephony on such a large scale, but that we did it with minimal customer impact.

And Now... A Word from Our Sponsors

"By moving aggressively to integrate IP communications throughout our global business, Cisco has realized a significantly lower total cost of ownership for voice communications while enabling new capabilities that are not possible with traditional TDM-based systems. We 'walked the talk' on IP communications, and as a result, we are enjoying the benefits of increased productivity, more effective communications between workgroups, and improved competitive advantage."

—Don Proctor, Cisco vice president of voice technology group

"Our conversion to VoIP has not only resulted in direct cost savings, but has also simplified the setup and maintenance of single back-end systems, such as databases. We no longer consider services such as voice, data, and storage as separate technology silos, but as services delivered over one converged, intelligent network. Looking back, it is hard for us to imagine doing it any other way. Looking forward, I think the biggest gains are yet to come as they lie in the applications associated with increasing employee productivity and improving services to our customers. We see this in our IP contact center applications and are just starting to see it in our IP phone service offerings. As Cisco continues to break new ground in the application of advanced technologies, I hope the industry will benefit from our experiences in ways we've only dreamed of before."

—Lance Perry, Cisco vice president of IT infrastructure

"It took two years to migrate Cisco to a full VoIP network. Today we have over 54,000 active IP phones. It has become an integral part of our IP communications network. We moved for several reasons: to showcase our technology, to improve employee productivity, and, of course, to reduce cost. During that migration process, we learned a lot about how to execute a company-wide cutover, including what to do and what not to do. This deployment has been a launching pad for many new services and conveniences that will enable Cisco to provide better service to its customers and greater flexibility for its employees. Cisco IT wants to share its implementation experience with Cisco customers and partners to aide in the deployment practices of new Cisco technologies. While conducting our own company-wide cutover, we learned a great deal about what to do and what not to do. This book shares our experiences. I encourage you to contact us and let us know how we can help share our best practices with you."

—Brad Boston, Cisco senior vice president and chief information officer

Lessons Learned

The following is a consolidation of the lessons we learned throughout each stage of the initiative, contributed by members of the Tiger Team who were front and center from beginning to end. Although I have delivered more than 400 customer briefings outlining the Cisco migration story, there are still key lessons and critical success factors that we have learned, including the following.

Communication

Without senior management support and sponsorship, the integration and acceptance of new world technology will ultimately fail or at least make it harder to gain acceptance. The technology strategy, your infrastructure, and the business strategy must be in synch toward a vision that will move all media and functional types of customer interactions to the next highest level, to a competitive advantage, to incremental improvements in customer satisfaction and loyalty.

Team/Relationships

Those involved in the original design and engineering of the new solution know the technology intimately. Involve the engineering team when making strategic implementation decisions to leverage their expertise for unique configurations and workarounds. Keep the engineering team close (and happy) because when you get into technical trouble, they will be your biggest allies.

Planning/Strategic

Starting the implementation before you know the "must-have" features is the ultimate mistake. Ensure that unique configurations are identified early. A mistake here can cause an immediate slowdown while fixes are developed and put into place. Know your users, and identify the product features that are "must have" versus "nice to have" before you begin. Also, do not forget your network readiness plan (IP Telephony ready infrastructure, QoS, inline power, security, LAN availability).

Strategic Placement of Equipment

Place servers in diverse data centers on campus, equally balancing the load and failover redundancy. Be sure to address your power backup requirements for the equipment.

Understand the Current Environment

Each department and group uses telephony differently. Study customer usage for usage patterns and requirements of the business. Conduct a user survey that identifies those "must-have" features, and review your PBX configuration report early to ensure that you do not have any surprises. Pay attention to the details, conduct a thorough site survey, and create a customer service model that minimizes end-user impact.

Migration Strategy

Create a plan that does not allow anyone to fall through the cracks. A phased migration is a great alternative to a flash cut when numerous users and solutions are involved. New buildings, new employees, and all adds, moves, and changes are a good start. Ensure that your schedule is realistic yet aggressive so that you keep the momentum going. If you do not have the expertise, get help. If the planning process is not well executed, you will see all the mistakes manifested throughout the migration. Pilots and time for proof of concept will flush out the surprises and create a standard for everyone to use during the installation phase.

Technology

The standard for desktop Ethernet service provides two 10/100 patches to each CAT 5 wall plate—one live jack for the IP phone with the PC connecting to the phone. We forgot to ask a basic question: "Tell us how you are using your phone today." We assumed we knew. What a big mistake that was. Global dial plan is a key watch for surprises: modems, faxes, operator consoles, call center applications. Special in-country ISDN signaling voice is a service, and CallManager is a server; you have to manage the relationship between the service and the server and bring an NT expert on board. (Availability and security are the keys.) Also, remember to certify those third-party applications that will hang off the CallManager. Get the vendors involved.

Process

Apply key rules of successful IT projects. Change management, organizational culture influences, and the governance board are critical. (Project tools, process, and change management are all components.) Remember that this is about service, not just technology (service, people, technology). Do not let the engineering team drive the project requirements because they are looking at the process from an engineering view, not from an end-user view (that is, phased migration versus flash cut). Use solid project management to determine when it is time to move to the next phase. Plan the plan, and always remember to communicate. Communication will save you every time!

Operations

Use the "clean network" philosophy when defining your implementation guidelines. The retrofit is a perfect opportunity to start out with a clean network. Focus on what you use, not what you have. Operational policies will accommodate the new voice and data converged network and keep it clean and stable.

Optimize

After the IP Telephony solution is up and running, keep it functioning at optimal levels. Use IP Telephony-enabled monitoring and troubleshooting tools that allow you to manage it reactively and proactively.

Get the Project Team Thinking

If you find yourself in a meeting with your project team, and you begin to feel overwhelmed as to the right questions you should be asking, just relax. Never let the team see you sweat; help is on the way. Take along my checklist of questions to ask your project team as a tool to jump-start the discussion. Be bold, and schedule a planning workshop to get the team thinking. Although this questionnaire does not cover everything (you will need to read the book for that), it does encompass the many key questions that customers continue to forget and can help you flush out key areas where project teams often get stuck.

Appendix 7-A: Stephanie's Checklist of Questions to Ask the Project Team

Use this questionnaire to jump-start your migration strategy discussions during your team planning workshop. Make sure you have answers before you begin the migration. You can offset this questionnaire by using the Cisco Services and Support Blueprint and Checklist, found on the Cisco Steps to Success site at http://www.cisco.com/go/stepstosuccess. (A Cisco.com login is required.)

Appendix 7-A is available at the following URL in its complete form for download: http://www.ciscopress.com/1587200880.

Planning

❑ How will you determine if the current network is ready for convergence?

❑ How will you navigate the change from the current network to a single IP infrastructure?

❑ What specific hardware, software, and infrastructure changes do you need for a converged network?

❑ What kind of experience, tools, and methodologies are necessary to take advantage of the converged technologies?

❑ How will the staff learn to manage the converged IP network? Who will manage it? Has time in the schedule been allocated for staff training?

❑ Have you established a training curriculum for the existing staff members? Have you met certification requirements for those resources?

❑ How will this new technology impact the end users? Have you interviewed the end users or conducted a voice of the client survey to determine their risk factors?

❑ Has anyone looked at your communication plan and what your key messaging should be?

❑ Have you created a governance model? What about a change management process?

❑ What does success look like? Have you incorporated additional tasks or deliverables that will contribute to the ROI?

❑ What does failure look like? How will you eliminate buyer's remorse?

❑ Who are the stakeholders? What are their high-risk factors? Which groups require zero failure rate?

❑ Have you conducted an IP Telephony assessment? How about an operational assessment?

❑ Are the goals and requirements for the rollout tied to another objective? (For example, increase productivity by 75 percent; increase efficiencies by 50 percent, and so on.)

❑ Has a financial controller been assigned to the project to keep cost at a minimum? Will the controller also track key savings and ROI considerations?

❑ Have you defined a migration strategy? What is driving the schedule? Is leased equipment involved? Are you considering a phased migration? Is there a timetable for when the project should be complete? Is there a penalty if the project runs late?

❑ Have you conducted an organizational change readiness review to determine your readiness scale or change tolerance?

❑ What is your content management plan? Have you established naming convention standards for easy access to all documents? Is the plan scalable and accessible to all team members? Do you have a project website to house this information? Can you password-protect sensitive documents?

❑ Are there gaps within the partner's ability to deliver? Are there gaps within the ability for Cisco to deliver? Are there gaps within the customer's ability to deliver?

❑ Has a clear path of responsibility been determined among Cisco, the partner, and the customer? Are there gray areas? Did you conduct a blueprint checklist of roles and responsibilities? Have you created an ongoing action plan or customer to-do list?

❑ Have you created a project alias so that timely information can be shared among the customer, Cisco, and the partner?

❑ Are you including the local site manager in the planning discussions? There might be some unusual considerations that only the site manager can flush out.

❑ Which tools will you use to ensure that the project says on track? Will you follow the standards already set by existing Cisco tools?

❑ Does the partner have an existing voice practice? Does the partner follow a planning, design, implementation, operations, and optimization (PDIOO) model? Have you reviewed it with Cisco and identified any gaps?

❑ Do you have a plan in place to address how to minimize customer impact? What about the customer service behavior each team should adhere to? Are your organizational culture standards an influencer here?

❑ Do you have a plan to automate all your standard processes? Will you take advantage of the web to make processes easily accessible? This will help with scale and consistently. Conduct a frequent review of these processes to flush out a problem that could be occurring every time you cut a site.

❑ Will you need to reinvest the savings that a new IP Telephony solution will deliver? Do you have a plan or process to capture these savings?

❑ Have you identified which services you need to offset the resource gaps? Have you begun discussions regarding the support strategy?

❑ Have you conducted a services and support checklist review to determine which services are required to support the migration?

Design

❑ What core functionality or design considerations do your key stakeholders/business units require?

❑ Has the customer provided a recent copy of the existing network topology? Who will create the newly proposed data network topology?

❑ Who are the high-risk users where failure is not an option? Have you established or discussed solutions or workarounds?

❑ Have you defined the core "must-have" functionality for the design? What unusual considerations must be addressed in the design?

❑ Will the implementation and support team be part of the design strategy? They should be.

❑ Does your design team include Cisco staff, the senior network design engineer, and the existing voice/data teams? Do they have concerns?

❑ Did you conduct an overall voice/network readiness and health review of your current infrastructure?

❑ Have you identified all the migration or integration considerations?

❑ Has someone interviewed or conducted a user survey of the stakeholders to ensure that the design requirements will meet their expectations?

❑ Did you compare the PBX dump with your new design? Are there gaps?

❑ Have you created a customer to-do list? What about a Cisco to-do list or a partner to-do list? Be sure to define all roles and responsibilities.

❑ Will your new design require users to change their phone numbers? How will you handle speed dial and distribution list conversions?

❑ Do you have a process for capturing all open technical issues? Is there a technical design issues log? Who is tracking the resolution of these issues to the entire design project team? Do you plan to ask Cisco or the partner for recommendations on how to resolve these technical design issues?

❑ Have you identified all the applications with which the new IP Telephony solution will have to integrate? Do you have a third-party application certification plan to ensure that the new solution will integrate? Have you contacted the vendors and gained their support for the point of contact?

❑ Have you conducted a user station review? Did it include attendants, administrative assistants, executives, standard users, and power users? Did you include those requirements in the design requirements?

❑ Have you contacted the third-party application vendors to gain their support for the point of contact and testing? Did you receive certification that the various applications will integrate with the new IP Telephony solution?

Implementation

❑ Who is the champion/sponsor of the migration? Have you begun communications that outline the reasons for this conversion?

❑ Have you established a project website that offers FAQs, a project schedule, training, two-way communication and feedback, and so on?

❑ Have you incorporated your culture into the migration plan? Culture dictates acceptance. Include all forms of familiarity in your plan.

❑ Do you have candidates/site locations for the pilot phase? Have you identified acceptance criteria for the pilot and proof of concept?

❑ What expectations do the users have? What is the training strategy for users and administrators? Have you established the training documentation requirements?

❑ Have you considered new employees as prime candidates for the new IP Telephony solution? You should, because change is already familiar to them.

❑ Have you identified a migration plan for your critical phone users? Does this include your senior management staff and their admin staff? Their needs are different and require extreme sensitivity.

❑ Does your migration plan include a crawl-walk-run approach?

❑ Do you have a plan to migrate the entire project team (including design and engineering, support, the installers, and the project management team) first so that they can get a better understanding of the new technology from a users' perspective?

❑ Does your implementation plan allow you to start with a bigger implementation team and scale back as the process becomes more fluid and streamlined?

❑ Do you have a plan to address user questions on Day after the cutover? Will you use your existing call center staff to manage calls, or will a special dedicated team be put in place? Do you have a transition plan to route all user calls to the support center on Day 2?

❑ Have you dedicated resources to manage the operations room (aka war room)? Will this be a virtual team, or will an onsite resource be required?

❑ Have you created a site escalation path for when something goes wrong during the cut? What about a backout procedure or a backup of key users who have unique configurations?

❑ Do you have a plan to measure the efficiencies of your installation team so that the migration process can go faster rather than slower as your experience level grows?

❑ Have you outlined the requirements for your cookbook that include the standards for which every site and theatre will follow?

❑ Have you considered how your culture dictates training? Use a method that is familiar and one that has worked in the past.

❑ Have you identified a test procedure for the placement of all new phones? Will you test each phone as you place it or utilize software that will do it after the fact?

❑ Have you selected a day of the week for when your site cutover will happen? Saturdays allow for minimum customer impact and also give you an extra day to fix a problem if something goes wrong.

❑ Do you have a selection process for the pilot site? How will you ensure that key members of the team participate and learn from the experience?

❑ Have you incorporated a training strategy for your administrators in your project plan? Make sure you allow time for this.

❑ Do you have a senior manager assigned to manage user escalations on Day 1? Make sure your policies are consistent.

❑ Does your training plan address the needs of your administrative assistant staff? Pay special attention to them because they can be your biggest supporter or nemeses if they cannot work their new phone.

Operate

❑ Have you created customer service standards for each deployment member? SLA is key here.

❑ How long will you manage the Day 1 activities (24 hours, 48 hours, and so on)? Do you have a solid hand-off plan? Be sure to capture the customer FAQs for the implementation and support teams.

❏ How will you capture your lessons learned so that the other sites can benefit from them?

❏ A converged network should also include a converged team. How will your network and voice teams work together? Will you cross-train the team on each other's jobs so that adverse mistakes do not bring down the network?

❏ During IT freeze cycles, what will the implementation team do to maintain momentum? What does your freeze policy say? What can or can't you do during the freeze that might halt the schedule?

❏ Do you have a backout process for when something goes wrong? How about an escalation path when problems occur? How will you keep documentation up to date and accessible?

❏ Will you require spares for each site? Have you identified a resource to allocate phones in a pinch?

❏ Do you plan to create a cookbook of standards for which each site and member will adhere?

❏ Will you require special monitoring and troubleshooting tools to manage your new network?

❏ What can you do to minimize a large flux of calls coming into the existing call center? FAQs, collaboration tools, special phone lines, special time of day/type of call routing, clear and concise communication, and training are all considerations.

❏ Have you addressed how to handle onsite adds, moves, and changes? Have you established a process or resource for managing the IP phone allocation for new employees? Will you require remote access to your network to create these?

❏ Does your new network allow you to grow? Does it have a balance of what you need versus what you use? Alternatively, does your network balance what you use versus what you need?

❏ Does your migration plan include the disconnection of all unused analog lines? How about unused and forgotten T1 and 1-MB lines? Use this time to clean up your network, and only migrate those lines that have been verified as valid.

❏ Have secondary phones been discussed? Who will receive them? Will the new network support them? How about a solution for your telecommuters? A new solution requires a new and updated policy.

❏ Will you assign floor walkers on Day 1 of the cutover to ensure that users have visible support? Have you created behavior standards for them and given them FAQ documents?

❏ Have you conducted a session to explain Day 2/Cisco TAC benefits and limitations based on your service contract? How, when, and who should engage operational support? What should you do prior to calling the operational Day 2 service provider?

❏ Who will be responsible for all project documentation? When will you give all the appropriate as-built documentation to the customer?

Optimizations

❏ When will you conduct or schedule performance audits of the customer's network?

❏ When will you schedule an optimization workshop to discuss optimization considerations?

❏ How will you schedule and plan major software/hardware upgrades as new releases become available?

❏ When will the customer see new XML applications that tie to his vertical and offer IP Telephony enhancements?

❏ When will the customer be ready to look at ways to improve call center optimization?

❏ Will you schedule optimization sessions to review and offer improvements to better manage your moves, adds, and changes? Have you considered making this function a remotely managed task?

NOTE   Be sure to use your Steps to Success Project Plan Poster to keep track of these and all the PDIOO deliverables that are associated with delivering your Cisco IP Telephony solution. The poster exists online under the original ISBN: ciscopress.com/1587200880 under the downloads link.

CUSTOMER CONCERNS

The Road to IP Telephony was developed in direct response to customer concerns of complexity, resources, timing, implementation, training, support, and other issues relative to deploying an enterprise-wide IPT solution throughout an organization. This book addresses a majority of concerns and questions that have been voiced by customers attending Executive Briefing Centers (EBCs) and via other methods of collecting feedback. Table A-1 provides a matrix that identifies some of the concerns and where you can find them in the book.

Table A-1 *IP Telephony Customer Concerns and Mapping to Book Chapter That Covers Them*

Customer Concern	Book Subtitle Location	Chapter Where the Answer Can Be Found						
		1	2	3	4	5	6	7
Getting the organization on board with the conversion	Executive Management Sponsorship		✔					
Managing accountability without sufficient resources, teams, and decision-making authority Insufficient coordination and teamwork	Importance of a Cross-Functional Team		✔					
Lack of communication	The Communication Plan			✔				
User acceptance and integration Managing employee expectations	Managing Change		✔					
Building a plan when you don't know when to start Managing project scope creep	Planning the Implementation: Steps to Success				✔			
Balancing current projects versus IP Telephony rollout requirements	Managing Change Where Do You Begin? The Engineering Story		✔					
Differentiating between a phased migration and a flash cut Developing migration strategy	The Migration Strategy (all of Chapter 3)			✔				

Table A-1 *IP Telephony Customer Concerns and Mapping to Book Chapter That Covers Them (Continued)*

Customer Concern	Book Subtitle Location	Chapter Where the Answer Can Be Found						
		1	2	3	4	5	6	7
Preparing the network for IP Telephony	Understand Your Infrastructure		✔					
Changing network designs, objectives, and policies	Identify Operational Policy Changes The Cisco LAN Infrastructure Preparing the WAN Provisioning the VLAN			✔	✔			
Returning current legacy equipment while maintaining relationship with vendor	Vendor Rules of Engagement						✔	
Managing PBX lease returns	PBX Lease Returns						✔	
Managing QoS*	QoS on the Cisco IT Network				✔			
What could go wrong during the deployment	The Good, the Bad, and the Ugly Project Risk Assessment			✔	✔			
Managing support of the new network Building a solid support model, team training requirements, and the right support tools	The Support Tools					✔		
User frequently asked questions	Appendix 3-E: User Frequently Asked Questions			✔				
Identifying training needs	User Training			✔				
Key lessons learned	Lessons Learned							✔
Key questions to ask the project team once they get started	Appendix 7-A: Stephanie's Checklist of Questions to Ask the Project Team							✔

continues

Table A-1 *IP Telephony Customer Concerns and Mapping to Book Chapter That Covers Them (Continued)*

Customer Concern	Book Subtitle Location	Chapter Where the Answer Can Be Found						
		1	2	3	4	5	6	7
Finding out about bug fixes and software upgrades	Software Upgrades						✔	
Special considerations when converting senior management staff	Best Practices: Converting Executive Row			✔				
Skill and experience requirements for building a team	AVVID Tiger Team		✔					
Managing change and setting the right expectations	Managing Change		✔					
Planning the network for the future	What's Next for Cisco							✔
Maintaining five 9s on the LAN network	Maintaining Five 9s on the New Network							✔
Standards guide used by implementation team	Retrofit Implementation Guide				✔			

* QoS = quality of service.

(356)

GLOSSARY

This glossary provides a table of prevalent acronyms in the book, along with their expansions and definitions. For a comprehensive list of IP Telephony terms and definitions, check out http://www.cisco.com/univercd/cc/td/doc/product/voice/ evbug14.htm#xtocid18819.

Acronym	Expansion	Definition
AVVID	Architecture for Voice, Video and Integrated Data	Cisco AVVID provides the baseline infrastructure that enables enterprises to design networks that scale to meet Internet business demands. Cisco AVVID delivers the e-business infrastructure and intelligent network services that are essential for rapid deployment of emerging technologies and new Internet business solutions.
BAT	Bulk Administration Tool	BAT is a plug-in application to the Cisco CallManager. BAT enables you to add up to 10,000 phones and users to the Cisco CallManager application. Using BAT, you can also perform bulk modifications to phones and delete several phones at one time.
BDF	Building Distribution Frame	BDF is the main wiring closet for a building. The other wiring closets in the building tie back to the BDF.
CDP	Cisco Discovery Protocol	CDP is used primarily to obtain protocol addresses of neighboring devices and discover the platform of those devices. CDP also can be used to display information about the interfaces that your router uses. CDP is media and protocol independent. It runs on all Cisco-manufactured equipment, including routers, bridges, access servers, and switches.

Acronym	Expansion	Definition
CDR	Call Detail Record (Cisco CallManager)	**1.** A record written to a database for use in post-processing activities. CDR files consist of several CDBs. These activities include many functions, but primarily include billing and network analysis. The Cisco CallManager writes CDRs to the SQL database as calls are made in a manner that is consistent with the configuration of each Cisco CallManager. **2.** Call detail record. Used in the original telephony networks and now extended to mobile wireless network calls, the CDR contains billing information for charging purposes. In a general packet radio service (GPRS) network, the charging gateway sends the billing information within a CDR to that subscriber's network service provider. **3.** call detail record. A Virtual Networking Services (VNS) record of voice or data switched virtual circuits (SVCs), which includes calling and called numbers, local and remote node names, data and time stamp, elapsed time, and call failure class fields.
DHCP	Dynamic Host Configuration Protocol	A protocol that provides a mechanism for allocating IP addresses dynamically so that addresses can be reused when hosts no longer need them.
DNS	Domain Name Service	A system used on the Internet to translate names of network nodes into addresses.
DTS	Defect Tracking System	The place where software defects are recorded. Each defect is defined with a number of attributes to describe the problem that was found. Those attributes provide the engineering leaders insight into the nature of the problem, where it was introduced, and the component where the problem occurred. Using the defect attributes, the team can ascertain whether the problem is systemic in nature, based on defect trends, or fairly unique. The trending information enables the team to drill down in their analysis to find the underlying causes of problems and use that analysis to repair the software and, if necessary, to improve the process that injected the problem.

continues

Acronym	Expansion	Definition
EPN	Expansion Port Network	EPN is an additional Avaya PBX cabinet(s) that does not contain CPU equipment and can be placed remotely from the Primary Port Network (PPN) cabinet.
IDF	Intermediate Distribution Frame	IDF is a secondary wiring closet for a building. The wall plates in cubes, offices, and other rooms tie back to an IDF. The IDF in turn ties back to a BDF.
IPT	IP Telephony	The transmission of voice and fax phone calls over data networks that use the Internet Protocol (IP). IPT is the result of the transformation of the circuit-switched telephone network to a packet-based network that deploys voice-compression algorithms and flexible and sophisticated transmission techniques. The IPT network delivers richer services using only a fraction of traditional digital telephony's usual bandwidth. IPT relies on an IP network to transmit voice. Voice is treated as the payload in an IP packet.
LAN	local-area network	A high-speed, low-error data network covering a relatively small geographic area (up to a few thousand square meters). LANs connect workstations, peripherals, terminals, and other devices in a single building or in another geographically limited area. LAN standards specify cabling and signaling at the OSI reference model's physical and data link layers.
MAC	moves/adds/changes (can also mean IP address)	For the purpose of this document, MAC means moves/adds/changes. It does not mean IP address in networking terms; it means Media Access Control. An Ethernet address would be a MAC address.
Mbit	Megabit	Approximately 1,000,000 bits.
MGCP	Media Gateway Control Protocol	A protocol that helps bridge the gap between circuit-switched and IP networks. A combination of Internet Protocol Device Control (IPDC) and Simple Gateway Control Protocol (SGCP). MGCP lets software programs externally control and manage data communications devices, or *media gateways,* at the edge of multiservice packet networks.
MTBF	mean time between failure	The average number of hours between failures for a particular device.

Acronym	Expansion	Definition
MTTR	mean time to repair	The average time needed to return a failed device or system to service.
NAT	Network Address Translation	A mechanism for reducing the need for globally unique IP addresses. NAT allows an organization with addresses that are not globally unique to connect to the Internet by translating those addresses into globally routable address space.
NOC	network operations center	An organization that is responsible for maintaining a network.
PBX	private branch exchange	A telephone switch used within an organization or company to connect private and public telephone networks. PBX is the preferred term in the United States, whereas private automatic branch exchange (PABX) is used in Europe.
PPN	Primary Port Network	The PPN is the first cabinet in an Avaya PBX that contains the CPU of the PBX and, depending on configuration, station and trunk ports.
PSTN	public switched telephone network (PBX)	A general term referring to the variety of telephone networks and services in place worldwide. Sometimes called plain old telephone service (POTS).
ROI	return on investment	ROI is used by the IT community to try to figure out if an IT investment can pay off the same or better than other investments a company might make. The traditional definition of ROI is that for a given use of money in an enterprise, the ROI is how much "return," usually profit or cost saving, results. Generally, companies try to calculate ROI based on hard benefits only. That is because these are the costs and benefits that are quantitative in nature and are easier to measure. Although ROI is most often considered a hard number, its definition can be extended to include any strategic business value created by the investment, whether quantifiable or not. Including the strategic value of an IT investment allows an organization to better understand how new technology can help them not only reduce costs and generate new revenue streams, but also increase employee productivity, enhance customer loyalty, and increase organizational flexibility.

continues

Acronym	Expansion	Definition
RTP	Real-Time Transport	**1.** A Virtual Integrated Network Service (VINES) routing protocol based on Routing Information Protocol (RIP). Distributes network topology information and helps VINES servers find neighboring clients, servers, and routers. Uses delay as a routing metric. **2.** Rapid Transport Protocol. A protocol that provides pacing and error recovery for Advanced Peer-to-Peer Networking (APPN) data as it crosses the APPN network. With RTP, error recovery and flow control are performed end to end rather than at every node. RTP prevents congestion rather than reacting to it. **3.** Real-Time Transport Protocol. A protocol commonly used with IP networks. RTP is designed to provide end-to-end network transport functions for applications transmitting real-time data, such as audio, video, or simulation data, over multicast or unicast network services. RTP provides such services as payload type identification, sequence numbering, time stamping, and delivery monitoring to real-time applications.
SNMP	Simple Network Management Protocol	A network management protocol used almost exclusively in TCP/IP networks. SNMP provides a means to monitor and control network devices and to manage configurations, statistics collection, performance, and security.
TFTP	Trivial File Transfer Protocol	A simplified version of File Transfer Protocol (FTP) that allows files to be transferred from one computer to another over a network, usually without the use of client authentication (such as username and password).
UDP	User Datagram Protocol	A connectionless transport layer protocol in the TCP/IP protocol stack. UDP is a simple protocol that exchanges datagrams without acknowledgments or guaranteed delivery, requiring that other protocols handle error processing and retransmission. UDP is defined in RFC 768.

Acronym	Expansion	Definition
VLAN	virtual LAN	A group of devices on one or more LANs that are configured (using management software) so that they can communicate as if they were attached to the same wire, when, in fact, they are located on a number of different LAN segments. Because VLANs are based on logical instead of physical connections, they are extremely flexible.
VoIP	Voice over IP	The capability to carry normal telephony-style voice over an IP-based Internet with POTS-like functionality, reliability, and voice quality. VoIP lets a router carry voice traffic (such as telephone calls and faxes) over an IP network. In VoIP, the digital signal processor (DSP) segments the voice signal into frames, which then are coupled in groups of two and stored in voice packets. These voice packets are transported using Internet Protocol (IP) in compliance with ITU-T specification H.323.
WAN	wide-area network	A data communications network that serves users across a broad geographic area and often uses transmission devices that common carriers provide. Frame Relay, Switched Multimegabit Data Service (SMDS), and Asynchronous Transfer Mode (ATM) are examples of WANs.

INDEX

A

acceptance letter, preparing, 146
accessing IP Telephony Readiness Audit, 41
accounting management, 233
adds, moves, changes, 87
ad-hoc team members (AVVID Tiger Team), 18–19
aliases (email), creating for team members, 98–99
Allred, Doug, 318
availability, five 9s, 240–242
    maintaining on new network, 334–335
AVVID (Architecture for Voice, Video and Integrated Data), 358
AVVID boot camp, 227
AVVID Tiger Team, 15
    ad-hoc team members, 18–19
    core team, 17
        roles and responsibilities, 55–56
    cross-functionality, implementing, 23–24
    engineering team, roles and responsibilities, 57
    executive management sponsorship, 24–26
    executive sponsor, 16
        roles and responsibilities, 53

finance track lead, roles and responsibilities, 62
LAN team, roles and responsibilities, 57–58
program manager, 17
    roles and responsibilities, 54–55
project tracks
    financial track, 22
    support track, 21
    technology track, 19–20
    theater track, 22–23
remote field office-theater implementation PM, roles and responsibilities, 59–61
steering committee, 16–17
    roles and responsibilities, 53
support track lead, roles and responsibilities, 61
team lead, 17, 54
theater implementation managers, roles and responsibilities, 58–59
third-party partners, 18

B

backing up device files, 242–243
BAT (Bulk Administration Tool), 168, 358

BDF (Building Distribution Frame), 358

best practices
- of change management, 35
  - *communicating change*, 37
  - *fostering cultural standards*, 36
  - *user familiarity*, 38
- support process, 232
  - *managing support team,* 229

Boston, Brad, 341

Bourdet, Reid, 280–282

building team cross-functionality, 23–24

business-critical phone users, identifying, 100–101
- best practices, 102–103
- call center agents, 101–102

C

calculating ROI for Cisco IP Telephony implementation, 5–7

call flow, design considerations, 67–68

CallManager
- monitoring network functions, 238
- providing access to Tier 1 support, 223
- software upgrade checklist, 246–249

CDP (Cisco Discovery Protocol), 358

CDR (Call Detail Record), 359

centralized call processing model, 41

certification, managing in support services, 226–227

Chambers, John, 25

Chancellor, Marisa, 104

change controllers, 254
- role in change management process, 262–263

change management, 27–28, 253
- best practices, 35, 274
  - *communicating change*, 37
  - *fostering cultural standards*, 36
  - *user familiarity*, 38
- change controllers, 254
- change planning, 261
  - *technical description of change*, 262
- change readiness, 29
- communication, importance of, 33–35, 264
- documentation, importance of, 266–267
- emergency change management, high-level process flow, 267–270
- in operate phase, 291–292
- IP Telephony Readiness Audit, sample assessment, 41–42
- managing change, 256
- network management update requirements, 266
- Organizational Change Plan, implementing, 30
- organizational culture, 28–29
- performance indicators, 271
  - *change history archive*, 272
  - *change planning archive*, 272
  - *metrics by functional group*, 271
  - *performance meetings*, 273
  - *targeting change success*, 272
- planning for change, 255
- planning for future growth, 43–44
- process flowchart, 254
- quarter end freeze policy, 273
- risk assessment, 257–258
  - *identifying risk level*, 259
- risk factor of changes, 258
- role of change controller, 262–263
- role of change management team, 263–264

role of implementation team, 264–265

scope of change, 257

team cross-functionality, importance of, 14

test and validation, 259–260

testing and verification procedures, 265–266

user familiarity, importance of, 32–33

Voice of the Client survey, 31–32

change planning, as part of change management process, 261–262

change request forms, recommended information, 261

checklist for successful migration strategies, 344–346

design-related issues, 347–348

implementation issues, 348–349

optimizations, 351

Cisco blueprint for Success, 297

Cisco CallManager 3.2 software upgrade checklist, 246–249

Cisco IP Phone test procedure template, 203–204

Cisco IP Telephony, operational benefits, 2–5

ROI, 5–7

Cisco IPCC Express, 321

Cisco LAN infrastructure, 149

Cisco Planning Workshop Template, 86

Cisco Services and Support Blueprint and Checklist, 344

Cisco Unity, migration, 335

architecture, 338

global strategy, 336–337

cleanup of retrofitted components, 285–286

communication

as part of successful migration, 95

best practices, 37, 99

creating e-mail aliases, 97–99

developing strategy, 96

initiating project website, 97

importance of in change management, 33–35, 264

IP-based, implementing, 296–297

conducting

planning meetings, 139

site surveys, 142–143

configuration management, 233

contact center migration strategies, 318–320

benefits of, 325–327

challenges encountered, 324–325

ICM project, 320

implementation approach, 322–324

site deployment design, 321

core team (AVVID Tiger Team), 17

roles and responsibilities, 55–56

corporate culture

change management, 28–29

fostering best practices, 36

CRC (customer response center), 321

cross-functionality

implementing in Tiger Team, 23–24

importance of, 14

customer concerns, 354–356

customer service, 177–179

D

decentralized call processing model, 42

deinstallation of PBX hardware, 280–281

deployment models, 41–42

design considerations, 66–67

call flow, 67–68

dial plans, 75–76

LAN, 70–72

needed features, 77–78

sites, 68

third-party special features, 76–77

user population, 68–69

voice mail, 79, 81
WAN, 72, 74–75
with Legacy PBXs, 67
developing
  support policies, 220
  three-tier support policy, 221
    AVVID boot camp, 227
    best practices, 229
    certification, 226–227
    documentation, 228–229
    SSM, 225
    Tier 1, 221–223
    Tier 2, 223
    Tier 3, 224–225
    training, 226
  vendor relationships, 93
device file backups, 242–243
DHCP (Dynamic Host Configuration Protocol), 359
dial plan
  design considerations, 75–76
  evaluating engineering needs, 42–43, 48
disaster recovery plans, 277–278
  best practices, 279
  resiliency and backup services, 278
disconnecting Cisco's non-IP PBX, 312–314
  Cisco PBX decommission team, 314
disposing of nonleased equipment, 283–284
DNS (Domain Name System), 359
documentation
  importance of in change management process, 266–267
  installation information, 140
  three-tier support policy development, 228–229
DTS (Defect Tracking System), 359

E

e-mail aliases, creating distribution lists for team members, 97–99
EMAN tool, monitoring support services, 235–237
emergency change management, high-level process flow, 267–270
employee mobility, effect on productivity, 311
end-user training, 147
engineering needs, evaluating
  data infrastructure, 40–41
    best practices, 47–48
  dial plan, 42–43
    best practices, 48
  PBX infrastructure, 40
    best practices, 46
engineering team (AVVID Tiger Team), roles and responsibilities, 57
EPN (Expansion Port Network), 360
escalation procedures, 139
establishing project milestones, 91
evaluating engineering needs, 42–43
  of dial plan, 42–43
    best practices, 48
  of network infrastructures
    data, 40–41, 47–48
    PBX, 40, 46
Event Viewer, 237
executing optimizations, 294–295
executive management sponsorship of AVVID Tiger Team, 24–26
"executive row," converting, 103
  best practices, 106–107
  providing support, 105–106
  scheduling, 104–105
executive sponsor (AVVID Tiger Team), 16
  roles and responsibilities, 53
export stations, 168

F

familiarity of users, importance of in change management, 32–33
FAQs, 134–135
  support-related, 244
fault management, 232
fault tolerance, file backups, 242–243
file backups, 242–243
financial track (AVVID Tiger Team), 22
  lead member, roles and responsibilities, 62
fiscal quarter end freeze policy, 273
five 9s, 240–242
  maintaining on new network, 334–335
flowchart for change management process, 254
fostering cultural standards, best practices, 36
future growth, planning for, 43–44

G

Garcia, Anthony, 161
GCC (Global Call Center), 321
Gibbs, LaVeta, 318
global contact centers, migration to Cisco IPCC Express, 321
Gross, Debbie, 106
GTRC (Global Technical Response Center), Tier 1 support, 221–223

H

help desk
  Tier 1 support, 221–223
  Tier 2 support, 223
  Tier 3 support, 224–225
high availability, maintaining five 9s on new network, 334–335

high-level process flow for change management, 257
  change planning, 261–262
  communication, importance of, 264
  documentation, importance of, 266–267
  emergency change management, 267–270
  identifying scope, 257
  implementation team, role of, 264–265
  network management updates, 266
  risk assessment, 257–259
  role of change controller, 262–263
  role of change management team, 263–264
  testing and validation, 259–260, 265–266
high-risk changes, planning for, 257
Holloman, Marc, 236
Huegen, Craig, 151

I–K

ICCIT (Internal Contact Center IT) business model, 235
ICM (Intelligent Call Management) project, 320
identifying
  business-critical phone users as part of successful migration, 100–103
  operational policy changes
    best practices, 114
    emergency phone lines, 113
    modem/analog policy, 111–112
    security policy, 113
  operations center, 93–94
  potential retrofit problems and improvements, 115–118
  risk level of intended changes, 259

IDF (Intermediate Distribution Frame), 360

implementation phase

closeout, 148

connecting to voice mail, 163

equipment, ordering, 140

escalation procedures, 139

establishing processes, 141–142

implementation team, role in change management process, 264–265

installation information, documenting, 140

installing equipment, 143–145

LAN architecture standardization, 150

network acceptance letter, preparing, 146

phone configurations, 166–167

planning meetings, conducting, 139

power supplies, 153

prelaunch tests, conducting, 146

QoS, 151–152

Retrofit Implementation Guide, 171

retrofit team, staffing, 172–174

risk assessment, 175

security, 154

site preparation, 141

site survey, conducting, 142–143, 164

system admin tools, 167–168

training class content, creating, 140

user training, 147

VLAN provisioning, 162–163

WAN preparations, 156

bandwidth, 156

cabling requirements, 159–160

upgrades, 157–158

implementing

IP-based communications, 296–297

Organizational Change Plan, 30

importance of team cross-functionality, 14

installing equipment, 143–145

IP phone configuration template, 132–133

IP Telephony customer concerns, 354–356

IP Telephony Readiness Audit template

accessing, 41

sample assessment, 41–42

IP Telephony Retrofit Efficiency Report, 204

IP Telephony Retrofit Project Gantt Chart, 205–211

IP-based communications, implementing, 296–297

IPCC (Cisco IP Contact Center) migration strategies, 318–320

benefits of, 325–327

challenges encountered, 324–325

ICM project, 320

implementation approach, 322–324

site deployment design, 321

L

LAN team (AVVID Tiger Team), roles and responsibilities, 57–58

LAN Upgrade Test Procedure, 182

LANs, 360

campus model, 41

design considerations, 70–72

LEAP (EAP-Cisco Wireless), 329

lease return dates (PBXs), 280

best practices, 281

deinstallation, 280–281

Legacy PBXs, design considerations, 67

lessons learned

about migrating to new technologies, 342–344

from IP Telephony implementation
communication, 302
operations, 306
placement of equipment, 304
relationships, 302–303
strategy, 303–304
technology, 305
*understanding current
  environment, 305*
Lowers, Bill, 39, 88, 112
low-risk changes, planning for, 258

M

MAC (moves/adds/changes), 360
**maintaining relationships with PBX
  vendors, 282–283**
managing
key network functions, 232–234
support services
  best practices, 229
  certification, 226–227
  monitoring tools, 235–238
  reporting tools, 234–235
  SSM, 225
  *three-tiered support model,
    230–231*
  training, 226
  *troubleshooting tools,
    238–239*
managing change. *See* **change
  management**
Marjaonovic, Vladeta, 310
Mbit (megabit), 360
McBrearty, Fran, 282
McKelvie, Jayne, 277
McQueen, Doug, 105, 275
Mercer, Tracey, 222
**MGCP (Media Gateway Control
  Protocol), 360**
Microsoft Event Viewer, 237

migration to new technologies
checklist for successful migration,
  344–346
  *design-related issues,
    347–348*
  *implementation issues,
    348–349*
  optimizations, 351
Cisco Unity voice mail, 335
  architecture, 338
  global strategy, 336–337
Cisco Wireless LAN, 328
  *architectural standards,
    329–330*
  benefits of, 330–331
  *future of wireless network,
    331, 334*
  pilot testing, 329
contact centers, 318–320
  benefits of, 325–327
  *challenges encountered,
    324–325*
  ICM project, 320
  *implementation approach,
    322–324*
  site deployment design, 321
enterprise-wide IP Telephony, 310
  benefits gained, 311–312
  project UTOPIA, 312
  *removal of non-IP PBX,
    312–314*
lessons learned, 342–344
planning workshops, 84–86
Mike, Cindy, 318
**moderate-risk changes, planning
  for, 258**
Molyski, Paul, 113
monitoring tools
CallManager, 238
Event Viewer, 237
managing support services,
  235–237
Performance Monitor, 237
**MTBF (mean time between
  failure), 360**
MTTR (mean time to repair), 361

N

NAT (Network Address Translation), 361
network infrastructures, evaluating engineering needs
    data infrastructure, 40–41, 47–48
    PBX infrastructure, 40, 46
network management, 232–234
    update requirements in change management process, 266
network-ready acceptance letter, preparing, 146
NOC (network operations center), 361
nonleased equipment disposal, 283–284

O

operate phase
    change management, 291–292
    performance management, 292–293
    system management, 289–290
operational benefits of Cisco IP Telephony, 2, 4–5
    ROI, 5–7
operations center, identifying, 93–94
optimize phase
    executing optimizations, 294–295
    optimization planning, 293–294
Organizational Change Plan, implementing, 30
organizational culture, change management, 28–29

P

pacing project initiatives, 90
    best practices, 94–95
    developing vendor relationships, 93
    establishing milestones, 91
    identifying operations center, 93–94
    removing obstacles, 92
    working with technology team, 91–92
PBX (private branch exchange), 361
    lease return dates, 280
        best practices, 281
        deinstallation, 280–281
    vendor relationships, maintaining, 282–283
PDIOO (planning, design, implementation, operations, and optimization), 295
    design, 298
    implementation, 298
    operational, 299–300
    optimization, 300–301
    planning, 298
performance
    five 9s availability, 240–242
    indicators for change management
        change history archive, 272
        change planning archive, 272
        metrics by functional group, 271
        performance meetings, 273
        targeting change success, 272
performance management, 233
    in operate phase, 292–293
Performance Manager, 237
performing site surveys, 164
Perry, Lance, 341
phases approach for successful migration, 86
    best practices, 90
    existing buildings, 88
    new buildings, 88
    new employees, 87
    relocations, 87
phone configuration template, 132–133
pilot testing of wireless LAN migration, 329

placement of CallManger servers,
44–45, 49

planning
for change, 255
for future growth, 43–44
performance optimization,
293–294

Planning Workshop Template,
84–86, 120
applications and feature
requirements, defining, 125–127
executive requirements and
expectations, 120
existing network review, 122–125
planning and strategy, 128, 130
technical requirements and
expectations, 121–122

power supplies, 153
backup, 239–240

PPN (Primary Port Network), 361

prelaunch tests, conducting, 146

preparing network-ready acceptance
letter, 146

Proctor, Don, 341

program manager (AVVID Tiger
Team), 17
roles and responsibilities, 54–55

Program Unity, 335
architecture, 338
global migration strategy, 336–337

Project Risk Assessment Table,
217–218

project tracks (AVVID Tiger Team)
financial track, 22
support track, 21
technology track, 19–20
theater track, 22–23

Project UTOPIA, 312–314

PSTN, 361

Q–R

QoS, 151–152

quarter end freeze policy, 273

remote field office-theater
implementation PM (AVVID Tiger
Team), roles and responsibilities,
59–61

removal of Cisco's non-IP PBX,
312–314

removing obstacles to successful
migration, 92

reporting tools, 234–235
managing support services,
234–235

responses to Voice of the Client
survey, "must have" features,
31–32

retrofit cleanup procedures, 285–286

Retrofit Implementation Guide,
171, 184
adding analog phones, 191
adding IP phones, 190–191
boss/admin phone configuration,
196–199
cutsheet requirements, 185–189
general phone information, 185
headset support, 196
IP Phone spreadsheet procedure,
192–194
phone installation notes, 195
phone tests, 191–192
restricted phone configuration
procedure, 195
retrofit project FAQ, 201–202
sample retrofit issues log
report, 202
staffing retrofit team, 172–174
troubleshooting Cisco IP
Phones, 200
voice-mail only configurations, 200
wall phone wiring punchdown, 196
war room FAQ, 201

risk assessment, as part of change
management process, 257–259
risk factor of changes, 258
risk management, power backup,
239–240
Robshaw, James, 23
ROI (return on investment), 361
of Cisco IP Telephony
implementation, 5–7
roles
in change management process
of change controller, 262–263
of change management team,
263–264
of implementation team,
264–265
of AVVID Tiger Team members,
53–62
Root, Darrell, 334
RTP (Real-Time Transport), 362

S

sample IP Telephony Readiness Audit
assessment, 41–42
sample project schedule, 212–216
sample users conversion notice,
130–132
scalability, planning for future
growth, 43–44
security management, 233
selecting CallManager server
location, 44–45, 49
server software, installing, 144–145
service requirements for success,
297–301
Silva, Dennis, 32, 161
site survey, performing, 164
during implementation phase,
142–143
site design considerations, 68
SMDI integration, 9

SMNP (Simple Network
Management Protocol), 362
sniffers, 238
software
installing, 144–145
upgrading, 274–275
best practices, 277
communication, importance
of, 276
sponsorship of AVVID Tiger Team,
24–26
SSM (Service and Support
Manager), 225
staffing, Tier 2 support, 223
staging tests, conducting, 143
standardization of LAN
architecture, 150
steering committee (AVVID Tiger
Team), 16–17
roles and responsibilities, 53
Steps to Success-IP Engagement
Guide, 138
strategies for successful migration
communication plan, 95
best practices, 99
developing strategy, 96
e-mail aliases, creating, 97–99
project website, initiating, 97
converting "executive row," 103
best practices, 106–107
providing support, 105–106
scheduling, 105
visual confirmation of phone
configuration, 104–105
holding planning workshops, 84–86
identifying business-critical phone
users, 100–101
best practices, 102–103
call center agents, 101–102
identifying policy changes
best practices, 114
emergency phone lines, 113
modem/analog policy,
111–112

operational security policy, 113
pacing the project, 90
 best practices, 94–95
 developing vendor relationships, 93
 establishing milestones, 91
 identifying operations center, 93–94
 removing obstacles, 92
 working with technology team, 91–92
phased approach, 86
 best practices, 90
 existing buildings, 88
 new buildings, 88
 new employees, 87
 relocations, 87
potential problems and improvements, identifying, 115–118
user training, 108–109
 best practices, 110–111
 operations center, 109
subject-matter experts, importance of, 38–39
success of change management, targeting performance indicators, 272
support policies, developing, 220–221
 AVVID boot camp, 227
 best practices, 229
 certification, 226–227
 documentation, 228–229
 SSM, 225
 Tier 1, 221–223
 Tier 2, 223
 Tier 3, 224–225
 training, 226
support services
 best practices, 232
 FAQs, 244
 managing with reporting tools, 234–235
 three-tiered model, 230–231

tools
 CallManager, 238
 Event Viewer, 237
 monitoring tools, 235–237
 network management, 232–234
 Performance Monitor, 237
 reporting tools, 234–235
 troubleshooting tools, 238–239
support track (AVVID Tiger Team), 21
 lead member, roles and responsibilities, 61
system admin tools, 167–168
system management, 289–290

T

team cross-functionality, building, 23–24
team lead (AVVID Tiger Team), 17
 roles and responsibilities, 54
technology team, maintaining relationship with, 91–92
technology track (AVVID Tiger Team), 19–20
Telang, Mike, 21, 220
testing and validation
 as part of change management process, 259–260
 importance in change management process, 265–266
TFTP (Trivial File Transfer Protocol), 362
theater track (AVVID Tiger Team), 22–23
 theater implementation managers, roles and responsibilities, 58–59
third-party partners (AVVID Tiger Team), 18

third-party special features, design
considerations, 76–77
three-tier support policy,
developing, 221, 230–231
AVVID boot camp, 227
best practices, 229
certification, 226–227
documentation, 228–229
SSM, 225
support process, best practices, 232
Tier 1, 221–223
Tier 2, 223
Tier 3, 224–225
training, 226
Tiger Team. *See* AVVID Tiger Team
training new users
as part of successful migration
strategy, 108–109
best practices, 110–111
operation center, 109
creating training class content, 140
in support services, 226
troubleshooting Cisco IP Phones, 200
troubleshooting tools, 238–239
Tsang, Mary, 33

U

UDP (User Datagram Protocol), 362
upgrading software, 274–275
best practices, 277
Cisco CallManager 3.2 software,
246–249
communication, importance
of, 276
UPS power, 239–240
user familiarity
best practices, 38
importance of in change
management, 32–33
user population, design
considerations, 68–69

user training as part of successful
migration strategy, 108–109
best practices, 110–111
operations center, 109
users conversion notice, example,
130–132
UTOPIA (Unity, Telephony, & Other
Powerful IP Applications)
project, 312
old world versus new world
network applications, 287

V

Vanderstraeten, Gert, 42
vendor relationships, developing, 93
VLANs, 363
provisioning, 162–163
voice mail
connecting, 163
design considerations, 79–81
Unity migration, 335–338
Voice of the Client survey, 63–65
responses to, "must have" features,
31–32

W–Z

WANs, 363
design considerations, 72–75
preparing during implementation
phase, 156
bandwidth, 156
cabling requirements,
159–160
upgrades, 157–158
websites, initiating for retrofit
project, 97
wireless LAN migration, 328
architectural standards, 329–330
benefits of, 330–331
future of wireless networks,
331, 334
pilot testing, 329